Communications
in Computer and Information Science 978

Commenced Publication in 2007
Founding and Former Series Editors:
Phoebe Chen, Alfredo Cuzzocrea, Xiaoyong Du, Orhun Kara, Ting Liu,
Krishna M. Sivalingam, Dominik Ślęzak, and Xiaokang Yang

Editorial Board

More information about this series at http://www.springer.com/series/7899

Sergio Nesmachnow · Luis Hernández Callejo (Eds.)

Smart Cities

First Ibero-American Congress, ICSC-CITIES 2018
Soria, Spain, September 26–27, 2018
Revised Selected Papers

 Springer

Editors
Sergio Nesmachnow ⓘ
Universidad de la República
Montevideo, Uruguay

Luis Hernández Callejo ⓘ
Universidad de Valladolid
Valladolid, Spain

ISSN 1865-0929   ISSN 1865-0937 (electronic)
Communications in Computer and Information Science
ISBN 978-3-030-12803-6   ISBN 978-3-030-12804-3 (eBook)
https://doi.org/10.1007/978-3-030-12804-3

Library of Congress Control Number: 2019930851

This Springer imprint is published by the registered company Springer Nature Switzerland AG
The registered company address is: Gewerbestrasse 11, 6330 Cham, Switzerland

Selected Articles from I Ibero-American Congress of Smart Cities

This CCIS volume presents selected articles from the I Ibero-American Congress of Smart Cities (ICSC-CITIES 2018), held in Soria, Spain, during September 26–27, 2018.

Smart Cities are the result of the increasingly urgent need to orient our lives toward sustainability. Therefore, these cities use infrastructure, innovation, and technology to reduce energy consumption and CO_2 emissions, in order to improve the quality of life of their citizens.

Being a strategic issue that brings new challenges, the I Ibero-American Congress of Smart Cities (ICSC-CITIES 2018) was a forum for discussion with the main goal of creating synergies among different research groups to favor the development of smart cities and contribute to their knowledge and integration in different scenarios, their possible development, and the strategies to address them.

Subject areas defined by the Steering Committee of ICCS-CITIES 2018 included energy efficiency and sustainability; infrastructures, energy and the environment; smart mobility; intelligent transportation systems; Internet of Things; and governance and citizenship.

The I Ibero-American Conference on Smart Cities was organized by the CITIES network, financed as part of the Ibero-American Program for Science and Technology Development (CYTED).

The conference received 101 submissions for peer review. The reviewing process followed a single-blind procedure using a panel of experts and external reviewers (outside the Program Committee). Each submission had an average of three independent reviews and each reviewer was assigned an average of two submissions. The best 15 articles were selected to be part of this CCIS volume.

January 2019

Sergio Nesmachnow
Luis Hernández Callejo

Organization

Conference Chairs

Luis Hernández Callejo   University of Valladolid, Spain
Sergio Nesmachnow   Universidad de la República, Uruguay

Program Committee

Rafael Asorey Cacheda   University Center for Defense/Marine Military School,
                             Spain
Jesús Vegas Hernández   University of Valladolid, Spain
Diego Alberto Godoy   University Gastón Dachary, Argentina
Luisenia Fernández   University of Zulia, Venezuela
Roberto Villafafila   Polytechnic University of Cataluña, Spain
Luis García Santander   University of Concepción, Chile
Ronney Mancebo Boloy   Federal Center of Technological Education Celso Suckow
                             Da Fonseca, Brazil
Javier Prieto   University of Salamanca, Spain
Vanessa Guimaraes   Federal Center of Technological Education Celso Suckow
                             Da Fonseca, Brazil
Javier Finat   University of Valladolid, Spain
Hortensia Amaris   University Carlos III of Madrid, Spain
Mónica Aguado   National Center for Renewable Energies, Spain
Claudia Liliana Zuñiga   University Santiago De Cali, Colombia
Carlos Méndez   National University of Litoral, Argentina
David Chinarro   University San Jorge, Spain
Ponciano Escamilla   National Polytechnic Institute, Mexico
Jorge Gómez   Complutense University of Madrid, Spain
Jorge Mírez   National University of Engineering, Peru
Fabian Castillo   University Libre, Colombia
Juan Leonardo Espinoza   University of Cuenca, Ecuador
Jose Antonio Ferrer   Research Centre for Energy, Environment
  Tevar   and Technology, Spain
Mª Del Rosario Heras   Research Centre for Energy, Environment
                             and Technology, Spain
Jaime Lloret Mauri   Polytechnic University of Valencia, Spain
Andrei Tchernykh   Centro de Investigación Científica y de Educación Superior
                             de Ensenada, Baja California, Mexico
Jamal Toutouh   University of Málaga, Spain

Financing Sponsors

Technical Sponsors

Non-Technical Sponsors

Contents

Study of the Influence of DC-DC Optimizers on PV-Energy Generation

Luis Hernández-Callejo$^{(\boxtimes)}$ ⓘ, Sara Gallardo-Saavedra ⓘ,
Alejandro Diez-Cercadillo, and Víctor Alonso-Gómez ⓘ

University of Valladolid, Campus Universitario Duques de Soria, Soria, Spain
{luis.hernandez.callejo,victor.alonso.gomez}@uva.es,
s.gallardosaavedra@gmail.com,
alejandro.diez.cercadillo@gmail.com

Abstract. The integration of renewable generation sources in cities is a reality. Specifically, photovoltaic technology is the most used (facades, roofs, urban spaces, etc.). The existence of buildings at different altitudes and other urban obstacles can cause shadows in the photovoltaic modules. These shadows will cause the decrease of photovoltaic efficiency. Therefore, the increase in photovoltaic efficiency is essential. This increase in efficiency can be achieved by associating DC-DC converters (DC-DC Optimizers) with photovoltaic modules. This work presents real results of the increase of efficiency of the photovoltaic modules, from the effect of the DC-DC Optimizers. In addition, the work shows simulations of the shadow effect on photovoltaic modules.

Keywords: Photovoltaic efficiency · DC-DC optimizers

1 Introduction

Smart City (*SC*) has emerged to solve the problems of population growth and urbanization [1]. However, this new concept of city must make changes to enable this evolution. The reality indicates that cities are evolving, for example in [2], 15 UK cities are analyzed, and the results are that carbon dioxide emissions do not grow/decrease linearly.

SC must adapt its existing infrastructures. A critical infrastructure is the electricity grid, as shown in [3]. In addition, as shown [4], the rapid increase in population and population flows require a complete modernization of existing infrastructures (electricity, water, gas, etc.).

Buildings are one of the most important infrastructures in the city. These buildings, like the city, must evolve, and they must integrate renewable sources and improve their energy efficiency [5]. This new building concept, called *Smart Building* (*SB*), will be responsible for increasing the efficiency and sustainability of the *SC*, since it will integrate renewable sources and other good practices [6–8].

As already mentioned, *SC* aims to improve efficiency at all levels. This increase in efficiency may affect the advanced programming of *SB* behavior [9]. Energy efficiency also refers to the sending of information through the *SC* [10, 11]. Another important

S. Nesmachnow and L. Hernández Callejo (Eds.): ICSC-CITIES 2018, CCIS 978, pp. 1–17, 2019.
https://doi.org/10.1007/978-3-030-12804-3_1

aspect of energy efficiency has to do with the reduction of peak demand and energy savings, as presented [12] through its new algorithm.

As presented in [13], the integration of large-scale renewable sources in cities is a reality. But this integration must be done in an efficient way, as mentioned in [14], and this efficient way refers to the way to install and improve the production of energy. Integration can be understood in a massive but small-scale way, as presented by the authors in [15], where small-scale integration is with photovoltaic (PV) and solar.

In this sense, the increase in efficiency in renewable systems is critical, as they reflect in [16, 17]. Therefore, this work is focused on demonstrating the increase of efficiency in the photovoltaic systems integrated in *SC*, since these renewable plants will be subject to numerous shadows (solids, obstacles, etc.). The use of optimizers at the photovoltaic module level will increase the efficiency of the overall system. The authors have developed several shadow scenarios, which have been validated with simulations and with a real environment. The rest of the document is as follows: Sect. 2 presents a theoretical review, Sect. 3 explains the methodology used, Sect. 4 shows the results, Sect. 4 discusses the results and Sect. 5 presents the conclusions of the work.

2   Theoretical Review

The performance of PV modules is inevitably decreased due to the different working conditions of each of the panels. The PV system output power will be reduced as a consequence of mismatch effects and environmental factors caused by partial shading, soiling, dirtiness, mismatch between PV cells generated during their manufacture or ageing mismatching, differences in the orientations and inclinations of solar surfaces, differences in temperature or irradiance in the modules. A lot of the available energy would be wasted since the shaded PV cells would be acting as passive charges and they would limit the output current of the unshaded ones [18]. These effects lead to the weakest PV cells determining the output power of the whole string of modules. Therefore, additional potential benefits of distributed power electronics include increased design flexibility by allowing mismatched or longer strings of PV panels, improved monitoring, and increased system availability [19].

In order to avoid this, DC-DC converters on PV module level can be added. These devices, commonly known as power optimizers, are mounted in each single module and minimise the impact that the different factors have on the performance of PV systems. Additionally, it allows testing the behaviour of each module by means of communications included into the electronic device, facilitating the operation and maintenance of PV arrays [20]. This is really beneficial in the cases of big PV plants, in which there are a large number of PV modules connected, because it helps to identify whether a PV module is working well. In case of absence of optimizers, it would be possible to identify the array in which is located the failure, but it would be more difficult to detect the single module or modules which fail. A quick detection of failures would avoid energy losses due to faults on the PV system.

Another appropriate application for this technology is the case of *Building Integrated Photovoltaic* (*BIPV*) systems, in which the environmental factors can be very significant in contrast with open-space plants. While a large PV plant is designed with the single aim of optimizing energy production, the goal of a *BIPV* system is not only electricity generation but also the achievement of aesthetical and functional objectives from an architectonic point of view [18]. The optimal orientation and inclination of BIPV systems are practically impossible, as well as avoiding partial shadows. Furthermore, having all the modules tested in *BIPV* systems is an enormous advantage, because in this case the access to PV panels can be very complex and it will incur heavy maintenance costs.

As a result of shadows or other failures, the P-V curve shows two *Maximum Power Points Tracking (MPPT)* values, one global and one local [20]. *MPPT* controllers find and maintain operation at the *MPP* using an *MPPT* algorithm. The modular converters incorporate this function. The literature proposed many of these algorithms. For instance, some MPPT methods such as fractional open circuit voltage and fractional short circuit current are simple to implement with moderate level of accuracy. The commonly used perturb & observe (P&O) technique produces oscillation around the maximum power point with a possibility of failure under partial shading condition. Other appliances employ PV power forecasting models to compute the reference value of the maximum PV power to be tracked by a direct power control scheme which of composed of a SEPIC converter [21].

The investigations through this topic started at the end of the 20th century [22]. First of all, in 1992, it was studied the incorporation of DC-AC converters in each module. In this way, each module will have a small inverter and the grid connection of the PV modules will be carried out directly in AC current, so the mismatch and environmental factors will not affect from one module to the rest of them. Some authors affirm that the peak efficiency of the system is 89% and that they have a lifetime of approximately ten years [23]. Nonetheless, it has some important disadvantages which inspire the study of alternative solutions. Firstly, it is quite difficult to reach efficiently and reliably the grid voltage from the output power of a module. Moreover, the use of several micro-inverters implies the duplication of protections and AC filters to offer the same quality and safety than a central inverter, which leads to a more expensive solution. Different micro-inverter efficiency are analysed in [24], in which a test circuit that can be used as efficient measure to analyze and compare different features of micro inverters is designed.

The necessity of micro AC inverters to boost the DC voltage and invert it leads to a lower efficiency and higher cost than DC-DC converters. Therefore, the implementation of DC-DC converters has been the main alternative studied during the last decade. During the first years of the 21st century the first application of this concept were proposed. In 2004, a cascaded DC-DC converter connection of PV modules was proposed [25]. It offers the advantages of modular converters approach without the cost or efficiency drawbacks of individual DC-AC grid connected inverters. Later experimental results show an efficiency of approximately 95% [26]. Nevertheless, the performance of converters depends on the operating conditions of the PV system along with the performance characteristics of the converter [19]. There are many different topologies which vary according to the complexity of circuits, stress on used components and quality of input and output power. Generally, a single-inductor, single-switch boost converter topology and its variations exhibit a satisfactory performance in the majority of applications where the output voltage is greater than the input voltage.

The performance of the boost converter can be improved by implementing a boost converter with multiple switches and/or multiple boost inductors. The two inductor boost converter exhibits benefits in high power applications high input current is split between two inductors, thus reducing power loss in both copper windings and primary switches. Furthermore, by applying an interleaving control strategy, the input current ripple can be reduced [27]. More recent developments carried out point to newer DC-DC technologies with low cost and high reliability. In the delta-conversion concept [28], the converters are only active when differences between substring and module output powers occur. This reduces the operation time and thereby increases the reliability.

3 Method

Experiments have been performed in the PV laboratory of the Campus Duques de Soria, University of Valladolid. This PV field is composed by two strings of eight Isofoton I-159 modules, with the same mechanical configuration and orientation. The main characteristics of the modules used in the tests are showed in Table 1.

Table 1. Isofoton I-159 module main characteristics.

	Main features
Pmax	159 Wp
Voc	21.6 V
Vmmp	17.4 V
Isc	9.81 A
Impp	9.14 A
Toll	±5%
ΔIsc	5.4 mA/°C
ΔUoc	−80 mV/°C

The first string is directly connected to a string inverter, SB 1.5-1VL40, which main characteristics are showed in Table 2.

On the other hand, the second string has optimizers TIGO TS4-O installed in each module, which characteristics are reviewed in Table 3. The eight optimizers are connected in series to a second inverter identical to the first string inverter (Table 2).

Six different tests have been studied to determine the influence of DC-DC optimizers in the production in case of shading. Different diagrams of the six shadings configurations are further analyzed in the results section.

1. One module affected, the shaded part will be 80% of three cells of the same circuit, leaving the rest of the module in standard conditions.
2. One module shaded in each string, affecting 50% of the surface of nine cells.
3. One module shaded in each string with 100% of the surface of thirty six cells belonging to the same circuit.

Table 2. SB 1.5-1VL40 main characteristics.

	Main features
V_{DC} max	600 V
V_{DC} MPP	160–500 V
I_{DC} max	10 A
I_{SC} pv	18 A
V_{AC}, r	230
P_{AC}, r	1500 W
Smax	1500 VA
F_{AC}, r	50 Hz
I_{AC}, max	7 A

Table 3. TIGO TS4-O main characteristics.

	Main features
Rated DC Input Power	475 W
Max Input Voltage @ Lowest Temperature	90 V
Isc	12 A
Max Voc @STC	75 V
Min Vmp @STC	16 V

4. Four modules of the string affected. In each module a line of 12 cells, belonging the same circuit, is shaded at 50% of its surface.
5. Whole string shaded in the same percentage as test 4, 12 cells in each module shaded at 50% of its surface.
6. One module affected, covering 80% of nine cells in the same column, affecting all three circuits.

As an example, Fig. 1 shows the shading configuration in test number 1 and Fig. 2 the shading configuration in test number 4.

Fig. 1. Shading configuration studied in case 1.

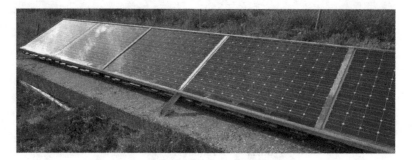

Fig. 2. Shading configuration studied in case 4.

All shading configurations have been simulated in LTSpice using the methodology proposed in reference [20], in order to obtain the theoretical IV curves to make possible the evaluation. Additionally, the real IV curves of the strings for each shading configuration have been experimentally obtained using the HT SOLAR IV-400 TRACER. The dimensions of the module used are presented in Fig. 3a and the electrical structure of the module simulated in LTSpice in Fig. 3b.

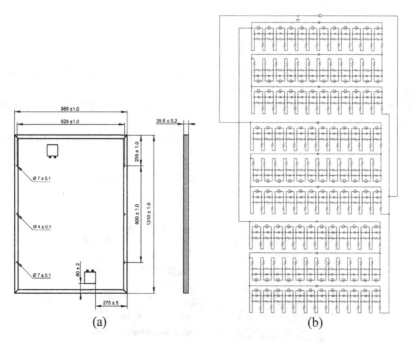

(a)   (b)

Fig. 3. Isofoton I-159 modules dimensions (a) and electrical structure of the module simulated in LTSpice (b).

Finally, all the results downloaded from the string inverters and the optimizers have been analyzed and compared considering the resultant theoretical and experimental IV curves of each shading configuration, and are presented in the results and discussion sections.

4   Results and Discussion

In this section we explain the two types of experiments that have been carried out. Firstly, computer simulations with LT Spice software and secondly field simulations in the PV laboratory of the Campus Duques de Soria (University of Valladolid) are displayed. Additionally, the results of the IV curve experimental tests in the field are shown and compared with LTSpice simulations.

4.1   LT Spice Experiments

LTSpice is a SPICE simulation freeware for analog circuits endowed with schematic capture and a wave form viewer. This software has been used to simulate the IV curves for each shading test proposed, which are presented in this section.

Benchmark. In benchmark simulation there is no shaded cells in order to see clearly the ideal graphics of both power and current, as showed in Fig. 4. Power curve has a maximum point at 1223.8 W.

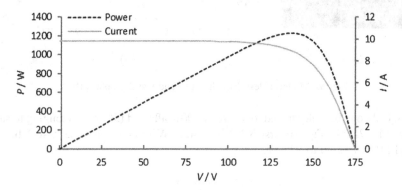

Fig. 4. Benchmark graphics.

Test 1. With only one module affected, the shaded part will be 80% of three cells of the same circuit, leaving the rest of the module in standard conditions (Fig. 5a). In this simulation two *MPP* appear clearly (Fig. 5b) with similar values of 1048.5 W and 1049.2 W.

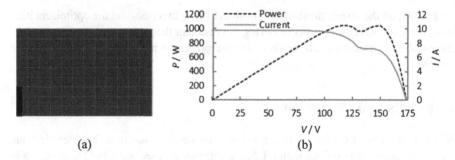

(a)   (b)

Fig. 5. Test 1 shaded module (a) and IV and power curve (b).

Test 2. It continues having only one module shaded in each string, affecting 50% of the surface of nine cells (Fig. 6a) belonging to three different circuits. Figure 6b shows how the power curve is affected by this new type of shadow, resulting in two *MPP* with values of 1048.5 W and 784.9 W.

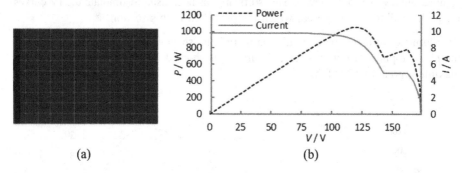

(a)   (b)

Fig. 6. Model of test 2 module (a), and test 2 graphics (b).

Test 3. Only one module shaded, one circuit 100% affected (36 cells belonging to same circuit, Fig. 7a). In Fig. 7b first MPP in 1048.9 W remains equal as test 2 but the second MPP rises up to 972 W.

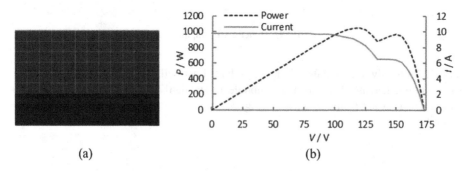

(a)   (b)

Fig. 7. Shaded test 3 solar module (a) and its simulation graphic (b).

Test 4. First one affecting 4 modules. In each module a line of 12 cells, belonging the same circuit, is shaded at 50% of its surface (Fig. 8a). In Fig. 8b, power graph exhibits two *MPP* at 1035.8 W and 1092 W.

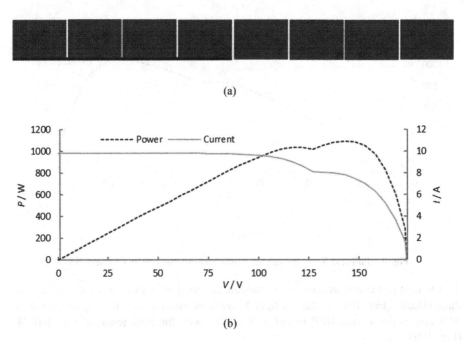

(a)

(b)

Fig. 8. Full test 4 string with half of its modules shaded (a) and graphics of test 4 (b).

Test 5. Continuing with the shadows of test 4, test 5 has the whole string shaded in the same way as the previous test, 12 cells in each module shaded at 50% (Fig. 9a). This power curve graph lowers the first *MPP* to 838.5 W but maintains the maximum in 1033.1 W (Fig. 9b).

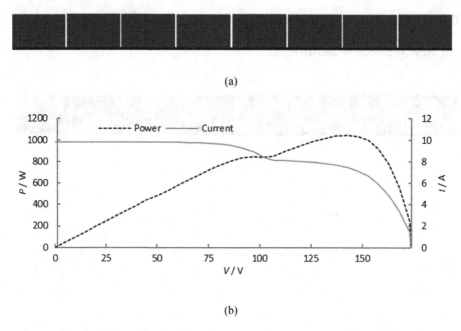

(a)

(b)

Fig. 9. Full test 5 string (a), and power and current curves of test 5 (b).

Test 6. Last test concerns only to one module covering 80% of nine cells, affecting all three circuits (Fig. 10a). Although tests 2 and 6 are similar, the shading difference of 30% causes the lowest *MPP* to fall to 306.5 W, with the high remaining at 1048 W (Fig. 10b).

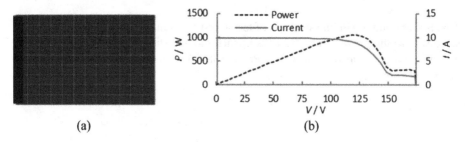

(a)   (b)

Fig. 10. Shaded module (a) and test 6 curves (b).

4.2 Laboratory Experiments

Tests were realized from May to June, with duration of one week for each, shadow position was changed every Monday. The day in which the shadows are changed is not counted in the tests, so there are six full days for each one.

Atypical weather (strong storms, cloudy and windy days) in certain days of tests 3, 4 and 6 generated graphics full of maximums and minimums instead of the standard production graph. Production data is monitored by each inverter, one mark every 5 min.

In order to simplify nomenclature, strings are numbered "String 1" and "String 2". String 1 worked with optimizers and String 2 worked without them.

There are natural shadows affecting both Strings in late afternoon and first evening hours.

Benchmark. Five days of benchmark data with similar production graphics in sunny days (Fig. 11) and disparate production charts on cloudy days (Fig. 12), left two recognizable patterns common to all days: string 2 starts sooner than string 1 and string 1 produces more than string 2 in the first hours of the morning. In cloudy days, string 1 has more difficulty reaching some of the production peaks after the cloud leaves (Fig. 12).

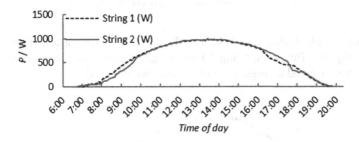

Fig. 11. Benchmark production graph on sunny day.

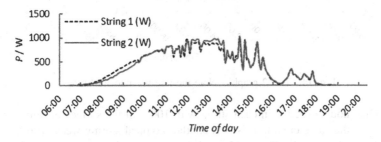

Fig. 12. Benchmark graphics in a cloudy day.

Test 1. Same shadow pattern as simulations with LTspice, one module shaded with 80% of three cells of the same circuit, leaving the rest of the string in standard conditions (Fig. 5a).

One cloudy and windy week collecting data show results like Fig. 13, full of maximums and minimums. Still there is the same pattern: String 1 starts later but rises first in early hours of the day.

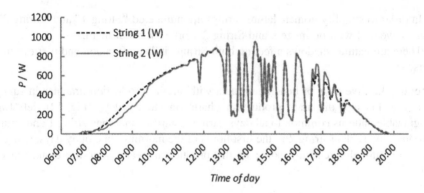

Fig. 13. Test 1 graphics, cloudy and windy days.

Test 2. One module shaded in each string, affecting 50% of the surface of nine cells as showed in Fig. 6a. This week string 1 had strange graphics that we attribute to some technical error or a bad configuration of the inverter (Fig. 14).

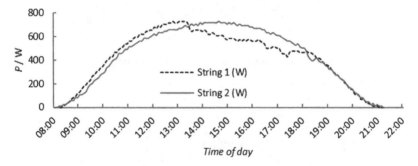

Fig. 14. Test 2 graphic. Note the rare behavior of String 1

Test 3. One module shaded in each string with 100% of the surface of thirty six cells belonging to the same circuit. This was another atypical stormy week with late afternoon heavy rain periods. Figure 15 displays String 2 higher production on cloudy periods before the storm.

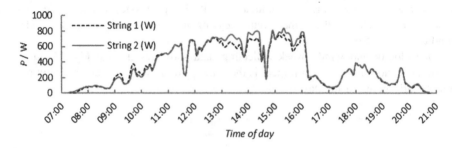

Fig. 15. Test 3 graphics.

Test 4. This week only 4 of 8 modules where affected with one line of 12 cells belonging to the same circuit, shaded at 50% of its surface (Fig. 8a). Another stormy week full of moments of sun left production peaks and long intervals below 400 W, as seen on Fig. 16.

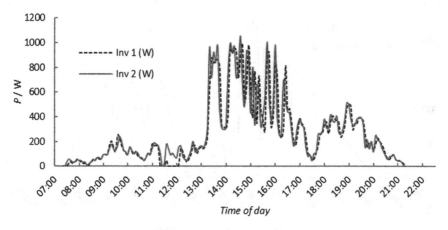

Fig. 16. Cloudy day on test 4 week.

Test 5. This test has the whole string affected, 12 cells in each module shaded at 50% (Fig. 9a). Graphics are very similar from string 1 to string 2 with only one common pattern: string 2 starts first but string 1 produces more in the first hours of the day (Fig. 17).

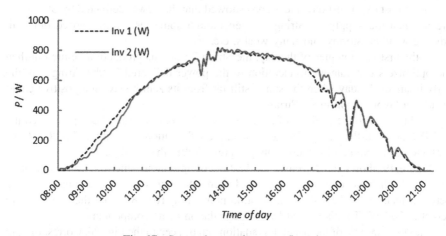

Fig. 17. Sunny day graph on test 5 week.

Test 6. With a similar pattern of test 2, test 6 has strong differences between the production of the two Strings which increases its value considering that it was a rainy week. Figure 18 shows a typical rainy day on Test 6 week.

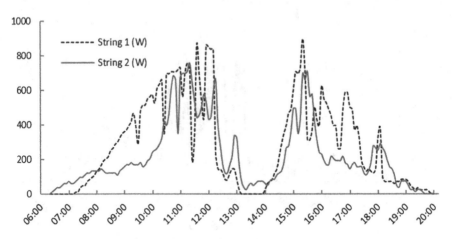

Fig. 18. Test 6 rainy day graph.

The optimal conditions to have being able to evaluate all the tests between them with larger amounts of data would have required more time with appropriated weather conditions. However, the comparison of the data has been made between the two strings of each test separately and although the meteorological conditions were not the most suitable, available data of the two strings of each test can be compared without any issue, as they have been taken in equal conditions.

On almost every test day, the graphs showed that the power delivered by String 1 is greater than the supply by String 2, even though some tests were carried out with adverse weather, stormy and rainy weeks, etc.

In the first few minutes of the day, the String 2 starts its production before but then the optimizers generate an acceleration to the power delivered by the String 1 in the early hours of the day when the sun is still far from its zenith leaving a positive count clearly in favor of optimized String.

Additionally to the analysis of the production introduced, it has been performed the real IV curves of the strings for each shading configuration using the HT SOLAR IV-400 TRACER. Some of these results are presented in this section.

Figure 19 shows the IV curve of Test 4 configuration which is really similar to Fig. 5b: Both have one lower MPP and then one higher MPP. The big difference between them is the first MPP: Simulation points it at 1035.8 W but the real measure sets it at 700 W. This is caused by the degradation of its components.

Another example of the panel degradation can be seen in the Fig. 20. Corresponding to Test 5, can be contrasted with Fig. 9b. First MPP on simulation was at 838.5 W but due to material decay the PV curve, first MPP in real conditions is at just 350 W.

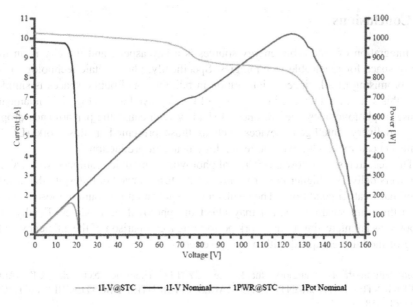

1I-V@STC   1I-V Nominal   1PWR@STC   1Pot Nominal

Fig. 19. IV Curve of test 4 shadow configuration.

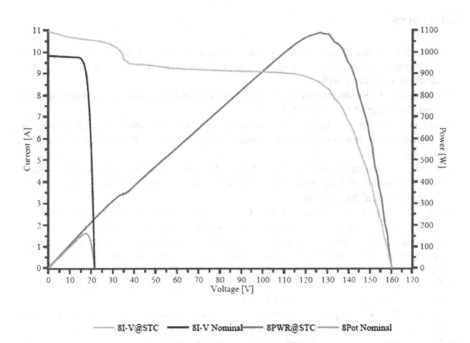

8I-V@STC   8I-V Nominal   8PWR@STC   8Pot Nominal

Fig. 20. Test 5 shadow configuration IV Curve.

5   Conclusions

The integration of renewable energy sources is a key aspect, and the city is an integrating space for renewable technologies. Specifically, photovoltaic technology is the most promising of all, since its integration in buildings and public spaces is simple.

In this sense, the increase in efficiency of the deployed technology is fundamental. In case of photovoltaics, the presence of shadows can cause the performance drop of energy delivery. Intelligent devices such as those presented in this work (DC-DC optimizer) can make photovoltaic technology better in production.

This research shows how the String of photovoltaic modules equipped with DC-DC optimizers delivers a higher power in most of the tests carried out, despite the absence of optimal weather conditions. The results must be taken into account in those locations where there are shadows, which may affect the photovoltaic modules. Finally, it is proposed as an interesting future work performing a comparison of the efficiency with a string of modules equipped with micro inverters.

Acknowledgment. The authors thank the CYTED Thematic Network "CIUDADES INTELIGENTES TOTALMENTE INTEGRALES, EFICIENTES Y SOSTENIBLES (CITIES)" n° 518RT0558.

References

1. Silva, B.N., Khan, M., Han, K.: Towards sustainable Smart Cities: a review of trend, architectures, components, and open challenges in Smart Cities. Sustain. Cities Soc. **38**(April), 697–713 (2018)
2. Yigitcanlar, T., Kamruzzaman, Md.: Does Smart City policy lead to sustainability of cities? Land Use Policy **73**, 49–58 (2018)
3. Anderson, A., et al.: Empowering smart communities: electrification, education, and sustainable entrepreneurship in IEEE Smart Village iniciatives. IEEE Electrification Mag. **5**(2), 6–16 (2017)
4. Kumar, H., Kumar, M., Gupta, M.P., Madaan, J.: Moving towards Smart Cities: solutions that lead to Smart City Transformation Framework. Technol. Forecast. Soc. Chang., Available Online 30 April 2018
5. García-Fuentes, M.A., González, I., Gordaliza, A., de Torre, C.: Retrofitting of a residential district under near zero energy buildings criteria. Proceedings **1**(7), 686–691 (2017)
6. Pooranian, Z., Abawajy, J.H., Vinod, P., Conti, M.: Scheduling distributed energy resource operation and daily power consumption for a smart building to optimize economic and environmental parameters. Energies **11**(6), 1348–1365 (2018)
7. Marinakis, V., Doukas, H.: An advanced IoT-based system for intelligent energy management in buildings. Sensors **18**(2), 610–626 (2018)
8. Moseley, Ph.: EU support for innovation and market uptake in smart buildings under the horizon 2020 framework programme. Buildings **7**(4), 105–129 (2017)
9. Wei, T., Zhu, Q., Yu, N.: Proactive demand participation of smart buildings in smart grid. IEEE Trans. Comput. **65**(5), 1392–1406 (2016)
10. Jiang, D., Zhang, P., Lv, Z., Song, H.: Energy-efficiency multi-constraint routing algorithm with load balancing for Smart City applications. IEEE Internet Things J. **3**(6), 1437–1447 (2016)

11. Li, Z., Shahidehpour, M.: Deployment of cybersecurity for managing traffic efficiency and safety in Smart Cities. Electricity J. **30**(4), 52–61 (2017)
12. Mahapatra, Ch., Kumar, A., Leung, V.C.M.: Energy management in Smart Cities based on Internet of Things: peak demand reduction and energy savings. Sensors **17**(12), 2012–2833 (2017)
13. Strzalka, A., Alam, N., Duminil, E., Coors, V., Eicker, U.: Large scale integration of photovoltaics in cities. Appl. Energy **93**, 413–421 (2012)
14. Harsha, P., Dahleh, M.: Optimal management and sizing of energy storage under dynamic pricing for the efficient integration of renewable energy. IEEE Trans. Power Syst. **30**(3), 1164–1181 (2015)
15. Kaygusuz, A., Keles, C., Baykant, B., Karabiber, A.: Renewable energy integration for Smart Cities. Energy Build. **64**, 456–462 (2013)
16. Gallardo-Saavedra, S., Hernández-Callejo, L., Duque-Perez, O.: Technological review of the instrumentation used in aerial thermographic inspection of photovoltaic plants. Renew. Sustain. Energy Rev. **93**, 566–579 (2018)
17. Gallardo-Saavedra, S., Hernández-Callejo, L., Duque-Perez, O.: Image resolution influence in aerial thermographic inspections of photovoltaic plants. IEEE Trans. Industr. Inf., 1–9 (2018). https://doi.org/10.1109/tii.2018.2865403
18. Alonso, R., Román, E., Sanz, A., Martínez, V.E., Ibañez, P.: Analysis of inverter-voltage influence on distributed MPPT architecture performance. IEEE Trans. Industr. Electron. **59** (10), 3900–3907 (2012)
19. Deline, C., MacAlpine, S.: Use conditions and efficiency measurements of DC power optimizers for photovoltaic systems. In: IEEE Energy Conversion Congress and Exposition (ECCE), Denver, CO, USA (2013)
20. Gallardo-Saavedra, S., Karlsson, B.: Simulation, validation and analysis of shading effects on a PV system. Sol. Energy **170**, 828–839 (2018)
21. Azab, M.: DC power optimizer for PV modules using SEPIC converter. In: The 5th IEEE International Conference on Smart Energy Grid Engineering, Oshawa, ON, Canada, pp. 74–78 (2017)
22. Orduz, R., Solórzano, J., Egido, M.A., Román, E.: Analytical study and evaluation results of power optimizers for distributed power conditioning in photovoltaic arrays. Prog. Photovoltaics Res. Appl. **2013**(21), 359–373 (2013)
23. Rodriguez, C., Amaratunga, G.A.J.: Long-lifetime power inverter for photovoltaic AC modules. IEEE Trans. Industr. Electron. **55**(7), 2593–2601 (2008)
24. Sadati, A.M., Krauter, S., Bendfeld, J.: Comparison of micro inverters based on practical analysis. In: 5th International Youth Conference on Energy (IYCE), Pisa, pp. 1–6 (2015)
25. Walker, G.R., Sernia, P.C.: Cascaded DC–DC converter connection of photovoltaic modules. IEEE Trans. Power Electron. **19**(4), 1130–1139 (2004)
26. Román, E., Alonso, R., Ibañez, P., Elorduizapatarietxe, S., Goitia, D.: Intelligent PV module for grid-connected PV systems. IEEE Trans. Industr. Electron. **53**(4), 1066–1073 (2006)
27. Elkamouny, K., Lakssir, B., Hamedoun, M., Benyoussef, A., Mahmoudi, H.: Simulation, design and test of an efficient power optimizer using DC-DC interleaved isolated boost PV-micro inverter application. In: International Multi-Conference on Systems, Signals & Devices (SSD), Marrakech, Morocco, pp. 518–525 (2017)
28. Bergveld, H.J., et al.: Module-level DC/DC conversion for photovoltaic systems: the delta-conversion concept. IEEE Trans. Power Electron. **28**(4), 2005–2013 (2013)

Smart Campus Human Tracking: The Case of University of Málaga

Jamal Toutouh$^{(\boxtimes)}$, Javier Luque, and Enrique Alba

Departamento de Lenguajes y Ciencias de la Computación,
Universidad de Málaga, Málaga, Spain
{jamal,eat}@lcc.uma.es, javierluque@uma.es

Abstract. Smart city initiatives have emerged to mitigate the negative effects of a very fast growth of urban areas. A number of universities are applying smart city solutions to face similar challenges in their campuses. In this study, we analyze the possibility of using low cost sensors based on detecting wireless signals of light commodity devices to track the movement of the members of the university community. This tracking information will help the university managers to provide the users with smart services. The first insight is that there were not detected barely movements through the campus during late-night/early morning hours (from 0:00H to 6:00H). In turn, the number of human flows sensed in a given direction is similar to the ones in the opposite one. The analysis of the sensed data has shown that the most mobility occurs during the opening and finishing school hours, as expected. Finally, we observed that the sensors are able to detect vehicular mobility.

Keywords: Smart city · Smart campus · Human tracking

1 Introduction

The concept of smart city has emerged to reduce the negative effects of a very fast growth in urban areas. With this purpose, countless new applications are appearing to improve our daily life [3,13,14,20,22]: parking, optimized routes, car charing, smart systems in buses, private models of mobility, signaling, lane decisions, social implications of mobility, energy consumption, etc. Most of these new applications use intelligent systems able to detect, predict, and efficiently manage different aspects of the city.

Most of these systems require accurate and up-to-date information based on actual data, such as, the origin/destination (OD) matrices of the city, pedestrian behavior or the number of cars per street. The access to these data is an issue today. Thus, there are some initiatives to advance in the knowledge of the city to build a minimum set of open data services to allow stakeholders to used them for final services. Traditional measurement systems [8] use to be expensive, traumatic to install, and scarcely available has been replaced with new technologies like sensors, cameras, etc. [6,21,24].

© Springer Nature Switzerland AG 2019
S. Nesmachnow and L. Hernández Callejo (Eds.): ICSC-CITIES 2018, CCIS 978, pp. 18–28, 2019.
https://doi.org/10.1007/978-3-030-12804-3_2

Smart solutions to be developed for our cities can be directly applied on the university campuses. The main reason is that universities and their campuses can be seen as urban areas with a reduced scale, but they have to face similar challenges than the city managers [27]. There are several initiatives aiming at applying intelligent systems to provide advanced services to the university community members, e.g., *Smart Campus of UMA*[1], *Smart Campus-Unicamp*[2] of Unicamp in Sao Paulo (Brasil), *DTU-Smart Campus*[3] of Technical University of Denmark, and *UIJ-Smart Campus*[4] of Universitat Jaume I in Castellón (Spain). These smart campus services range from a smart classrooms, which benefits the teaching process within a classroom, to an intelligent campus that provides lots of proactive services in a campus-wide environment [27].

In this context, we focus on the analysis of the spatio-temporal behavior of the people through the Campus of Teatinos of the University of Málaga (UMA). We used the data captured by a cyber-physical system based on a wireless sensor network (WSN) installed along the campus. This system was devised in the context of Smart Campus Project of UMA [21]. These sensors are able to detect the Bluetooth and Wi-Fi wireless signals of the devices carried by the people and extract the hardware MAC (Media Access Control) addresses to identify them individually. This low cost alternative is experiencing a fast development, since it is very cheap and easy to maintain [15].

The main goal of this study is to perform an analysis of the data captured by the sensors installed in the campus in order to evaluate people movement. The extracted knowledge would be very interesting for the university managers since they would know how many people are in the different areas of the campus depending on the time and how they move. This knowledge could be used to design and to assess the services provided according to the influx of the people, to take decisions about the schedules to avoid overcrowding, etc.

In the next section, we summarize a set of different studies that deal with human tracking. Section 3 describes the experiments carried out. Section 4 presents the experimental results and their main findings. Finally, conclusions and future work are considered in Sect. 5.

2   Related Work

During the last decades, collecting data about the spatio-temporal behavior (movement) of individuals has got the attention of academia and industry, since it provides useful information to be used in a number of domains, such as, crowd management, safety management or consumer research [26].

Traditionally, the human tracking studies were performed by the application of some slow and inefficient methods such as shadowing [12], collecting

---

[1] https://www.uma.es/smart-campus/.

[2] http://smartcampus.prefeitura.unicamp.br/.

[3] http://www.smartcampus.dtu.dk/.

[4] http://smart.uji.es/.

travel diaries [2], and surveys [9]. All these methods require the direct interaction between humans to get the required data. This methodology was improved by applying more technologically advanced methods, such as light curtains [11], which is very limited due to the impossibility to identify individually each person to develop human paths, to calculate the duration of the movement or to get more complex information about the behavior of the people. The advances in image processing methods facilitated the emergence of video tracking methods based on image and behavior recognition [18].

Nowadays, a number of applications and services are based on the user identification by using Radio Frequency Identification (RFID) technologies taking the advance of the common use of smart cards, smart wearables, and other type of smart devices equipped with such technology [4]. Besides, Global Positioning System (GPS) based approaches are also applied to track and to analyze the movement of people [19].

Finally, a set of new proposals are based on identifying people by getting wireless signals of the Bluetooth and the Wi-Fi interfaces of the devices carried by the humans. This is a very promising approach because most of smartphones are equipped with both type of network interfaces. Individual identification is carried out by registering the unique MAC address of the devices. Thus, different authors have applied such idea in various domanis and settings: to measure throughput time in airport security, on a large scale open air festival, on a trade fair, in an office setting, and to study the movements of tourists in a city amongst others [15].

When using Bluetooth to track individuals, Bluetooth scanners are being installed at locations of interest. These scanners continuously scan for Bluetooth signals emitted by the devices and register every detection. The method is based on the *proximity principle*. Thus, it is assumed that the device is located close to the scanner. In practice, the scanners register in the log when a device is detected (i.e., they store the scanner id, the time stamp, and the MAC address). The path can then be reconstructed by combining the logs of all scanners, where the location of each scanner is added as the location of the device.

The main issue when using Bluetooth is that the interface has to be in *mode on* to be scanned, so only a ratio of the population can be tracked. Various works showed that the detection ratio ranges between 7% and 11% [5,23,24].

Tracking by detecting Wi-Fi signals is very similar to the same by using Bluetooth. Thus, different researches have analyzed this technology since it critically improves the detection ratio [1]. The detection of Wi-Fi has been applied in tracking people in large outdoor areas [17], managing human queues [25], tracking humans in indoor environments [16], detecting pedestrian flows in different contexts as in metro areas [7], etc.

In the present study, we evaluated the applicability of Wi-Fi tracking to evaluate the spatio-temporal behavior of the members of the university community. Thus, we analyzed the data captured by the sensors installed in the context of Smart Campus of UMA.

3   Experimental Design

To carry out this work, we used a WSN installed in the university campus. The system is composed by a set of sensors connected to a central server that receives the captured data [21]. These sensors principally measure the environmental noise at the streets and detect humans by sensing the wireless devices carried by them. The data captured by this system were satisfactory used in a study about the environmental noise in the campus of UMA [10].

In order to detect humans, the sensors apply a procedure to extract MAC addresses from wireless signals sniffed by using their specialized wireless interfaces. As the MAC addresses are unique, they allow us to identify individually each device or human. The MAC addresses are stored together with a time stamp that indicates the moment when the device was detected. Thus, in this work, we used such a data to detect human flows.

In this work, we analyzed the data of two sensors: *Sensor 1* and *Sensor 2*. The first sensor is located in the facade of the School of Science and the *Sensor 2* in the facade of the School of Humanities. Both schools are located at the Boulevard Louis Pasteur, the main street that crosses the campus. The distance between the two analyzed sensors is 183 m. Figure 1 shows the location of both sensors. The used data cover the months of May and June of 2018 (from May 13, 2018 to June 30, 2018), so in the study we used the data of 61 days.

Thus, we analyzed the human movement (flows) through the university campus. With this purpose, we performed a first study about the number of devices/humans detected by each sensor. Second, we extracted and analyzed the flows of people who move through both sensors. As we have two sensors, we studied two different flows (see Fig. 1) *Flow A*, which considers the devices moving from *Sensor 1* to *Sensor 2* (i.e., from left to right), and *Flow B*, which takes into account the devices moving in the opposite direction (i.e., from right to left).

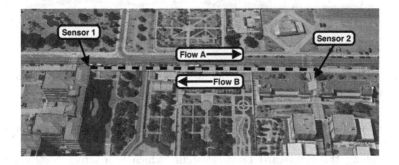

Fig. 1. Sensors location.

4   Results and Analysis

This section presents the main results and analyses. First, we study the devices (humans) detected by each sensor individually in order to evaluate the variability in the number of people that pass through the sensing points during the day. Then, we analyze different spatio-temporal aspects of the detected human flows by using the sensed data.

In this study, a given movement from the sensor s_i to the sensor s_j is detected when a given device (MAC address) is registered in s_i in a time t_{si}, and after a time Δt, the same device is detected in s_j, i.e., $t_{sj} = t_{si} + \Delta t$.

4.1   Human/Devices Detection

In order to evaluate the number of devices detected over time by the two sensors, we group the results each ten minutes. Thus, Figs. 2 and 3 shows this sensed data for the *Sensor 1* and the *Sensor 2*, respectively.

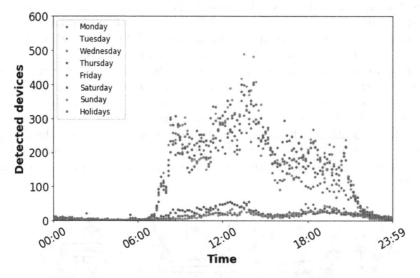

Fig. 2. Number of devices detected by *Sensor 1* over the day grouped by the week day. (Color figure online)

For both sensors, the number of sensed devices is significantly low from midnight to 7:00H. This is principally due to the location of the sensors. They are installed along the Boulevard Louis Pasteur, which is a street basically used by the university community to move through the campus. Thus, this street is marginally crossed during late night/early morning hours.

Considering the data patterns from 7:00H, when the number of detected devices increases dramatically, we can observe two main groups of data: *working days*, which includes the data from Monday to Friday, and *no working days*,

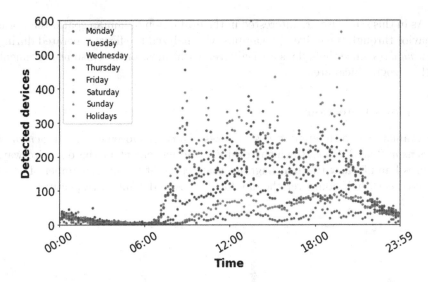

Fig. 3. Number of devices detected by *Sensor 2* over the day grouped by the week day. (Color figure online)

which includes the data of the Saturdays, the Sundays, and the holidays. These patterns are much more clear in the results of the *Sensor 1* (see Fig. 2).

Table 1 summarizes the detection results by presenting the mean and the coefficient of variation of the detected devices each ten minutes for each data group. These results show that *Sensor 1* detects more devices than *Sensor 2* during *working days*. This is mainly because *Sensor 1* is located closer to the side walk than *Sensor 2*. In turn, this longer distance from side walk provokes that *Sensor 2* presents more difficulties to detect the devices carried by humans, generating very scattered results (see Fig. 3) with higher coefficient of variation.

In contrast, during *no working days*, *Sensor 2* sensed more devices than *Sensor 1*. This is principally due to a surface parking that is located close to the School of Humanities, which is used during the whole week to park the cars. Therefore, even during weekends there are a number of people crossing through this sensor.

Table 1. Mean and coefficient of variation results of the detected devices each ten minutes grouped by *working days* and *no working days*. *All data* represents the results without any group.

Patter type	Sensor 1	Sensor 2
	Mean ± CV	Mean ± CV
Working days	112.084 ± 126.66%	100.929 ± 130.69%
No working days	15.098 ± 121.74%	45.823 ± 116.40%
All data	78.462 ± 158.97%	82.214 ± 140.24%

As in this study we are interested in the evaluation of human spatio-temporal behavior through the university campus, we analyzed the flows generated during *working days* since these days critically represent most of the existent movement in this geographical area.

4.2 Flows Detection

We evaluated two different types of flows: *Flow A*, movement from *Sensor 1* to *Sensor 2*, and *Flow B*, which considers the movement in the opposite way. Figures 4 and 5 show two bar diagrams that represent the mean number of flows detected each half hour over the day for *Flow A* and *Flow B*, respectively.

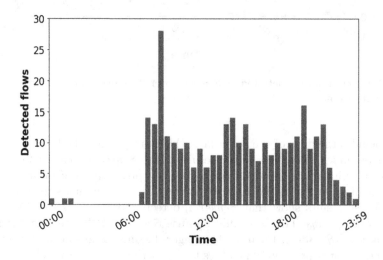

Fig. 4. Mean number of detected *Flow A* flows over the day for *working days*.

As it is shown in the figures, the distribution of the results of both types of flows are similar. In average, there were detected 244.92 movements per day from *Sensor 2* to *Sensor 1* (*Flow B*) and 229.112 *Flow A* flows, i.e., there were sensed 6.45% more *Flow B* flows than *Flow A* ones.

As it was expected, the system was not able to detect flows during late night/early morning hours. During the time period between 0:00H and 7:00H there were detected just three *Flow A* flows and two *Flow B* ones. These results are consistent with the previously presented findings in Sect. 4.1, since during that period of time the number of detected devices was negligible.

The system sensed the highest number of movements between both sensors (for both flow types) at the period of time between 8:30H and 9:00H, which corresponds to the school opening hours (i.e., most of school hours start at 8:30H or 8:45H).

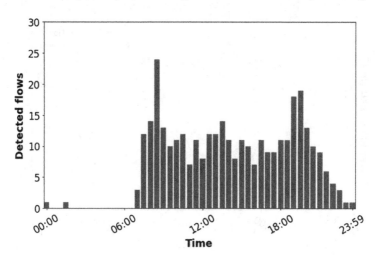

Fig. 5. Mean number of detected *Flow B* flows over the day for *working days*.

Besides, both flow types exhibited two different less marked peaks: the first one around 14:00H and the second one around 19:30H. These times correspond to school end times for the morning and late shift classes, respectively.

According to these results, in which there were a high amount of detected devices at opening hours and two lower and two noticeable rises during both school end times, we can conclude that there exists a set of people that arrives at morning and stays at the campus until late afternoon. This is quite common at UMA since there are a number of students that have to attend classes during morning and afternoon (or stays in the libraries). In general, these students use to eat in the canteen of their faculties. For this reason there were not peaks of movement during lunch time.

These insights have a direct benefit for the university managers, since they are able to show that the selection of the same opening and ending school hours for different university schools provokes the highest movement of students at similar hours. Thus, some crowding and congestion problems could be mitigated by shifting the scholar schedules.

Finally, we analyzed the speed of the detected movements. Figure 6 illustrates the mean speed detected during every half hour. There is not values during the period of time between midnight and 7:00H because there were not registered representative flows. As it can be observed, these speeds are in average relatively high for people moving by foot, about 2.8 m/s (10.1 km/h) and 3.1 m/s (11.2 km/h). This is mainly because the sensors were able to detect flows of people moving by using vehicles, e.g., bikes and cars, and people running. The movement with maximum speed sensed by our sensor was of 13.1 m/s (47.2 km/h), which would correspond to a car moving in a urban area.

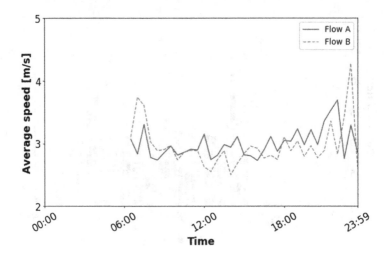

Fig. 6. Average speed of *Flow A* and *Flow B* over time.

5   Conclusions and Future Work

In this paper we studied the human spatio-temporal behavior (movement) in the Campus of Teatinos of UMA by using a WSN installed in specific locations of interest in the campus. The main aim of this study is to understand the behavior and movement of the people of the university community through the campus, which can be helpful for the university managers.

As it has been shown, the data registered by the system regarding Wi-Fi devices were useful to analyze the human flows in the campus. The results obtained confirmed numerically important intuitive observations about the movement of the people of the university community.

Thus, we showed that the are not barely people crossing the campus during late-night/early mornings hours (from 0:00H to 7:00H). In turn, the most mobility occurs during the opening (about 8:30H) and ending (about 14:00H and 19:30H) school hours. This is principally due to that the street analyzed (Boulevard Louis Pasteur) corresponds with a specifically university area (no residential area). Therefore, the system captures data from people of the university community during class schedule. Besides, we observed that there was a similar amount of flows in both studied directions (*Flow A* and *Flow B*). Finally, it is noticeable that the sensors are able to register vehicular mobility data.

As future work we plan to extend the proposed methodology by analyzing spatio-temporal behavior through the campus by combining the information of more installed sensors, applying a specific methodology to identify pedestrian and individuals moving by using vehicles, and studying together the movement knowledge extracted with other data registered by the sensors (e.g., environmental noise).

Acknowledgements. This research has been partially funded by the Spanish MINECO and FEDER projects TIN2017-88213-R (http://6city.lcc.uma.es) and TIN2016-81766-REDT (http://cirti.es). University of Malaga. International Campus of Excellence Andalucia TECH.

References

1. Abedi, N., Bhaskar, A., Chung, E., Miska, M.: Assessment of antenna characteristic effects on pedestrian and cyclists travel-time estimation based on bluetooth and WiFi MAC addresses. Transp. Res. Part C Emerg. Technol. **60**, 124–141 (2015)
2. Axhausen, K.W., Zimmermann, A., Schönfelder, S., Rindsfüser, G., Haupt, T.: Observing the rhythms of daily life: a six-week travel diary. Transportation **29**(2), 95–124 (2002)
3. Camero, A., Toutouh, J., Stolfi, D.H., Alba, E.: Evolutionary deep learning for car park occupancy prediction in smart cities. In: Battiti, R., Brunato, M., Kotsireas, I., Pardalos, P.M. (eds.) LION 12 2018. LNCS, vol. 11353, pp. 386–401. Springer, Cham (2019). https://doi.org/10.1007/978-3-030-05348-2_32
4. Fujino, T., Kitazawa, M., Yamada, T., Takahashi, M., Yamamoto, G., Yoshikawa, A., Terano, T.: Analyzingin-store shopping paths from indirect observation with RFIDtags communication data. J. Innov. Sustain. RISUS **5**(1), 88–96 (2014). ISSN 2179-3565
5. Hagemann, W., Weinzerl, J.: Automatische erfassung von umsteigern per bluetooth-technologie. Nahverkerspraxis, pp. 31–68. Springer, Heidelberg (2008)
6. Haseman, R., Wasson, J., Bullock, D.: Real-time measurement of travel time delay in work zones and evaluation metrics using bluetooth probe tracking. Transp. Res. Rec. J. Transp. Res. Board **2169**, 40–53 (2010)
7. Husted, N., Myers, S.: Mobile location tracking in metro areas: malnets and others. In: Proceedings of the 17th ACM Conference on Computer and Communications Security, pp. 85–96. ACM (2010)
8. Leduc, G.: Road traffic data: collection methods and applications. Working Papers on Energy, Transport and Climate Change, vol. 1, no. 55 (2008)
9. Liebig, T., Wagoum, A.U.K.: Modelling microscopic pedestrian mobility using bluetooth. In: ICAART, vol. 2, pp. 270–275 (2012)
10. Luque, J., Toutouh, J., Alba, E.: Reduction of the size of datasets by using evolutionary feature selection: the case of noise in a modern city. In: Herrera, F., Damas, S., Montes, R., Alonso, S., Cordón, Ó., González, A., Troncoso, A. (eds.) CAEPIA 2018. LNCS (LNAI), vol. 11160, pp. 230–239. Springer, Cham (2018). https://doi.org/10.1007/978-3-030-00374-6_22
11. McMichael, I., Khoshnevisan, M.: Uniform sensitivity light curtain, 23 July 1996. uS Patent 5,539,198
12. Millonig, A., Gartner, G.: Shadowing-tracking-interviewing: How to explore human spatio-temporal behaviour patterns. In: BMI, pp. 1–14. Citeseer (2008)
13. Mir, Z.H., Toutouh, J., Filali, F., Alba, E.: QoS-aware radio access technology (RAT) selection in hybrid vehicular networks. In: Kassab, M., Berbineau, M., Vinel, A., Jonsson, M., Garcia, F., Soler, J. (eds.) Nets4Cars/Nets4Trains/Nets4Aircraft 2015. LNCS, vol. 9066, pp. 117–128. Springer, Cham (2015). https://doi.org/10.1007/978-3-319-17765-6_11
14. Nesmachnow, S., Rossit, D., Toutouh, J.: Comparison of multiobjective evolutionary algorithms for prioritized urban waste collection in montevideo, uruguay. Electron. Notes Discret. Math. **69**, 93–100 (2018)

15. Oosterlinck, D., Benoit, D.F., Baecke, P., Van de Weghe, N.: Bluetooth tracking of humans in an indoor environment: an application to shopping mall visits. Appl. Geogr. **78**, 55–65 (2017)
16. Pirzada, N., Nayan, M.Y., Hassan, F.S.M.F., Khan, M.A.: Device-free localization technique for indoor detection and tracking of human body: a survey. Procedia Soc. Behav. Sci. **129**, 422–429 (2014)
17. Sapiezynski, P., Stopczynski, A., Gatej, R., Lehmann, S.: Tracking human mobility using WiFi signals. PloS one **10**(7), e0130824 (2015)
18. Saxena, S., Brémond, F., Thonnat, M., Ma, R.: Crowd behavior recognition for video surveillance. In: Blanc-Talon, J., Bourennane, S., Philips, W., Popescu, D., Scheunders, P. (eds.) ACIVS 2008. LNCS, vol. 5259, pp. 970–981. Springer, Heidelberg (2008). https://doi.org/10.1007/978-3-540-88458-3_88
19. Van der Spek, S., Van Schaick, J., De Bois, P., De Haan, R.: Sensing human activity: GPS tracking. Sensors **9**(4), 3033–3055 (2009)
20. Stolfi, D.H., Alba, E.: Smart mobility policies with evolutionary algorithms: the adapting info panel case. In: Proceedings of the 2015 Annual Conference on Genetic and Evolutionary Computation, GECCO 2015, pp. 1287–1294. ACM, New York (2015)
21. Toutouh, J., Arellano-Verdejo, J., Alba, E.: Enabling low cost smart road traffic sensing. In: The 12th edition of the Metaheuristics International Conference (MIC 2017), pp. 13–15 (2017)
22. Toutouh, J., Rossit, D., Nesmachnow, S.: Computational intelligence for locating garbage accumulation points in urban scenarios. In: Battiti, R., Brunato, M., Kotsireas, I., Pardalos, P.M. (eds.) LION 12 2018. LNCS, vol. 11353, pp. 411–426. Springer, Cham (2019). https://doi.org/10.1007/978-3-030-05348-2_34
23. Versichele, M., Neutens, T., Claeys Bouuaert, M., Van de Weghe, N.: Time-geographic derivation of feasible co-presence opportunities from network-constrained episodic movement data. Trans. GIS **18**(5), 687–703 (2014)
24. Versichele, M., Neutens, T., Delafontaine, M., Van de Weghe, N.: The use of bluetooth for analysing spatiotemporal dynamics of human movement at mass events: a case study of the ghent festivities. Appl. Geogr. **32**(2), 208–220 (2012)
25. Wang, Y., Yang, J., Chen, Y., Liu, H., Gruteser, M., Martin, R.P.: Tracking human queues using single-point signal monitoring. In: Proceedings of the 12th Annual International Conference on Mobile Systems, Applications, and Services, pp. 42–54. ACM (2014)
26. Yamin, M., Ades, Y.: Crowd management with RFID and wireless technologies. In: First International Conference on Networks and Communications, NETCOM 2009, pp. 439–442. IEEE (2009)
27. Yu, Z., Liang, Y., Xu, B., Yang, Y., Guo, B.: Towards a smart campus with mobile social networking. In: 2011 International Conference on Internet of Things and 4th International Conference on Cyber, Physical and Social Computing, pp. 162–169 (2011)

A New Model for Short-Term Load Forecasting in an Industrial Park

Luis Hernández-Callejo$^{(\boxtimes)}$ (iD), Angel García-Pedrero$^{(\boxtimes)}$ (iD),
and Víctor Alonso Gómez$^{(\boxtimes)}$ (iD)

Universidad de Valladolid, Campus Universitario Duques de Soria, Soria, Spain
{luis.hernandez.callejo,angelmario.garcia,
victor.alonso.gomez}@uva.es

Abstract. Nowadays, industrial parks are seen as spaces for the integration of demand and electricity generation. The proximity of the industrial parks to the Smart City, makes possible the employment of advanced techniques for the prediction of the demand and electric generation. This paper presents a complete experiment to choose a model of Short-Term Load Forecasting in industrial parks. The models used are based on artificial intelligence, and different input variables have been tested on all models.

Keywords: Short-Term Load Forecasting · Industrial park ·
Artificial intelligence · Smart City

1 Introduction

In recent times, the technological advances applied to cities and their surroundings have led to the Smart City concept. The sustainability of cities and their surroundings is one of the main interests at present [1].

As shown in [2], one of the important pillars of Smart City is energy, but this area is expanded thanks to the Smart Energy Systems concept (electricity, heating, cooling, industry, buildings and transportation). In other words, the electrification of cities and their surrounding areas is critical for the development of a society, as it appears in [3].

One of the areas close to the city with the most electricity consumption is an industrial park. These integrate a variety of industrial sectors with a very different consumption behavior. Despite new paradigms such as eco-industrial parks [4], these scenarios are in need of electrical power, and in some cases elevated.

In addition to the above, the current trend towards the integration of renewable generation sources in cities must be taken into account. This integration will be in: Smart Buildings [5], microgrids [5, 6] and industrial parks [7, 8].

In these scenarios, an industrial park is considered a microgrid, since it has distributed generation, distributed storage and loads. An emerging actor in an industrial park will be the aggregator, whose responsibility is to adjust generation to demand [9]. In order to achieve a balance of power, it is necessary to have forecasting tools, for generation and demand. Specifically, in order to operate distributed storage, it is

S. Nesmachnow and L. Hernández Callejo (Eds.): ICSC-CITIES 2018, CCIS 978, pp. 29–37, 2019.
https://doi.org/10.1007/978-3-030-12804-3_3

necessary to have short-term forecasting tools, and in the case of demand, Short-Term Load Forecasting (STLF) tools.

As it appears in [10], the forecast of the demand is already a very old challenge. These authors also show the need for new models applied to disaggregated environments, such as microgrids, industrial parks or Smart Buildings. Another of the conclusions obtained is that the models most used in the last two decades are those based on Artificial Intelligence (AI).

With respect to models based on AI for STLF in microgrids, the works found are numerous and varied. The authors in [11] present a one-stage model, where they use a Multi-Layer Perceptron (MLP), which is a model based on Artificial Neural Network (ANN). Following the ANN, other authors use two stages to finalize the prediction [12, 13].

Regardless of the chosen model, for the prediction of electrical demand it is fundamental to choose the input variables to the model correctly. Some authors focus their efforts on locating the climatic variables that most relate to the electrical demand [14]. However, other authors [15] focus their attention on the climatic variables, but also on the relationship itself with previous values of the electricity demand.

Therefore, this work presents a new model for STLF in a real industrial park. There have been numerous experiments, with several models based on AI, each of which has been tested with input variables that have been increasing in number. The final results have been satisfactory and the model obtained has a high efficiency.

The work is structured as follows. In Sect. 2 the data used are presented as well as the methodology used. Section 3 shows the results of the experiments. In Sect. 4 the results are discussed to conclude with some conclusions and future works.

2 Data and Methods

2.1 Data Description

In order to carry out this work, it was necessary to have data from a real location. The Spanish electricity company Iberdrola has provided the data to be able to do the experiment. Specifically, the data is from an industrial park located in Burgos (Spain), called "Gamonal".

The data of Iberdrola are those corresponding to the power consumption of the industrial park. The company has provided a total of 4 years. Figure 1 shows the power demand along time during the complete time under study. In order to facilitate the visualization of the data, they have been aggregated on a daily basis. Therefore, the available data set has the following information: day, month, year, 24 values of electricity demand, as well as the maximum, average and minimum temperature. These data of the electric company have been completed with the variable that indicates whether the day is workable or not.

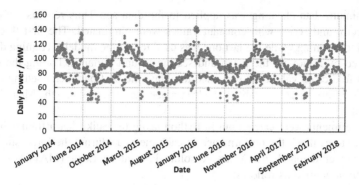

Fig. 1. Daily power demand from January of 2014 to March of 2018.

2.2 Methodology

The ability of four types of algorithms to predict the next day's hourly power demand was evaluated:

- Decision Tree Regression (DTR) [16];
- Multi-Layer Perceptron Regressor [17] with three activation functions which are ReLu (MLP_{ReLu}), Logistic ($MLP_{Logistic}$), and hyperbolic tan (MLP_{tanh});
- Support Vector Regressor [18] with three kernels which are Linear (SVR_{Linear}), Polynomial ($SVR_{Polynomial}$), and Radial Basis Function (SVR_{RBF}); and
- Gradient Boosting Trees [19] for three types of regressions which are Linear ($XGBR_{Linear}$), Gamma ($XGBR_{Gamma}$), and Tweedie ($XGBR_{Tweedie}$).

To determine the predictive capacity of the aforementioned methods, different experiments were carried out. Each experiment corresponds to different combinations of features which serve as input to these methods. The different combinations are described in Table 1.

Table 1. Features used in each experiment.

Features	Experiments						
	0	1	2	3	4	5	6
24 hourly electricity demand values for the current day	■	■	■	■	■	■	■
Is the current day a working day? [0,1]		■	■	■	■	■	■
Is the next day a working day? [0,1]			■	■	■	■	■
Weekday of the current day [1-7]				■	■	■	■
Weekday of the next day [1-7]				■	■	■	■
Minimum temperature of the current day					■	■	■
Maximum temperature of the current day					■	■	■
Average temperature of the current day						■	■
Minimum temperature of the next day							■
Maximum temperature of the next day							■
Average temperature of the next day							■

A minimum data cleaning was applied to the data set. Thus records with values equal to zero, and series with constant values were eliminated. The first three years were used for training while the last one was used to test the models. Training data was standardized by removing the mean and scaling to unit variance. During the training phase, a 3-fold cross validation was used to obtain the best parameter setting for each model. The criteria used to establish the best model was to minimize the Mean Squared Error (MSE).

All experiments were carried out in Python using the Scikit-learn framework [20].

In order to evaluate the performance of each methods during the forecasting of the electrical power demand, the Mean Absolute Percentage Error (MAPE) was used. The MAPE is defined as follows:

$$MAPE = \frac{100\%}{n} \sum_{t=1}^{n} \left| \frac{A_t - F_t}{A_t} \right| \tag{1}$$

where A_t is the actual value, F_t is the predicted value, and n is the total of observation in time series.

3   Results and Discussion

The results expressed in MAPE of all experiments are shown in Fig. 2. Logically, the MAPE is greater on those hours which have more standard deviation and lower on those with less standard deviation. It can also be seen that for some methods, like SVRLinear, MLPtanh and, especially, $XGBR_{Gamma}$, the dependence of the experiment assumptions for training the network is not very significant. On the other hand, other methods, like MLP_{ReLu}, $XGBR_{Linear}$ and $XGBR_{Tweedie}$ are very sensible to those kind of information. As the shape of all graphs is smooth and consistent, it is possible to leave just the best experiment (or experiments if they are nearly) in each of the method for a better comparison between them. Due to that, it is also possible to average the daily error, probed that all the methods have maximums and minimums at similar time intervals.

Figure 3 shows the daily average of the hourly MAPE values displayed in Fig. 2 for all methods and experiments. In Fig. 4, worse methods have been removed for each experiment, i.e. $SVR_{Polynomial}$, DTR, MLP_{tanh} and $XGBR_{Gamma}$. There clearly can be seen that experiments 3 to 6 has obtained better results than 0 to 2 so, finally, in Fig. 5, just the experiments and methods which have obtained significantly better results than the rest, are shown. These three methods, MLP_{Relu}, $XGBR_{Linear}$ and $XGBR_{Tweedie}$, are the best for our dataset. Additional studies over other similar datasets are necessary to conclude if they are significantly better always or just in this case. Moreover, if the results crown them as always the best, it would be interesting to look inside their basics and find if there is some logical reason in order to extrapolate this conclusion over a more general dataset of energetic demand as residential or heavy industrial scenarios.

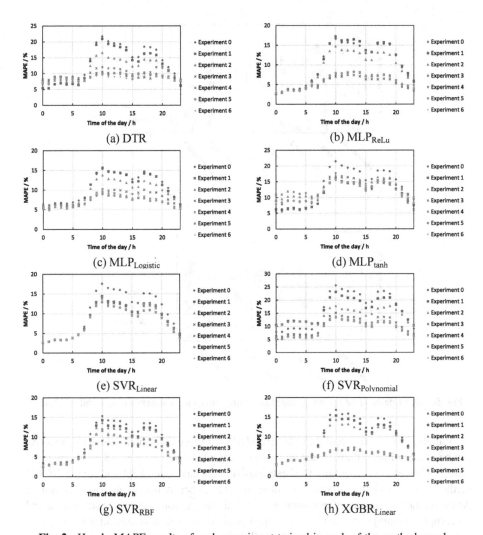

Fig. 2. Hourly MAPE results of each experiment trained in each of the methods used.

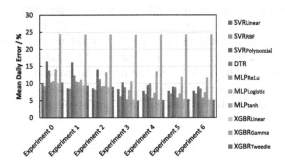

Fig. 3. Mean daily error (in percentage) for all methods and experiments.

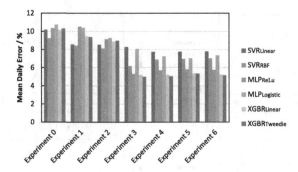

Fig. 4. Mean daily error (in percentage) excluding worse methods.

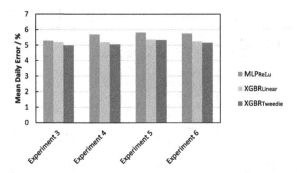

Fig. 5. Mean daily error (in percentage) including only the best experiments and methods.

Finally, in Figs. 6, 7 and 8 the hourly MAPE of these three methods are shown. As can be seen, in Fig. 6 there is just one experiment while in Figs. 7 and 8, there are three or four. The reason is that only the bests experiments have been kept and for the XGBR methods, the difference between some of the experiments is almost negligible. Anyway, the conclusion of our study is that without previous classification of data and no complex assumptions, we have obtained predictions with less than an 8% error over the real power necessities anytime. And all these finally selected models have between 3% and 5% of error over 10 h of the 24 of the day. This can seem not very accurate, but taking into account that the standard deviation of the mean consumption for each hour goes from 11% to 25%, it is a very good result. Even more if we think that this precision probably cannot be achieved by an experienced human without a lot of hours of effort and that, this technique, can be automatized (and retrained if it is needed) with much less effort and cost. It would be interesting for future works study if a clusterization of data previously to the training gives better results and which kind of patterns is able to detect which, surely, we have not took into account.

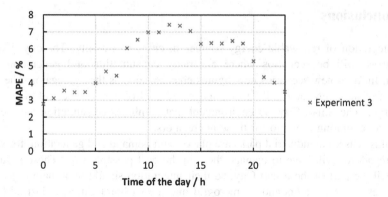

Fig. 6. MAPE (%) obtained by MLP$_{ReLu}$ in Experiment 3

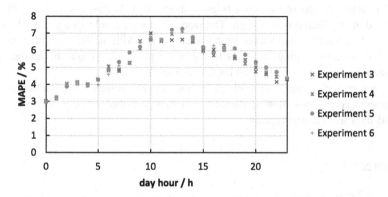

Fig. 7. MAPE (%) obtained by XGBR$_{Linear}$ in Experiments 3, 4, 5, and 6.

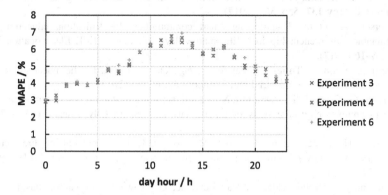

Fig. 8. MAPE (%) obtained by XGBR$_{Tweedie}$ in Experiments 3, 4, and 6.

4   Conclusions

The integration of renewable energy sources in cities is a reality. The city, like the microgrids, will be scenarios where electricity consumption and generation must coexist. In these new scenarios new figures emerge, such as the aggregator. The main function of the aggregator will be to manage and control the demand and the existing generation. The Smart City, an environment that combines consumption and generation, is an operating scenario for these aggregators.

In this sense, the industrial parks are places with demand and generation, for which the agregadores will have to manage them in the best possible way. These industrial parks will be part of the Smart City, so their integration should be a main objective.

Therefore, aggregators and/or microgrid managers (Smart Cities, Industrial Parks, etc.) will need forecasting tools, both demand and generation.

New models of electric demand prediction must be tested and validated (for industrial parks). In this sense, this work has shown that AI-based models are of great interest and their effectiveness is high. The work shows the results of a group of models to make STLF, and the results have been presented. In addition, the work demonstrates the need to have interesting variables to solve the problem, so that the models have been tested for different input variables (experiment).

The authors will continue to work on finding better solutions for prediction in these environments. The application of climatic variables to improve the problem is a next step, and then use clustering tools.

References

1. Lazaroiu, G.C., Roscia, M.: Definition methodology for the smart cities model. Energy **47**(1), 326–332 (2012)
2. Lund, H., Østergaard, P.A., Connolly, D., Mathiesen, B.V.: Smart energy and smart energy systems. Energy **137**, 556–565 (2017)
3. Anderson, A., et al.: Empowering smart communities: Electrification, education, and sustainable entrepreneurship in IEEE smart village initiatives. IEEE Electrification Mag. **5**(2), 6–16 (2017)
4. Valero, A., Usón, S., Torres, C., Valero, A., Agudelo, A., Costa, J.: Thermoeconomic tools for the analysis of eco-industrial parks. Energy **62**, 62–72 (2013)
5. De Luca, G., Fabozzi, S., Massarotti, N., Vanoli, L.: A renewable energy system for a nearly zero greenhouse city: case study of a small city in southern Italy. Energy **143**, 347–362 (2018)
6. Mirez, J., Hernandez-Callejo, L., Horn, M., Bonilla, L.-M.: Simulation of direct current microgrid and study of power and battery charge/discharge management. DYNA **92**(6), 673–679 (2017)
7. Timmerman, J., Vandevelde, L., Van Eetvelde, G.: Towards low carbon business park energy systems: classification of techno-economic energy models. Energy **75**, 68–80 (2014)
8. Jin, D.-G., Choi, J.-C., Won, D.-J., Lee, H.-J., Chae, W.-K., Park, J.-S.: A practical protection coordination strategy applied to secondary and facility microgrids. Energies **5**(9), 3248–3265 (2012)

9. Gkatzikis, L., Koutsopoulos, I., Salonidis, T.: The role of aggregators in smart grid demand response markets. IEEE J. Sel. Areas Commun. **31**(7), 1247–1257 (2013)
10. Hernandez, L., et al.: A survey on electric power demand forecasting: future trends in smart grids, microgrids and smart buildings. IEEE Commun. Surv. Tutor. **16**(3), 1460–1495 (2014)
11. Hernández, L., et al.: Artificial neural network for short-term load forecasting in distribution systems. Energies **7**(3), 1576–1598 (2014)
12. Amjady, N., Keynia, F., Zareipour, H.: Short-term load forecast of microgrids by a new bilevel prediction strategy. IEEE Trans. Smart Grid **1**(3), 286–294 (2010)
13. Hernández, L., Baladrón, C., Aguiar, J.M., Carro, B., Sánchez-Esguevillas, A.: Classification and clustering of electricity demand patterns in industrial parks. Energies **5**(12), 5215–5228 (2012)
14. Vu, D.H., Muttaqi, K.M., Agalgaonkar, A.P.: A variance inflation factor and backward elimination based robust regression model for forecasting monthly electricity demand using climatic variables. Appl. Energy **140**, 385–394 (2015)
15. Hernández, L.: Experimental analysis of the input variables relevance's to forecast next day's aggregated electric demand using neural networks. Energies **6**(6), 2927–2948 (2013)
16. Breiman, L., Friedman, J.H., Olshen, R.A., Stone, C.J.: Classification and Regression Trees. Wadsworth International Group, Belmont (1984)
17. Rumelhart, D.E., Hinton, G.E., Williams, R.J.: Learning representations by back-propagating errors. Nature **323**(6088), 533 (1986)
18. Vapnik, V.: The Nature of Statistical Learning Theory. Springer, New York (2013)
19. Friedman, J.H.: Greedy function approximation: a gradient boosting machine. Ann. Stat. **29**, 1189–1232 (2001)
20. Pedregosa, F., et al.: Scikit-learn: machine learning in Python. J. Mach. Learn. Res. **12**, 2825–2830 (2011)

PVCOM Project: Manufacture of PV Modules Encapsulated in Composite Materials for Integration in Urban Environments

Elena Rico[1], Irene Huerta[1(✉)], Teodosio del Caño[1], Loreto Villada[1],
Ángel Gallego[1], Vicente Velasco[1], Oihana Zubillaga[2],
José María Vega de Seoane[2], Igor Arrizabalaga[2], Naiara Yurrita[2],
Jon Aizpurua[2], Gorka Imbuluzketa[2], and Francisco J. Cano[2]

[1] Onyx Solar Energy S.L., Rio Cea 1, 05004 Ávila, Spain
ihuerta@onyxsolar.com
[2] Parque Científico y Tecnológico de Gipuzkoa,
Mikeletegi Pasealekua 2, 20009 San Sebastian, Spain

Abstract. PVCOM project has as objective the development of new solutions for the integration of PV technology in urban applications. Despite traditional glass-glass configuration, the use of composite materials for encapsulation is proposed because its high transparency, low weight and great integration possibilities. Four solutions, a solar table, a solar slate tile, a PV shelter and an electric vehicle roof are proposed. For each proposed application conceptual designs using c-Si and CIGS technologies are done. Conceptual designs are based on legal and end-user's requirements and involved technologies limitations. More appropriated resin systems and PV system configuration have been also defined. Conceptual designs will be used as reference for the manufacturing of conceptual-proof specimens, testing and the detailed design of final prototypes.

Keywords: Photovoltaic · Composite materials · BIPV · CIGS

1 Introduction: State of Art of the Photovoltaic Technology in Urban Environments

Use of BIPV in urban elements is a reality. There are many examples of PV technology integrated as building elements but also in urban furniture or vehicles, boosted by the BIPV modules adaptability to end-user's requirements regarding transparency, colour or glass treatments.

Specifically for the proposed applications, the attempts for the integration of PV elements are especially numerous for vehicles and roof tiles to the point that, nowadays, several solutions are already available. For PV solutions for roof applications, some representative examples are the products developed by Solardachstein [1], Solarcentury [2], Lumeta [3], SRS Energy Solutions [4] and Tesla [5].

S. Nesmachnow and L. Hernández Callejo (Eds.): ICSC-CITIES 2018, CCIS 978, pp. 38–52, 2019.
https://doi.org/10.1007/978-3-030-12804-3_4

To date, there are no commercial full-solar vehicles, although some conceptual designs [6–8] and prototypes have been shown, such as the solar vehicles of Sono-Motors [9] and Lightyear [10] that are expected to be ready for market by 2019. Integration of PV solutions in vehicles is strongly limited by geometry of PV traditional solutions and their characteristics (fragility, weight, etc....) which limit the amount of PV elements that can be integrated and, in consequence, the power obtained is relatively low. Usual efforts for the integration in vehicles have been done to incorporate photovoltaic technology as a complement of the main energy source or to feed secondary systems such as air conditioning system or auxiliary lights [11].

Regarding the urban furniture, examples found during state of the art revision are fewer. For the PV shelter, several attempts for PV integration can be discussed: PV canopy installed in Canary Wharf (London) [12], tree-like street furniture, equipped with solar panels, provides free-of-charge services developed by JCDecaux [13], and LED elements powered by PV technology in San Francisco promoted by SFMTA and the organization Clear Channel Outdoor (CCO) [14]. Onyx Solar has experience in the design and development of PV shelters. Among all the projects carried out to date two of them stand out: the Union City Station PV shelter installed in San Francisco (USA) with a total area about 1.600 m^2 and a power over to 170.000 kWh per year [15] and the PV shelter developed and installed in the district Cuatro de Marzo in Valladolid (Spain) in the frame of the project R2Cities (European Union's Seventh Programme with Grant Agreement No 314473) for the development of district renovation strategies to achieve nearly zero energy cities [16].

Onyx Solar has already developed a product for the integration of PV technology in urban and outdoor furniture [17]. It consists of a photovoltaic glass module and the electric equipment needed for the connection of electronic devices that can be easily installed in the furniture element [18].

2 PVCOM Project: Objectives, Methodologies and Challenges

Onyx Solar participates as coordinator of PVCOM Project (Multifunctional Photovoltaic Devices Based on Transparent Composite and CIGS for Integration) in consortium with FLISOM AG (Switzerland) assuming partner role and with Tecnalia (R&I) (Spain) as a subcontracted research centre. PVCOM is co-funded by the European Union Horizon 2020 Research and Innovation Programme, the Eurostars Programme, the State Secretariat for Education, Research and Innovation (SERI) of Switzerland and the Centre for the Development of Industrial Technology (CDTI) of Spain.

PVCOM targets the development of new applications based on multifunctional materials to enhance the utilization of photovoltaic solutions in the framework of the specifications and requirements of BIPV (Building Integrated Photovoltaic) and Smart Cities sectors.

Although glass-glass encapsulated traditional photovoltaic (PV) solutions are frequently and successfully used in BIPV, some of their characteristics, such as the restricted flat geometry, relatively high weight and mechanical restrictions can limit their use and complicate a complete integration.

To navigate through the limitations of the actual market-available photovoltaic solutions, PVCOM proposes the utilization of composite materials as encapsulation media. The use of composite materials would allow the manufacture of PV modules with more complex geometries and reduced weight (about 43% if compared with single-glass solutions of equivalent thickness and about 60% with respect to double-glass products) but keeping the mechanical and optical properties of glass-glass encapsulated modules. In this encapsulation method c-Si cells or CIGS submodules are completely embedded in the composite resulting in a monolithic unit combining photovoltaic and structural properties that both protect PV elements against the environment and facilitate integration, replacing original components instead of placing/attaching the modules onto pre-existing surfaces. In addition to the advantages regarding the final product, composite manufacturing is based on a one-step process (cell encapsulation and final product manufacturing is done in the same step) without extra stages for lamination or composite substrate manufacturing which reduce the costs and simplify the processes.

PVCOM developments are focused on three specific sectors: building envelopes, urban mobility and urban furniture for which four different products are defined, namely, a solar tile, a photovoltaic roof for an electric vehicle, a photovoltaic shelter and a solar table.

2.1 Objectives

The goals of PVCOM are not just the development of a new technology for the composite encapsulation of photovoltaic elements but also to produce prototypes for specific and real applications with the perspective of a future commercialization. To ensure the success of the project, several intermediate goals and objectives have been defined related to the technical but also to the economic challenges of the project.

- The identification of the key requirements and limitations for the integration of the photovoltaic elements in each sector regarding the final product with consideration of the materials, the manufacturing processes and the market demands and legislations.
- The attainment of new photovoltaic materials based on CIGS and c-Si cells encapsulated in composite materials with the necessary properties in terms of durability, design flexibility, lightweight, optical and mechanical properties, aesthetic and market acceptance.
- The development of an encapsulation system for the manufacturing of CIGS and c-Si modules that responds to all the requirements identified.
- The building and testing of several prototypes to demonstrate the technical viability (including electrical efficiency, mechanical and optical properties, durability and sustainability) but also the social, economic and environmental benefits related to the use of PV technologies in urban applications.
- The development of an adequate dissemination plan to enhance the interest and the awareness about the use of photovoltaic technologies in urban applications.

2.2 Methodology

The consecution of the objectives of the project demands a double methodology: one for the design and definition of prototypes for each specified application and one for the manufacture of the innovative PV modules.

Methodology for the design and definition of the prototypes for the specific applications is based on the periodic identification and evaluation of those requirements and limits that could be considered critical for the obtaining of a suitable design but also for its acceptance by the end-users. During the project, especially during the conceptual phases of the design, a deep analysis of the state of the art, the market expectations and the legislation related to each application is done. Using the information gathered as a baseline it is possible to determine which requirements are mandatory for the design (e.g. legal limitations regarding the normative and standards or stability against environmental agents) and which, although important, could be considered as desirable but not strictly necessary. An adequate design and an appropriate identification of the requirements expected for the prototypes can reduce the impact and/or the probability of that could jeopardize the success of the project:

- Regulatory framework, standards and certifications.
- Quality levels and end-users' expectations.
- Market barriers.

Methodology for the manufacture of innovative PV modules is based on a patent application of Tecnalia R&I (WO2016/038000 and EP3006181) [19]. Patents describe not only the method of manufacturing composite-encapsulated PV modules but also include important information about the resins, the fibres and the additives that are used as reference for the selection of the most appropriate materials for each prototype.

Manufacturing of the composite PV modules is summarized in Fig. 1. A mould is used to fix the shape and geometry of the piece over which the fibre layers that are going to be the front part of the unit are placed. Once these fibres are placed and perfectly adapted to the mould, the PV elements (c-Si in the example or CIGS submodules) are positioned and electrically connected. Then, fibre layers for the backside of the piece are added until the desired thickness is obtained. This way, it is possible to use different fibre materials for the front and backside of the modules, enhancing the possibilities of functionalization and customization of the final product.

An auxiliary ply is used to facilitate the removal of the vacuum bag and ensure a good finish, the vacuum points, the resin channels and the vacuum bag are assembled and sealed. Finally, vacuum is created inside the bag to feed the mixture of resin and additives into the piece. Once the infusion is completed, the piece is left on the mould until curing is finished. If necessary, an oven can be used during the curing stage.

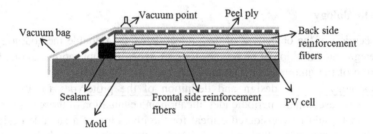

Fig. 1. Diagram of the encapsulation of the PV modules (Adapted from [19]).

Range of reinforcements and resins systems for composite manufacturing available in the market is huge. Although a detailed selection of the most appropriate ones have to be done according to the specified requirements defined for each prototype, general criteria for selection has been fixed regarding:

– Chemical compatibility and stability among composite and electrical components.
– Final transparency and optical properties of the composite, especially for those materials that are going to compound the frontal side of the module.
– Resistance against external agents.
– Density and viscosity of the resin system to ensure the correct flux along the piece and the wetting of the fibres.

The use of composite materials for the encapsulation of photovoltaic elements allows the creation of new types of modules with special characteristics such as more complex geometries and shapes, special surface finishes and features, reduced weight and increased resilience. However, it also implies some technological challenges that should be considered to guarantee the success of the developments. Some of the main challenges that PVCOM has to deal with are:

– The difficulty of manufacturing large size units with complex geometries while maintaining adequate quality levels.
– The manufacture of modules with curved surfaces.
– Optimization of the amount of fibre layers.

During the project, specimens, proof-of-concepts and prototypes generated as the results of the work done will be tested and characterized to validate the progress and, if necessary, correct deviations or mistakes that could risk the success of the project and the prototypes. Methodologies and designs would be modified in consequence.

3   Project Progress

PVCOM started in May 2017 and has a total duration of 30 months. The results and preliminary designs discussed below correspond to the project progress done until the submission of this paper and may vary depending on the evolution of the project.

3.1 Definition of the Photovoltaic Elements

Each specimen and prototype developed in this project will be composed of two differentiated integrated elements: the PV element and the composite system. Regarding the photovoltaic technology, a double approximation is proposed using crystalline silicon cells and CIGS modules. This double approximation aims not just to guarantee the project success but also the demonstration of new applications for the technologies involved in the project and identification of synergies and incompatibilities.

Regarding the c-Si technology, the selection is justified due to the high efficiency, acceptability and availability on the market. Specific pseudosquare monocrystaline silicon cells with a dimension of 156 mm × 156 mm and a thickness of 180 μm are used for this project. The main electrical properties of these c-Si cells are summarized in Table 1. Ranges are given since these c-Si cells can be provided with different electrical properties.

Table 1. Electrical properties of c-Si cells used in PVCOM project.

Properties at standard test conditions			
Fill factor (%)	79.08–79.98	I_{mpp} (A)	8.65–8.80
V_{oc} (V)	0.654–0.664	P_{mpp} (W)	4.59–5.04
I_{sc} (A)	9.19–9.33	Efficiency (%)	19.18–21.06
V_{mpp} (V)	0.550–0.563		

Configuration (number and distribution) of the c-Si cells for each prototype was realized with the objective of maximizing the surface covered but keeping a certain degree of transparency. Appropriate distances between cells and between strings have been defined to ensure enough space to allow the resin flux along the piece.

Besides the use of these c-Si cells, the use of back contact c-Si cells was also considered and analysed although it was finally dismissed. Dismissing was based on the fact that back contact cells need a special welding procedure that could complicate the development of the prototypes, the cost is relatively higher than for regular monocrystalline cells and that the introduction of a third PV technology would increase the complexity of the project further than the defined scope and objectives.

Despite the good performance of c-Si cells, a new generation of PV technologies is becoming more and more promising reaching values of performance and efficiency that could compete with traditional technologies. On this new generation different technologies are included such as dye sensitized cells (DSSC), perovskites, organic photovoltaic, tandem cells and CIGS technology. For this project, CIGS technology for the development of the proposed applications was selected.

CIGS submodules developed and manufactured by FLISOM are supported by flexible substrates that simplify the fabrication, potentially reduce the cost (compared to 1st and 2nd generation) and facilitate integration by allowing more complex designs perfectly fitted to each specific application. FLISOM has developed proprietary machinery and roll-to-roll production technology for low-temperature deposition of

CIGS and multiple thin film layers on high-grade plastic substrate. Monolithic inter-
connections are done by laser patterning technology, which allows FLISOM to adapt
the shape and electrical output of a module to customer requirements.

FLISOM's manufacture procedure allows the customization of the submodules to
adapt them to the end application requirements. Based on that, the most appropriate
submodules with respect to their dimensions but also the separation lines and the
contact areas are discussed and defined for each prototype. Where possible, standard
CIGS submodules used for the commercial module eFlex 0.8 m have been selected to
be used for the prototypes. The decision is based on the fact that standard submodules
are optimized regarding the surface coverage and the CIGS foil usage. Electrical and
thermal characteristics as well as dimensions of the module are summarized in the
specification sheet available at FLISOM's web page [20] (Fig. 2).

Fig. 2. Flexible solar panels developed by FLISOM [20].

For the solar tile prototype it is not possible to use standard submodules due to
incompatible dimensions and geometry of the design. In this case, non-standard submodules sized 170 mm × 170 mm are proposed. More details about the solar tile
prototype are discussed in further sections.

3.2 Definition of the Composite System

A typical composite system includes different elements. The main ones are the resin
system and the reinforcement fibres, but other additives can be needed or added
depending on the resin and fibres used and the final target application of the composite.

A detailed analysis of alternatives available for each element of the composite
system was done to determine the most adequate one. The selection was done
according to the requirements defined for each prototype with regard to general
knowledge about composite material, commercial availability and Tecnalia's previous
experience. After analysis of the requirements, prototypes were divided into two categories: one for the solar table and one for the PV shelter, the solar tile and the solar
roof for electrical vehicles. Division is based on special requirements regarding abrasion and cleanability defined for the solar table prototype. Table 2 summarizes the
encapsulation system defined for each prototype.

Table 2. Composite system proposed for each prototype.

	Solar tile, PV shelter and electrical vehicle roof	Solar table
Resin system	Type: Epoxy	Type: Epoxy
Reinforcement	Type: E Glass Areal weight: 160 g/cm^2 Fabric type: Woven fabric, 0/90°	Type: E Glass Areal weight: 160 g/cm^2 Fabric type: Woven fabric, 0/90°
Surface finish	Type: Polyurethane-acrylic varnish	Type: Thin-glass

For the solar table, an ultra-glass is proposed as the protection material to guarantee enhanced resistance against abrasion and wear expected from regular use.

Customization and aesthetic finishing are key requirements for all prototypes since acceptance by the end-users ultimately depends on them. Alternatives for aesthetic finishes have been evaluated and defined. Composite materials can be customized in various ways by the selection of paints, pigmented resins, coloured fibre or veils. For the prototypes planned in this project, the following selections have been considered: coloured glass fibre, coloured carbon-kevlar fabric and coloured/patterned veils.

Use of carbon or Kevlar fibres can be especially of interest for some applications where mechanical strength is necessary such as for the electrical vehicle roof. Combinations of different kinds of fibres, although possible, are not obvious and some difficulties may appear during manufacturing (delamination and distortion), so further essays and tests have to be done before considering to include them in the prototypes designs.

Independently of the procedure detailed in Tecnalia's patents [19], there are different composite manufacturing methods that could be used for the prototypes defined for this project. Vacuum bag resin infusion and resin transfer moulding (RTM) were analysed to qualify their viability. Selection of the most appropriate manufacturing method depends not just on the final application of the unit but also its size, geometry, quality and batch size. Initially a vacuum bag resin infusion method is proposed for all the prototypes, thereafter, for the development of first specimens and prototypes the use of RTM technology will be evaluated (Table 3).

Table 3. Comparison of resin infusion and RTM processes

Resin infusion	RTM
(−) Only one side of the module has a moulded finish.	(+) Both sides of the module have a moulded finish.
(+) Much lower tooling cost due to one half of the mould being a vacuum bag, and less strength required in the main tool.	(−) Tooling is expensive, and heavy, in order to withstand pressure.
(−) Unimpregnated areas can occur resulting in very expensive scrap parts.	(+) Possible labour reductions.
	(−) Unimpregnated areas can occur resulting in very expensive scrap parts.
	(+) High fibre volume laminates can be obtained with very low void contents.
	(+) Better health and safety, and environmental control due to enclosure of the resin.

3.3 Conceptual Designs

For each prototype, the conceptual design has been defined using specifications and requirements identified, the composite system and the PV elements discussed previously.

Photovoltaic Shelter

The proposed prototype is a modular photovoltaic shelter. Photovoltaic behaviour is obtained by replacing elements of the existing cover with a new photovoltaic cover formed by PV cells or CIGS submodules encapsulated between a fibre-reinforced composite. The PV cover will be attached to the shelter structure mechanically using standard elements such as rivets or bolts.

The conceptual design has dimensions of 1 m × 1.5 m with a bending curvature of 0.2 m. Total longitude of the prototype can be modified by increasing or decreasing the number of units. Dimensions were selected to be representative of the huge variety of designs and models of shelters already available on the market although they could be easily adapted to specific requirements. The entire surface will be covered by PV elements even for CIGS and c-Si design. The curvature radius has been carefully estimated to minimize the risk of cracking or damage of the cells, but this aspect of the design could be modified according to the results of preliminary tests. If necessary, c-Si cell positions could be limited to zones with smaller curvature radii.

For this prototype, semitransparency has been considered to be desirable requirement and as a consequence no aesthetic elements that could reduce it will be used. For the same reason, c-Si cells and CIGS submodule configurations have been done with the objective of maximize photovoltaic capacity while keeping a proper degree of transparency. For crystalline technology, 40 cells with a configuration of 8 × 5 (cells x strings) was defined resulting in a transparency of 65% and a power of 184–198 Wp (123–132 Wp/m^2). For CIGS technology, prototypes will have three standard submodules with a 54% of transparency and a power about 75–90 Wp (50–60 Wp/m^2).

Expected generated energy could be enough to feed (directly or using batteries) smart urban elements, such as signals, traffic lights, lamp posts or even electrical car recharging points, but also to be fed to the energy grid. Final electric applications will depend on the demands of final applications (Fig. 3).

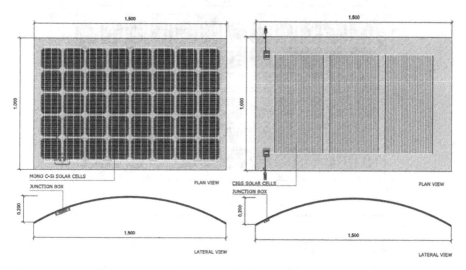

Fig. 3. Conceptual design for PV shelter, c-Si configuration (left) and CIGS configuration (right)

Electric Vehicle Roof

The proposed prototype consists of several PV cells or CIGS submodules encapsulated in an E-glass fibre reinforced composite and fully integrated as the roof of a semi-industrial electrical vehicle. The prototype is designed to be part of the vehicle structure while generating electrical energy that could be used by the vehicle to feed secondary systems (such as illumination or air conditioning) or as a complement to the primary driving system (electrical battery charging during parking periods). This dual purpose prototype requires appropriate mechanical and resistance properties as well as electrical compatibility with the vehicle electric systems.

Dimensions of conceptual design were defined according to a pre-selected vehicle model for demonstration: a semi-industrial four-wheel vehicle manufactured by ALKE. Demonstration will be done on a cargo bed roof, as the surface is greater than for the driver cabin. The conceptual design has dimensions of 2.28 m × 1.14 m, large enough surfaces to place 5 CIGS standard submodules and 72 c-Si cells (6 × 12 layout). Electrical power obtained for CIGS and c-Si alternative is 125–150 Wp (48.3–57.9 Wp/m^2) and 330–356 Wp (127.4–137.4 Wp/m^2).

For these prototypes transparency has not be identified as a desirable parameter so, besides protective elements previously discussed, alternative aesthetics coatings or reinforcements will be used to enhance the acceptability of the product and adapt it to colours and finishing qualities for the large catalogue and manufacturers of electrical vehicles. Prototypes will be attached to the vehicle structure by mechanically fixing elements like rivets, bolts or inserts (Fig. 4).

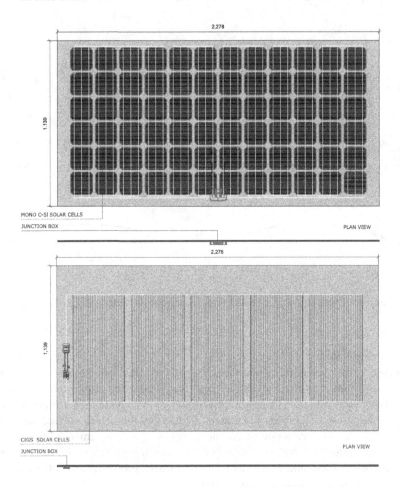

Fig. 4. Conceptual design for PV shelter, c-Si and CIGS configuration

Solar Table

The proposed prototype is a photovoltaic table made with composite material to be used as an urban furniture table. The solar table is formed by two main elements: table-top and table legs. Table-top is the main element of the prototype and constitutes the photovoltaic element. It consists of several PV cells or CIGS submodules embedded into a fibre-reinforced composite. Conceptual design includes curved zones to differentiate it from other solar tables already on the market and to show the potential of composite technology to the manufacturing of pieces with curves or complex geometries.

Preliminary approximations for the design of the solar table were done including c-Si cells on curved zones, although after preliminary analysis, this idea was dismissed because the risk of c-Si cells' cracking was too high. When CIGS submodules are used, no limitations are expected since CIGS submodules are flexible. Conceptual design dimensions (1.773 m × 0.8 m × 0.705 m) are fixed according to end-use sector and end-users' requirements, including accessibility recommendations, typical dimensions of tables of urban furniture sector, composite manufacturing expected limitations and photovoltaic performance optimization.

PV configuration has been done to maximize the photovoltaic capacity. For c-Si technology 24 cells are placed with a 4 × 6 configuration with a power or 110–119 Wp (77.7–83.9 Wp/m^2). CIGS configurations have four standard submodules to generate a power of 100–120 Wp (70.5–84.6 Wp/m^2). Transparency is kept on conceptual design, since it can be considered as a valuable element that differentiates this design from others, although alternatives for opaque or coloured designs are considered (Fig. 5).

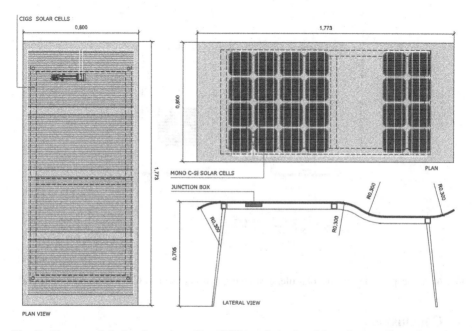

Fig. 5. Conceptual design for solar table, CIGS configuration (plan view), c-Si configuration (plan view) and lateral view

Photovoltaic Slate Tile

Proposed conceptual design of prototype consists of a rectangular slate tile in which a squared formed cast has been created. Onto the cast, a composite piece with a PV cell or a 170 mm × 170 mm CIGS submodule (depending on the PV technology used) is placed. The composite piece is fully integrated with tile structure and it is fixed using mechanical elements or adhesives.

The tile dimensions and position of each PV element on the tile are based on the cell dimensions and the tiles' pattern on the roof. For the standard pattern just the bottom third of each tile remains uncovered by other tiles; this means that the tile dimension should be big enough to accommodate a PV element on the bottom third. Taking into account these limitations, among the regular slate tile models available on the market, the selected tile dimensions for this application are 600 mm × 300 mm.

Each tile will have just one c-Si cell or a 170 mm × 170 mm CIGS submodule; individual electric power of each tile is lower if compared with other BIVP solutions (2.67 Wp/tile for CIGS technology and 4.59–4.94 Wp/tile for c-Si cells) but enough to provide a high power when installed as part of a complete roof installation.

Suitability of the proposed conceptual design depends on handling capabilities of the tiles without damaging them, keeping an adequate value of their mechanical properties and with an affordable cost and the simplification of the electrical connection system to ensure compatibility with installation procedures and regular tiles (Fig. 6).

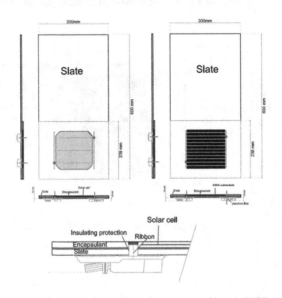

Fig. 6. Conceptual design for solar tile, c-Si configuration (left) and CIGS configuration (right)

4 Conclusions

The use of composite material for the encapsulation of c-Si cells or CIGS submodules can facilitate obtaining a new kind of PV module and the integration in urban environments. Modules obtained with composite material will have enhanced properties, like lighter weight, increased mechanical resistance, complex geometries and customization possibilities, but keeping optical transparency and electrical characteristics of traditional BIPV solutions.

Although, some approximations for the encapsulation of PV elements in composite material have been already done, further development of the technical aspects and the procedures has been analysed and realized, since there are still several barriers and challenges to be overcome such as the encapsulation of CIGS submodules and the manufacture of large and/or curved pieces.

An analysis of the state of art and other solutions developed for the integration of photovoltaic technology in buildings and other elements of the urban environment was used to set the starting point for the project and to select the kind of solutions that are going to be developed. Based on it, four solutions have been proposed to be developed during this project: a solar tile, a photovoltaic roof for an electric vehicle, a solar table and a photovoltaic shelter.

Conceptual designs, one with monocrystalline silicon cells and other with CIGS submodules manufactured by FLISOM, have been done for each proposed application. Designs include the identification of the most important requirements regarding the normative and legislation but also the end-users and stakeholders. Besides dimensions and geometry, a discussion of the most appropriate cell lay-out to maximize electrical performance and the composite system for each prototype has been included.

Conceptual designs will be used as reference for the detailed designs and the manufacturing and testing of the prototypes.

Acknowledgment. Authors of this paper like to thank FLISOM for its collaboration and participation in the development and procurement of the results here summarized.

This project has been co-funded by the European Union Horizon 2020 Research and Innovation Programme, the Eurostars Programme, the State Secretariat for Education, Research and Innovation (SERI) of Switzerland (Exp. 1315001145) and the Centre for the Development of Industrial Technology (CDTI) (CIIP – 20171010) of Spain.

Schweizerische Eidgenossenschaft
Confédération suisse
Confederazione Svizzera
Confederaziun svizra

References

1. SRT- Solar Roof Tile: Sed.at (2018). https://bit.ly/2rKKBII. Accessed 4 June 2018
2. Sunstation Solar Panels | Solar Roof Tiles | Solarcentury UK: Consumer Homes UK (2018). https://bit.ly/2L3YwBB. Accessed 4 June 2018
3. For Tile Roofs: Lumeta Solar (2018). https://www.lumetasolar.com/service/tile-roofs. Accessed 4 June 2018
4. Solar Roof Tiles | Solar Roof Shingles | SRS Energy: SRS Energy Solutions (2016). http://srsenergysolutions.com/solar-roof-tiles/. Accessed 4 June 2018
5. Tesla Solar Roof: Tesla.com (2018). https://www.tesla.com/solarroof. Accessed 4 June 2018
6. Zoe Z.E. Concept (2009) - My Renault ZOE electric car: My Renault ZOE electric car (2014). https://bit.ly/2rJip90. Accessed 4 June 2018
7. SsangYong e-XIV concept - SsangYong GB: Ssangyonggb.co.uk (2018). http://www.ssangyonggb.co.uk/news/ssangyong-e-xiv-concept/6902. Accessed 4 June 2018
8. Let the Sun In: Ford C-MAX Solar Energi Concept Goes Off the Grid, Gives Glimpse of Clean Vehicle Future | Ford Media Center: Media.ford.com (2018). https://ford.to/2LVAE3Cl. Accessed 4 June 2018
9. Sono Motors - Solarauto Sion: Sono Motors (2018). https://sonomotors.com/. Accessed 4 June 2018
10. The electric car that charges itself with sunlight | Lightyear: Lightyear (2018). https://lightyear.one/. Accessed 4 June 2018

11. Prius Plug-in | Overview & Features | Toyota UK: Toyota UK (2018). https://www.toyota.co.uk/new-cars/prius-plugin/. Accessed 4 June 2018
12. Polysolar install the UK's first solar photovoltaic glass bus shelter: Buildingcentre.co.uk (2018). https://bit.ly/2IKgaMk. Accessed 4 June 2018
13. Street furniture goes sustainable and self-sufficient with JCDecaux: Jcdecaux.com (2018). https://bit.ly/2Ir5hfc. Accessed 4 June 2018
14. Urban Solar deploys solar bus stops in San Francisco - Urban Solar: Urban Solar (2016). https://bit.ly/2Kt33fP. Accessed 4 June 2018
15. Onyxsolar.com (2018). https://www.onyxsolar.com/union-city-station. Accessed 20 June 2018
16. R2Cities: Residential Renovation towards nearly zero energy cities: R2cities.eu (2018). http://r2cities.eu/. Accessed 20 June 2018
17. Onyxsolar.com. https://bit.ly/2L7ltUC. Accessed 4 June 2018
18. Looknphil.com (2018). https://bit.ly/2JfBKW4. Accessed 4 June 2018
19. Fundación Tecnalia Research & Innovation: Method of encapsulating photovoltaic cells and encapsulated modules. EP3006181 (A2) (2018)
20. Flisom - Lightweight Thin Flexible Solar Panels: Flisom.com (2018). https://flisom.com/. Accessed 4 June 2018

Services of Energy Storage Technologies in Renewable-Based Power Systems

Francisco Díaz-González[✉], Eduard Bullich-Massagué, Cristina Vitale,
Marina Gil-Sánchez, Mònica Aragüés-Peñalba, and Francesc Girbau-Llistuella

Centre d'Innovació Tecnològica en Convertidors Estàtics i Accionaments
(CITCEA-UPC), Universitat Politècnica de Catalunya ETS d'Enginyeria
Industrial de Barcelona, C. Avinguda Diagonal, 647, Pl. 2, 08028 Barcelona, Spain
`francisco.diaz-gonzalez@upc.edu`

Abstract. Due to the vast deployment from distributed to large-scale renewable generation, electrical power systems are being equipped more and more with tools improving the controllability of power flows and state monitoring and prospective. In this regard, future power networks are evolving into smart grids. One of the tools for the modernization and decarbonization of power networks is the field of Energy Storage Systems (ESSs). This paper proposes a classification for the many services the ESSs can provide in power systems dominated by renewable-based generation. Three categories of services are defined in terms of the power and energy ratings of the ESS and the main type of beneficiary in each case. For each service, the most suitable type of ESS is identified, exemplary projects are noted and key regulatory issues are highlighted.

Keywords: Smart grids · Energy storage ·
Renewable-based power plants

1 Introduction

Electrical power systems are holding an increasing penetration of renewable-based generation. The intrinsic variability of wind-based and photovoltaic systems –integrated at large scale and also at the consumer level– impose diverse challenges for the planning and the operation of future power networks, e.g. the achievement of the required balance between generation and demand at all time, and the security of supply to customers. To do so, power networks should be equipped with new tools in many technological areas to improve controllability of power flows and the state monitoring and prospective. In this regard, future power networks are evolving into smart grids [1].

One of the tools for the realization of smart grids is the field of ESSs. ESSs can effectively be controlled so as to integrate renewables at the different scale levels, from the customer domain to the large-scale level, thus facilitating a transition to a decarbonized power system and society in general.

S. Nesmachnow and L. Hernández Callejo (Eds.): ICSC-CITIES 2018, CCIS 978, pp. 53–64, 2019.
https://doi.org/10.1007/978-3-030-12804-3_5

The ESSs can provide numerous services in power systems with high penetration of renewable generation. The present paper presents a classification of such services, contributing to the various approaches proposed in literature [2–4]. In the present paper, services are distributed in three main categories. Each category is defined by the power and energy ratings of the ESS to manage, as well as by the main type of beneficiary of such services. The first category is the one involving so-called small-scale ESS (see Fig. 1). In here, relatively small storages in power and energy ratings mainly enable the active participation of individuals, domestic end users, in electricity markets. Thus, keywords such as self-consumption and off-grid operation (energy independency) come into play here. Then, the second category is characterized by involving mid-size ESS, reaching up to few MW in power and few MWh in energy storage capacity. Services related here refer to the management of relatively important amount of power, flowing through distribution systems. Thus, the main beneficiaries here are the actors in the distribution domain (i.e. distribution system operators (DSO)). Finally, the third category of services is the one involving large-scale ESSs. Here, bulk energy storage capacity is required to enable the integration of large renewable-based power plants in power systems and related markets. Keywords such as system ancillary services and generation time-shifting are addressed. Without any doubt, the main beneficiaries here are the wind and photovoltaic power plants. Figure 1 graphically depicts the classification of services described above.

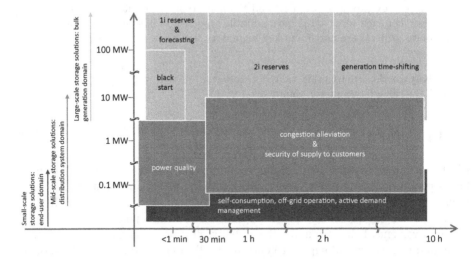

Fig. 1. Catalog of services for energy storage systems in renewable-dominated power systems.

Following sections describe each of the services in Fig. 1, highlighting the suitable energy storage technologies, representative projects and related regulatory issues.

2 Small-Scale Energy Storage Solutions: The End-User Domain

Small-scale energy storage can be used to improve the self-consumption performance and to provide services to the end user. In this case, the storage device is installed at local residences or small facilities such as town-hall, municipal sports center, etc. Below, the different services that small-scale energy storage technologies can provide are explained.

2.1 Services: Self-consumption, Off-Grid Operation and Active Demand Management

Self-consumption. Local small installations commonly present variable consumption profiles. When renewable energy production is installed in these sites, during some periods the electrical production will be higher than the consumption and vice-versa. When the local generation is higher than the consumption, the excess have to be injected to the grid (or wasted, losing efficiency). Contrarily, when the energy production is lower than the consumption, the end-user needs to buy electricity from the grid. Small energy storage devices can mitigate this effect, storing energy when there is excess production and delivering it when there is a lack of production.

Off-Grid Operation. Commonly, it is desirable to be connected to the main distribution network. Nevertheless, any fault on the system can produce an outage of this network, which can last several minutes, hours or even days. In this case, energy storage devices, combined with other generation sources such as photovoltaic, diesel engines, and etcetera, can help the operation in islanded (or off-grid) mode.

Active Demand Management. Small-scale storage devices could manage the load demand by storing or injecting active power according to the electricity price signals. In essence, it consist on increasing the total load (store energy) during low electricity price periods, and reducing it (supply energy) during high price periods. On the other hand, batteries from electrical vehicles can also buy the electricity during low price periods or when there is excess of production from local generation.

2.2 Suitable Technologies and Representative Projects

The small-scale storage devices should be sized considering the local consumption profiles, the local generation profiles (if exist) and the desired service. Nevertheless, the size of these systems are in the scale of few kW to hundreds of kW in power and of few tens of kWh to hundreds of kWh (for community scale installations). The suitable energy storage technologies for this application are mainly secondary batteries. Lead-acid ones have dominated the market for decades because of their commercial availability and low cost, while Lithium-ion and flow batteries are gaining momentum progressively [5,6].

Table 1 lists exemplary projects around the application of small-scale energy storages for the services discussed above.

Table 1. Small-scale energy storage examples

Project	Loc.	Size	Tech.	Description	Status	Ref.
ENDESA HQ B2G	Spain	20 kW 20 kWh	Li-ion	Install batteries close to EV charging points and on-site renewable generation. Uses: electric energy time shift, load following, on-site renewable generation shifting	ON dec 2013	[7]
Duke Energy Charlotte	US	6 kW 11.5 kWh	Li-ion	Residential energy storage in combined with local solar power generation. Uses: Renewable energy time shift, back-up power supply	ON dec 2013	[8]
NRECA/ CRN	US	4.6 kW 11.8 kWh	Lead-acid	Storage installed at utility office building. Uses: demand charge reduction, back-up power supply, electric energy time shift	ON aug 2013	[9]
PVCROPS	Portugal	5 kW 60 kWh	Flow	Demonstration project: Develop control strategies to store energy in building integrated PV installations. Uses: renewable capacity firming, renewable energy time-shift	ON oct 2013	[10]

2.3   Snapshot on Regulatory Issues

One of the main barriers for further integration of small-scale energy storage technologies is the regulation. For example, in the case of Spain, self-consumption regulation changes are continuously announced each time the political party that governs changes. This leads to uncertainty, turning the investments in self-consumption installations unattractive to the end user. Currently, the European Union is trying to encourage countries to develop regulatory frameworks that incentives the self-consumption installations. This is, in fact, one of the hot topics for the transition towards a decarbonized energy sector [11].

3   Mid-scale Energy Storage Solutions: The Distribution System Domain

Mid-scale energy storage solutions will enable the distributed generation and electrical vehicle integration. These mid-solutions are designed to be deployed along the low and medium voltage networks. They may provide diverse services to the grid operator and end users. The most representative mid-scale services are described in the following.

3.1   Services: Power Quality Improvement, Congestion Alleviation and Security of Supply

Power Quality Improvement. A power system with a high number of renewable sources and non-linear and non-resistive consumptions (such as electrical vehicles, LED lighting solutions, among others) might increase electrical losses and lead to voltage variations. The causes can be diverse, but the most usual are directly related to the presence of harmonic and reactive currents, unbalances and reverse power flows. A suitable mid-scale storage system may revert this situation balancing power flows, canceling current harmonics and reactive currents, reducing the voltage variability through active power injection, etc.

In practice, the storage solution collects data from the field continuously quantifying power quality issues. Then, it corrects them compensating reactive power and current harmonics, as well as balancing downstream consumptions. Additionally, it is able to inject or consume active/reactive power according to predefined droops in order to regulate the voltage at its point of common coupling.

Based on experience, it can be estimated that the power ratings for the storage solution so as to provide the above services should reach up to 66% of maximum power flow at its connection point, e.g. at a secondary substation feeding a neighborhood [12]. To provide the services above, energy storage is in fact not strictly needed, but are the power capabilities of the associated power electronics what determines the performance of the storage solution. However, having some energy storage can be beneficial for also exchanging active power with the grid for voltage control purposes in networks with relatively important resistive behavior (e.g. rural grids).

Congestion Alleviation in Weak Grids. Power systems with a high number of renewable sources and high power demand may experience critical situations such as congestions. Suitable storage systems may revert this situation charging and discharging energy when needed. Dedicated management with certain forecasting capability is required to do so. Forecast could be performed based on historic data on power flows, calendar and weather data, among others. Based on this, the schedule for the storage can be solved.

Security of Supply for Customers at District or Neighborhood Level. The reliability of a network can be measured by the average number and duration of supply interruptions [13]. According to [14], a supply interruption is "a condition in which the voltage at the supply terminals is lower than 1% of the declared nominal voltage of the system". There are two types of supply interruptions: prearranged interruptions, that can be due to planned maintenance works of a part of the network and accidental interruptions, usually caused by a fault of different natures (external event, equipment failures or interferences).

Distributor System Operators (DSOs) are encouraged to increase the reliability of the grid they operate through incentives and penalties. For this purpose, standards entail the continuity of supply and set specific limits based on maximum duration and frequency of the interruptions, imposing penalties if the requirements are not fulfilled [13].

In this context, energy storage systems can play a key role for enhancing the security of supply for customers (enabling shorter or less frequent interruptions) and leading to economic savings for the DSO. One strategy to ensure the continuity of supply is through the so-called "network reconfiguration".

The grid is reconfigured by bypassing the fault that is creating the interruption. The DSO can utilize the sensing distributed infrastructure to localize the fault and then calculate the new grid arrangement to redirect the power flow. Controlled islanding can be created (intentionally) in order to keep supplying the customers that got isolated from the main grid. When islanding is planned, a schedule for power management should be provided to ensure adequate balancing, coordinating all the network equipment.

The energy storage system will receive the appropriate signals from the management system of the DSO to provide an optimal and secure schedule of the island operation, utilizing the energy forecast, grid configuration information and status of the monitored grid elements.

3.2 Suitable Technologies and Representative Projects

The power rating and energy capacity of the energy storage system will depend on the type of customers willing to profit from these service, which could be connected either to LV or MV networks. The power rating of the power electronic equipment will be in the range of a few tens kW to few MW. The energy storage capacity will depend on the interruption time allowed in the installation and is in the range of tens of kWh to few MWh and this depends on the time a grid congestion occurs and its severity, for instance.

So the most suitable storage technologies for mid-scale energy storage solutions for the above explained services are secondary batteries and flow batteries. Specifically, Lithium-ion and Lead-acid batteries are being widely employed. Lithium-ion batteries offer large energy density for their size, fast charging/discharging and long lifetime, compared to Lead-acid batteries. However, the latter are less expensive. Also for services related to power quality improvement, energy storages with very short time response and large cyclability may be needed. In this sense, not batteries but supercapacitors and flywheels are best addressed [2].

See representative examples of projects adopting mid-scale ESSs in Table 2.

Table 2. Mid-scale energy storage examples

Project	Loc.	Size	Tech.	Description	Status	Ref.
Nice grid	France	250 kW 479 kWh	Li-ion	Develop a smart grid that integrates solar panels, energy storage batteries and smart meters. Uses: microgrid capability, on-site renewable generation shifting, grid upgrade deferral	ON sep 2013	[15]
Horse Island Microgrid	UK	12 kW 60 kWh	Lead-acid	Reduce residents reliance on their two diesel generators. Uses: electric supply capacity, microgrid capability, on-site renewable generation shifting	ON aug 2009	[16]
Smart Rural Grid	Spain	40 kW 40 kWh	Li-ion	Develop a smart grid that integrates distributed generation, power electronics and storage in rural grids. Uses: Power quality improvement, microgrid capability, on-site renewable generation shifting	ON sep 2017	[12]
Trolleybus facility	Germany	5 kW 5.7 kWh	Li-ion Supercap.	Fully static supercapacitor-based storage technology installed in Cologne. Uses: Compensation of resistive voltage drops in transportation networks	ON sep 2017	[17]

3.3   Snapshot on Regulatory Issues

The separation of activities for the different agents in the electrical sector in Europe is mandatory, as stated in the Directive 2003/54/Eg [18]. This Directive establishes that the operation and ownership of electrical grids should be fully regulated: there should not be competence here. In turn, these activities should be separated from those concerning generation and commercialization to customers, which functioning should be based on competitive market-based rules.

So at the end, and in regard of energy storage, it can be deduced that a DSO could not participate in markets managing an energy storage device. This is in fact explicited in the European Directive 2009/72/Ec [19]. This Directive forbids distributors –and the operators of the transmission networks also– to own and operate generating assets. By generating assets one can also intend energy storages, but this word did not even appear in the Directive in 2009.

Nowadays, it is hard for a DSO to take advantage of managing energy storage systems. Anyhow, research is focused on identifying the benefits of doing so and, respecting the requirements of the regulation, the applications aimed for such energy storages are not related with the electricity market, but with the improvement of the quality of service the DSO offers to its customers instead (e.g. power quality issues, reduction of interruptions of supply, etc.)

4   Large-Scale Energy Storage Solutions: The Bulk Generation Domain

Large-scale energy storage solutions enable the integration of bulk renewable generation. The most representative large-scale services are described in the following.

4.1   Services: Grid Ancillary Services, Enhancement of Generation Controllability

Grid Ancillary Services: Primary and Secondary Power Reserves, Voltage Control, Power Ramp-Rate Limitation and Black Start Capability. The variability of renewables impacts on required power reserves in the network. Such reserves are needed to ensure the required balance between generation and demand at all time. Energy storage can be a provider of such power reserves in the different time frames, i.e. the so-called primary and secondary reserves [20]. They also can contribute to the grid integration of renewables by providing the services of black start support and voltage control. These services in the frame of renewables integration are known as grid ancillary services and are described in the following.

Primary reserves refers to the so-called primary frequency control. Primary reserves from a generator group represents the ability of its system to modify its current active power in-feed to the grid in a short period of time (seconds to minutes). It can be either generation increase or decrease depending on the grid frequency fluctuation, this way, the frequency perturbations in the grid due to unbalances in the power supplied can be balanced. It can be achieved by a droop control (power output/frequency function) as can be deduced from Fig. 2.

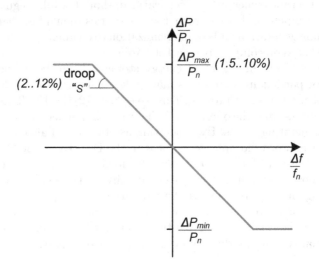

Fig. 2. Power-frequency droop characteristic for primary frequency control according to EU network code [21].

The next control to be taken is the one activating secondary reserves. Secondary reserves progressively replaces primary reserves (and this process takes from minutes to hours) to be available for future grid imbalances; it maintains the generation-demand balance previously supported by inertia and primary reserve and it initiates the process of restoring the frequency level back to the nominal value, i.e. 50 Hz in Europe.

Along with the provision of primary and secondary reserves, energy storage can provide renewables with black start capability. This is the first step in the process of system restoration in the unlikely event of a black-out. This service is supplied by local power plants that have the capability to start up its main generator(s) and carry out initial energization of sections of the electricity transmission system and distribution network.

Further even, ESSs can also provide the service of power ramp-rate limitation in renewable-based power plants. This is a service being progressively introduced in grid codes. The idea here is to smooth out fast power fluctuations of PV and wind power plants for a better grid integration. Some exemplary studies by the authors of the present work can be found in [22–24].

Finally, energy storage, since connected to the grid through fully controlled power electronics can facilitate the task of voltage control by renewables. This control is provided by generating units or static equipment capable of exchange reactive power. This requires generating equipment to measure a voltage, compare the measurement to a reference and increase/decrease the reactive power flow out of the generating equipment. This can be achieved changing the excitation in the field winding in a synchronous generator or changing the angle of a power inverter.

Enhancement of Generation Controllability (Time Shifting and Compensation of Forecasting Errors for Renewables). The difficult prediction nature of the energy resource may affect the electricity sale scheduled in the day-ahead market, where the producer estimates the energy generation. This prediction has to be performed as closer as possible to the real operation of the power plant, since in case of forecasting error, that is a difference between the programmed generation and the effective power consumption, the market participation profit is dramatically affected. On one hand, the producer incurs in economic penalizations imposed by the system operator, while, on the other hand, the last is forced to take relative precautions for sudden events of power output, such as allocating more energy reserves, thus increasing balancing costs. In order to encourage producers to participate into the electricity market ensuring the profitability provided by this service, the implementation of an energy storage system can be offered as a solution. This device, indeed, is able to provide that energy needed to balance estimation and effective power plant generation.

Apart from the forecasting error reduction, energy storage system is an appropriate technology for the field of time shifting, which involves storing energy during low price times and discharging it during high price times, maximizing the power plant income. Surplus of renewable energy generated during valley hours can be indeed stored to be used in peak hour periods, avoiding curtailments and operation of fuel-based generators, thus improving carbon footprint.

4.2 Suitable Technologies and Representative Projects

Usual capacity requirements for the above explained services are between few MW to hundreds of MW in power, with a response operation up to diverse hours [2]. The most suitable technologies implemented for this type of service are compressed-air energy storage, pumped-hydro installations, hydrogen and secondary batteries, especially lithium-ion, lead-acid or sodium ones for systems rated at tens of MW. Flywheels, because of their easy scalability, enabling the realization of systems rated at tens of MW in power can be also suitable for these services.

See representative examples of projects adopting mid-scale ESSs in Table 3.

4.3 Snapshot on Regulatory Issues

As stated in the Clean Energy for All Europeans package, the implementation of energy storage systems alone is not enough to improve the participation of renewables in the electricity market; their penetration, indeed, can be increased switching from a day-ahead programming dispatch, with maximum probability of incurring in prediction error (long term basis), to a short term electricity

Table 3. Large-scale energy storage examples

Project	Loc.	Size	Tech.	Description	Status	Ref.
Stephentown Spindle	New York, US	20 MW 25 MWh	Flyw.	The ESS provides frequency regulation service (primary and secondary) to the NYISO. Fast response (4 s). It is connected at 115 kV to NYSEG grid.	ON jun 2011	[25], [26]
Notrees Wind Storage	Texas, US	36 MW 24 MWh	Li-ion	ESS is located at substation and tied to the distribution side. Uses: Frequency regulation, voltage control, wind firming, curtailment mitigation	ON jan 2013	[27], [28]
Jeju SmartGrid Jocheon	South Korea	4 MW 8 MWh	Li-ion	The ESS connected to 154 kV grid. Black start, frequency regulation, ramping, capacity firming and voltage support	ON jul 2013	[29], [30]
Tehachapi Wind ESS	California, US	8 MW 32 MWh	Li-ion	This ESS is connected to a WPP. Uses: Capacity firming, congestion alleviation, upgrade deferral and voltage support	ON jul 2014	[31], [32]
Hydroelectric Cardos Valley	Spain	134 MW - MWh	Pumped hydro	This ESS is connected to a WPP. Uses: Capacity firming, transm. congestion alleviation, upgrade deferral and voltage support	ON jul 2014	[33]

market creating an intraday approach with higher accurate predictions. So energy storage, also at bulk scale, should be exploited in synergy with other sources of flexibility of the system.

In regard of the application of energy storage in renewable-based power plants, operational rules and related control algorithms should be explored according to the previously mentioned grid codes. The applicable grid code regulation in Europe that determines the requirements for the grid connection of renewable-based power plants and the ancillary services they should provide is the European Commission Regulation 2016/631 of 14 April 2016 [21].

5   Conclusions

This paper proposed a classification for the many services the ESSs can provide in power systems dominated by renewable-based generation. Three categories of services are defined in terms of the power and energy ratings of the ESS and the main type of beneficiary. Small-scale ESSs (in the range of few kW to hundreds of kW in power and of few tens of kWh to hundreds of kWh in energy) are best intended for the provision of services to the end-user. Analogously, mid-scale ESSs (in the range of few tens kW to few MW in power and of few tens of kWh to few MWh in energy) are best intended for the provision of services to the distribution domain. For both cases (small and mid-scale ESSs) the exploitation of related businesses is bounded by remarkable regulatory issues. Finally, large-scale ESSs (in the range of few MW to hundreds of MW in power, with a response operation up to diverse hours) are primarily intended for the provision of services for bulk renewable-based power plants.

Acknowledgments. This work was supported by the Ministerio de Economia, Industria y Competitividad (Spanish government), under the grant agreement number ENE2017-86493-R.

References

1. Fang, X., Misra, S., Xue, G., Yang, D.: Smart grid, the new and improved power grid: a survey. IEEE Commun. Surv. Tutorials **14**(4), 944–980 (2012)
2. Díaz-González, F., Sumper, A., Gomis-Bellmunt, O.: Energy Storage in Power Systems. Wiley, Hoboken (2016)
3. Energy Storage Association: Energy Storage, Case Studies (2000). http://energystorage.org/energy-storage/case-studies/delivering-100-commercial-reliability-aes-los-andes-battery-energy. Accessed June 2018
4. Zame, K.K., Brehm, C.A., Nitica, A.T., Richard, C.L., Schweitzer, G.D.: Smart grid and energy storage: policy recommendations. Renew. Sustain. Energy Rev. **82**, 1646–1654 (2018)
5. Parra, D., Swierczynski, M., Stroe, D.I., et al.: An interdisciplinary review of energy storage for communities: challenges and perspectives. Renew. Sustain. Energy Rev. **79**, 730–749 (2017)
6. Díaz-González, F., Sumper, A., Gomis-Bellmunt, O., Villafáfila-Robles, R.: A review of energy storage technologies for wind power applications. Renew. Sustain. Energy Rev. **16**, 2154–2171 (2012)
7. Endesa HQ B2G project (2013). https://www.endesa.com/es/proyectos/todos-los-proyectos.html. Accessed June 2018
8. Duke Energy Charlotte Residential ESS (2013). https://www.duke-energy.com/home. Accessed June 2018
9. NRECA/CRN Distributed Energy Storage Research Project (2013). https://www.smartgrid.gov/files/NRECA_DOE_Energy_Storage.pdf. Accessed June 2018
10. PVCROPS Evora Demonstration Flow Battery Project - REDT (2013). https://redtenergy.com/pv-crops-press-release-strong-irish-involvement-new-solar-energy-project/. Accessed June 2018
11. European Commission: Markets and consumers. Integrated energy markets for European households and businesses (2016). https://ec.europa.eu/energy/en/topics/markets-and-consumers. Accessed June 2018
12. Girbau-Llistuella, F., Díaz-González, F., Sumper, A., Gallart-Fernández, R., Heredero-Peris, D.: Smart grid architecture for rural distribution networks: application to a Spanish pilot network. Energies **11**(4), 844 (2018)
13. CEER: 6th CEER benchmarking report on the quality of electricity and gas supply (2016). https://www.nve.no/energy-market-and-regulation/latest-news/ceer-6th-benchmarking-report-on-the-quality-of-electricity-and-gas-supply/. Accessed June 2018
14. CENELEC: UNE-EN 50160, European Standard, Voltage characteristics of electricity supplied by public distribution systems (2006)
15. NICE GRID project (2014). https://www.energystorageexchange.org/projects/1599. Accessed June 2018
16. Horse Island Microgrid Project - Aeolus Power (2009). http://www.windandsun.co.uk/case-studies/islands-mini-grids/horse-island.aspx#.U35T1PldXXo. Accessed June 2018

17. Rufer, A., Hotellier, D., Barrade, P.: A supercapacitor-based energy storage substation for voltage compensation in weak transportation networks. IEEE Trans. Power Deliv. **19**(2), 629–636 (2004)

18. European Commission: Directive 2003/54/EC of the European Parliament and of the Council of 26 June 2003 (2003). https://eur-lex.europa.eu/legal-content/en/TXT/?uri=CELEX:32003L0054. Accessed June 2018

19. Directive 2009/72/EC of the European Parliament and of the Council of 13 July 2009. https://eur-lex.europa.eu/legal-content/EN/ALL/?uri=celex%3A32009L0072. Accessed June 2018

20. ENTSO-E: Operational handbook; policies; load-frequency control and performance (2009). https://www.entsoe.eu. Accessed June 2018

21. European Commission: Commission Regulation (EU) 2016/631 of 14 April 2016 establishing a network code on requirements for grid connection of generators (2016). https://eur-lex.europa.eu/legal-content/EN/TXT/?uri=OJ%3AJOL_2016_112_R_0001. Accessed June 2018

22. Cabrera-Tobar, A., Bullich-Massagué, E., Aragüés-Peñalba, M., Gomis-Bellmunt, O.: Review of advanced grid requirements for the integration of large scale photovoltaic power plants in the transmission system. Renew. Sustain. Energy Rev. **62**, 971–987 (2016)

23. Díaz-González, F., Bianchi, F.D., Sumper, A., Gomis-Bellmunt, O.: Control of a flywheel energy storage system for power smoothing in wind power plants. IEEE Trans. Energy Convers. **29**(1), 204–214 (2014)

24. Bullich-Massagué, E., Aragüés-Peñalba, M., Sumper, A., Boix-Aragones, O.: Active power control in a hybrid PV-storage power plant for frequency support. Sol. Energy **144**, 49–62 (2017)

25. Beacon Power LLC: Operating Plants (2018). http://beaconpower.com/stephentown-new-york/. Accessed June 2018

26. Rockland Capital: Stephentown Spindle (2018). http://www.rocklandcapital.com/portfolio/stephentown-spindle-llc/. Accessed June 2018

27. Ratnayake, A.: Notrees Wind Storage Project Description. Duke Energy (2011) http://www.sandia.gov/ess/docs/pr_conferences/2011/3_Ratnayake_Notrees.pdf. Accessed June 2018

28. Duke Energy Coorporation: Wind Energy, Notrees Battery Storage Project (2018). https://www.duke-energy.com/our-company/about-us/businesses/renewable-energy/wind-energy/notrees-battery-storage-project. Accessed June 2018

29. Del Castillo, J.M., Gun-Pyo, L., Yongbeum, Y., Byunghoon, C.: Application of Frequency Regulation Control on the 4MW/8MWh Battery Energy Storage System (BESS) in Jeju Island, Republic of Korea (2014). http://ethanpublishing.com/uploadfile/2015/0106/20150106024232688.pdf. Accessed June 2018

30. KEPCO Smart grid and ESS Department: Kepco's SG Biz Model and Strategies for Expanding (2014). http://www.nedo.go.jp/english/ired2014/program/pdf/s3/s3_5_keun-seong_kim.pdf. Accessed June 2018

31. Campbell, D., Pinsky, N.: Tehachapi Wind Energy Storage Project Technology Performance, Report 2. 2015 (2015). https://www.smartgrid.gov/files/OE0000201_SCE_TSP_InterimRep_2016_02_12.pdf. Accessed June 2018

32. Kimberly, N., Naum, P.: Southern California Edison Company Tehachapi Wind Energy Storage Project (2015). https://www.smartgrid.gov/files/OE0000201_SCE_FactSheet.pdf. Accessed June 2018

33. Cardos Valley Hydroelectric Complex (1971). http://tavascan.wixsite.com/tavascan/tavascan. Accessed June 2018

Crowdsourcing Optimized Wireless Sensor Network Deployment in Smart Cities: A Keynote

Rafael Asorey-Cacheda[1(✉)], Antonio Javier Garcia-Sanchez[2],
Claudia Zúñiga-Cañón[3], and Joan Garcia-Haro[2]

[1] Centro Universitario de la Defensa (University of Vigo), Escuela Naval Militar,
Plaza de España, s/n, 36920 Marín, Spain
`rasorey@cud.uvigo.es`
[2] Department of Information and Communication Technologies, Technical University
of Cartagena, ETSIT, Campus Muralla del Mar 1, 30202 Cartagena, Spain
{`antoniojavier.garcia,joang.haro`}`@upct.es`
[3] Research Group COMBA R&D, Santiago de Cali University, Cali, Colombia
`claudia.zuniga00@usc.edu.co`

Abstract. The deployment of wireless sensor networks in smart cities for environmental monitoring is a complex issue. One of the main problems is to determine the most appropriate places for these tasks. This paper proposes the use of information from crowdsourcing to identify places of interest from the environmental point of view to deploy the sensor network.

Keywords: Wireless sensor networks · Crowdsourcing · Optimization

1 Introduction

This paper presents the context in which the *Crowdsourcing Optimized Wireless Sensor Network Deployment* (CrOWD) project is being developed. The CrOWD project proposes the use of data sources from crowdsourcing for the design, characterization, integration and analysis of wireless sensor network (WSN) architectures for environmental monitoring in the context of smart cities. Crowdsourcing is based on the power of the crowd to solve problems or carry out smart tasks [4]. In the context of the CrOWD project, crowdsourcing allows citizens to identify those places where they perceive environmental problems as those where it may be more useful to install an environmental monitoring node.

The paradigm of the Internet of Things (IoT) and the reduction of costs of wireless sensor technology have driven the popularization of the WSN. The implementation of WSN on a large scale faces non-trivial problems such as useful network time or capacity. To address these problems, many authors have proposed different algorithms and optimization frameworks that improve routing, energy consumption, deployment of nodes or the implementation of communication protocols, among others.

S. Nesmachnow and L. Hernández Callejo (Eds.): ICSC-CITIES 2018, CCIS 978, pp. 65–79, 2019.
https://doi.org/10.1007/978-3-030-12804-3_6

A WSN can be defined as a large number of connected nodes that detect some kind of physical magnitude [1]. In these networks, the position of the nodes does not need to be predetermined for a large number of applications. This fact allows a random implementation of the nodes, but requires that the network protocols have self-organization capabilities similar to those of ad-hoc wireless networks. However, the classic protocols for ad-hoc wireless networks are not suitable for WSNs [3,5].

This document is organized as indicated below. Section 2 shows a summary of the Urb@nEcoLife and CAMoN projects. Section 3 presents the proposal to optimize the deployment of the WSN for environmental monitoring based on information from crowdsourcing sources. Finally, Sect. 4 presents the conclusions and future lines.

2   The Urb@nEcoLife and CAMoN Projects

Within the context of the CrOWD project there are ongoing projects within this line of research. In particular, the projects "Development of an environmental control platform in urban environments using crowdsourcing (Urb@nEcoLife)" and "Co-Creative Air Monitoring Network (CAMoN)".

The Urb@nEcoLife[1] and CAMoN[2] projects are quite similar to each other. In fact, the CAMoN project can be considered as a sister project of Urb@nEcoLife. The Urb@nEcoLife project is a collaborative initiative between Spanish universities (University of Vigo and University Center of Defense) and Colombian universities (Santiago de Cali University). The project is supported by Colombian institutions and its scope of action are smart cities and environmental control. It is based on an original idea that consists of combining the information generated by citizenship (crowdsourcing[3]), the information generated by a WSN and information from open sources (meteorology, traffic, etc.) to alert the public of problems in their cities and help the authorities to urban management. The scope of the project is to establish the basic points and define the main areas of development that should be carried out a complete system. The project is structured in the following modules:

– *Crowdsourcing:* Getting citizen collaboration to obtain information on the state of the environment is not easy. It is necessary that the citizen has a tool that allows him to generate reports in a simple way and motivate him to use it. In addition, it is necessary to previously categorize the problems that the citizen (air quality, water quality, garbage, etc.) so that this information can be processed and used in other areas.

---

[1] http://urbanecolife.org.

[2] http://camonproject.eu.

[3] Crowdsourcing consists of outsourcing tasks that, traditionally, employees or contractors perform, leaving them in charge of a large group of people or a community, through an open call.

- *Sensor network:* Citizen information has a subjective nature and may have reliability problems. One way to increase reliability is to complement citizen information with a WSN. In this way, WSNs and crowdsourcing become complementary techniques with a greater potential than the use of each of them separately.
- *Data processing:* The data obtained from crowdsourcing and the WSN is useless if it is not processed and knowledge and new services are generated based on them. In this sense, it is necessary to address the use of big data techniques to handle a large volume of data and also assess the use of machine learning and deep learning for the interpretation of information and for the generation of new knowledge. The processing of the data has two aspects that are explained below:
    1. Information for the citizen: The citizen obtains a benefit by having access to the reports of other citizens and those captured by the WSN. In addition, based on the data, new services can be offered as historical data, recommenders to improve the quality of life (healthy routes, good practices, etc.) or generation of alerts.
    2. Information for the authorities: The authorities benefit because they can know first-hand the concerns of citizens in relation to environmental problems. In addition, thanks to the processing of data services could be generated that help urban management indicating areas on which it would be advisable to limit vehicle traffic, areas on which to develop green areas or strengthen or implement new public transport lines.

The Urb@nEcoLife project laid the foundations for the development of the European CAMoN project. In particular, this project is funded through a call made from the OrganiCity[4] project. The components of this project are the Santiago de Cali University, the Technical University of Cartagena, the University of Vigo and the University Center of Defense. The objectives in this project, based on the ideas put forward in Urb@nEcoLife, were:

- Delimit, in this phase, the environmental problem to the monitoring of air quality.
- Develop a crowdsourcing mobile app (Fig. 1).
- Define a WSN topology for the deployment of air quality monitoring devices. In this case, to reduce costs, WiFi technology was chosen despite not adapting well to the WSN and having a limited coverage.
- Build a device to monitor air quality and integrate it into the topology of the WSN. The philosophy was to design a device of low cost and small size that could be mounted on public transport or installed in public buildings or authorized locations.
- Deploy the experiment in the cities of Santiago de Cali (Colombia) and Cartagena.

---

[4] http://organicity.eu.

Fig. 1. Screenshot of the crowdsourcing mobile application.

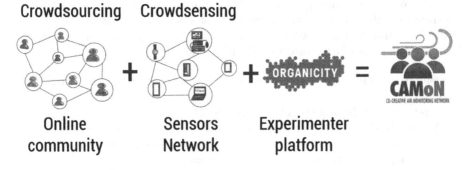

Fig. 2. Graphic summary of the CAMoN project.

In addition, the CAMoN project is integrated with the OrganiCity experimentation framework. This framework allows to store data from the experiments on this platform and facilitates the creation of services based on them. Figure 2 is a graphic summary of the CAMoN project.

Figure 3 represents the internal architecture of the air quality monitoring device [6]. The chosen sensors correspond to the criteria pollutants defined by

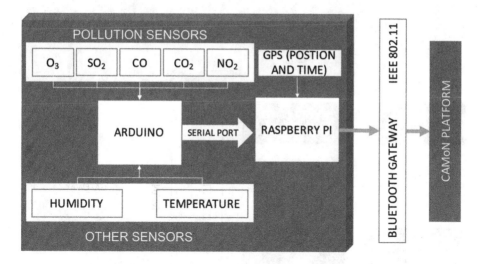

Fig. 3. Internal architecture of the air quality monitoring device.

the World Health Organization (WHO). The platform is based on an Arduino Nano microcontroller that digitizes the signals from the sensors and transmits them to a Raspberry Pi 3, which has a GPS and a temperature and humidity sensor. The collected data can be transmitted through the WiFi interface or the Bluetooth interface.

Regarding the architecture of the network, Fig. 4 represents the software architecture of the operation of the network. The data obtained is dumped on a delay-tolerant network (DTN)[5]. This decision was made because it was assumed that most of the time the devices would be disconnected. On the other hand, an mobile ad-hoc network (MANET) was chosen for the network topology in order to facilitate the routing of the data and not depend on the deployment of a specific infrastructure. The Bluetooth interface, on the other hand, allows the deployment of dynamic gateways for the transfer of data using mobile phones. This functionality is integrated into the crowdsourcing application.

Figure 5 shows an example of what would be the complete operation of the CAMoN project. It shows the integration of the system with the OrganiCity experimentation framework.

The image in Fig. 6 shows one of the air quality monitoring prototypes. These devices have been tested with satisfactory results in the streets of Santiago de Cali and Cartagena.

---

[5] A DTN is a network architecture approach that seeks to address the technical problems in heterogeneous networks that may lack continuous network connectivity. Examples of such networks are those that operate in extreme mobile or terrestrial environments or planned networks in space.

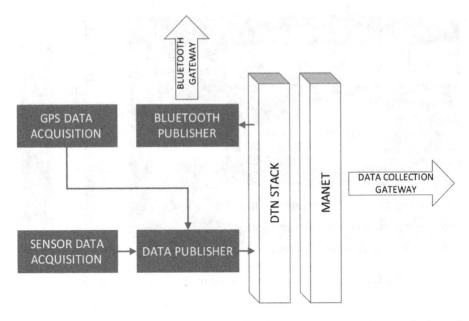

Fig. 4. Software architecture of the network in the air quality monitoring devices of the CAMoN project.

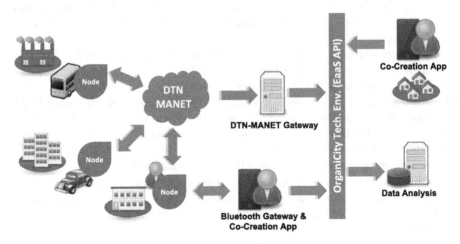

Fig. 5. Example of the operation of CAMoN.

2.1   The Future of Urb@nEcoLife and CAMoN

Urb@nEcoLife and CAMoN are part of a long-term strategy of collaboration between research groups from different universities. With these projects the first steps have been taken to develop a complete system that takes advantage of the potential of the masses (crowdsourcing) to complement the WSN and with the information obtained from both sources, together with other open sources, to

Fig. 6. Image of one of the air quality monitoring prototypes.

offer services that improve the life of citizens and help the authorities in the management of smart cities.

One of the issues related to these projects that has only been treated in a basic way and that requires attention is the processing of data. Figure 7 shows the general idea of the architecture of data processing where it is necessary to develop big data and machine learning techniques to handle the foreseeable large volume of data that the platform will collect.

There are several topics that will be addressed in the immediate future:

- Improve the crowdsourcing application to make it easier to use. It is also important to look for ways that encourage its use, such as gamification[6].
- Achieve a more compact device design and develop an architecture that allows the installation of other types of sensors. In the short term, it is proposed to integrate sensors to measure water quality, which would be a very interesting complement to the monitoring of air quality. It is also proposed to replace the Arduino and Raspberry Pi platform with another more compact and optimized for the IoT.
- Use a new topology for the WSN that is not based on WiFi. The objective is to facilitate data transfer and reduce consumption. One technology that is considered adequate is LoRa and LoraWAN [2]. In practice, LoRaWAN

---

[6] The gamification is the use of techniques, elements and dynamics of games and leisure in non-recreational activities in order to enhance motivation, as well as to reinforce behavior to solve a problem, improve productivity, obtain an object, activate learning and evaluating specific individuals.

would allow maintaining the DTN, which is considered a necessary element in the context of this project.
- Advance in the processing of data and the development of services based on them. The management of the data will be what provides added value to the project.

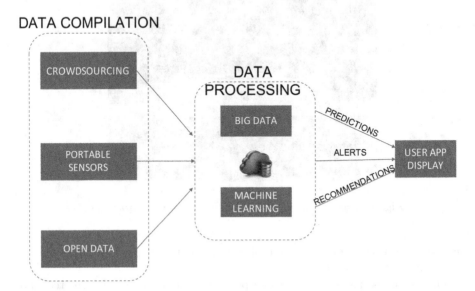

Fig. 7. General outline of the data processing for the future of Urb@nEcoLife and CAMoN.

3 Optimization of WSNs Based on Crowdsourcing

So far, crowdsourcing and WSNs, as proposed in the Urb@nEcoLife and CAMoN projects, are complementary elements that produce data that, when combined, allow the development of advanced services that, separately, would not be possible. To the best of our knowledge, there are no other works in the academic literature with a similar approach. Therefore, this proposal is sufficiently novel to warrant attention.

In the context of this research project, it is proposed to go further with this idea and take advantage of the information provided by crowdsourcing to optimize the deployment of the WSN in smart cities. There are several reasons that justify further research on this idea:

- This topic has not been addressed previously in the academic literature up to where the authors have been able to investigate.

– WSN optimization focuses mostly on energy efficiency, location, positioning and capacity. All these optimizations are done mostly from the WSN point of view but it does not take into account where it is useful to capture the information from the medium.

Thus, in environmental issues, it can be assumed that citizens make reports from places where they perceive problems, beyond the accuracy of this information. Therefore, following this reasoning, it seems logical that in areas where there is a greater number of reports, it is where a greater number of measures should be taken. Figure 8 shows a screenshot of the crowdsourcing application that indicates reports received by area.

By way of example, Fig. 9 shows a possible optimized deployment for a WSN based on the data received through the crowdsourcing of Fig. 8. The deployment of Fig. 9 can be compared with another example deployment in which there has not been taken into account the crowdsourcing in Fig. 10. Thus, it can be seen that many nodes are deployed in areas of little interest and that as it has to cover the entire area it has been necessary to place a larger number.

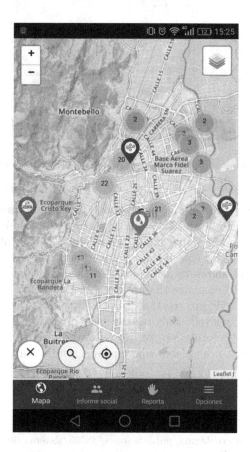

Fig. 8. Locations from where people generated reports in the CAMoN project.

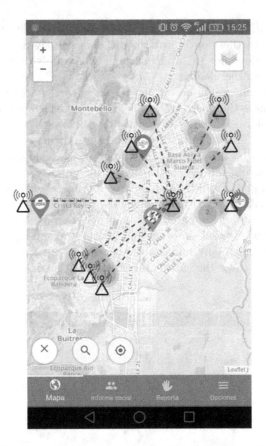

Fig. 9. Example of an optimized deployment of a WSN based on crodwsourcing sources.

The crowdsourcing data of Fig. 8 correspond to real reports sent by citizens in the city of Santiago de Cali (Colombia). Likewise, the Administrative Department of Environmental Management of the Mayor's Office of Santiago de Cali offers the possibility of consulting the location of the air quality measuring stations. Figure 11 shows measurements of these stations taken on May 24, 2018[7]. It is easy to compare the positions of the meters with the locations since the reports arrive to see that there is little correlation between where the stations are deployed. This can be seen in Fig. 12. Probably, based on the crowdsourcing information, we would have opted to install the stations in locations closer to the places where people send reports.

---

[7] http://www.cali.gov.co/dagma/publicaciones/38365/sistema_de_vigilancia_de_calidad_del_aire_de_cali_svcac/.

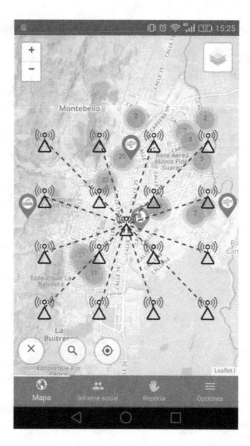

Fig. 10. Example of a WSN deployment not based on information from crowdsourcing.

- Using the information from crowdsourcing to optimize WSNs has multiple
  advantages:
  - *Cost reduction:* Many times the WSN deployment and maintenance costs
    are not taken into account. If the operation of the WSN is optimized to
    take measures mainly in the places of interest, there should be a significant
    reduction both in the deployment of the network and in its subsequent
    maintenance.
  - *Improved data processing:* As already indicated, the potential of the
    Urb@nEcoLife and CAMoN projects lies in the combination of crowd-
    sourcing data with those of the WSN. These results can be even better if
    the capture of WSN data is done based on the reports received from the
    crowdsourcing system.
  - *Improvement of data-based services:* As a consequence of the improvement
    in data processing, more efficient and useful services can be created both
    for citizens and for public authorities.

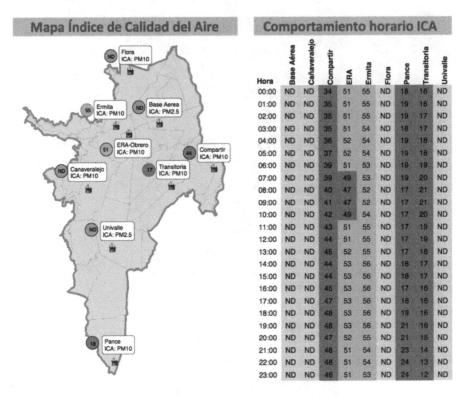

Fig. 11. Information produced by the air quality measuring stations in Santiago de Cali corresponding to May 24, 2018.

In addition to the technical advantages and the academic interest of the idea, this proposal has a clear focus on generating knowledge and transferring results obtained in the form of:

- Generation of publications in indexed journals. The research topic is novel and, therefore, the results are relevant for the academic community.
- Generation of patents from publications (or vice versa). This research project is focused on the generation of new knowledge that is patentable.
- Transfer of results to companies through the exploitation of patents or through the creation of spin-offs. The ultimate goal of the project is to generate wealth in society through knowledge and research.

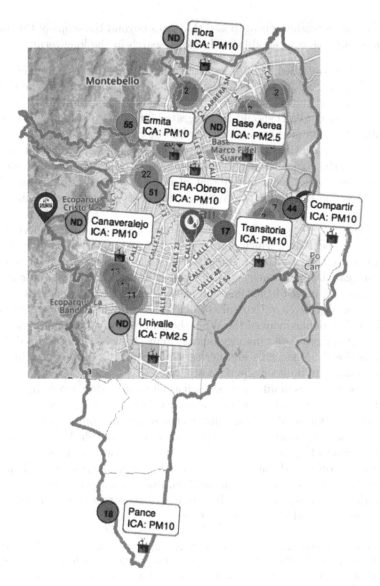

Fig. 12. Location of the air quality measuring stations compared to the places where citizens' reports are received.

4   Conclusions and Future Lines

The CrOWD project is not an isolated proposal. CrOWD is part of and is a natural continuation of the Urb@nEcoLife and CAMoN projects, which are currently being executed. For all this, the CrOWD project is one more step towards the construction of comprehensive and efficient monitoring and environmental management systems in smart cities.

As a result, a roadmap is proposed that goes beyond the scope of this project and whose purpose is to establish a line of research in the long term:

- The results obtained should be integrated into the Urb@nEcoLife and CAMoN projects. As already indicated in Sect. 3, the scope of the CrOWD project was not initially present in the roadmap of these projects. Therefore, the results of CrOWD should be integrated into this roadmap, which in turn should review its medium and long-term objectives.
- Dynamic optimizations of the WSN architecture should be taken into account in terms of the evolution of crowdsourcing. Environmental problems can have many causes and appear in different places as time passes. This fact should allow reconfigurations of the WSN deployments that adapt to changes in situations:
  - In the case of opting for the installation of sensors on transport lines, it can be decided on which transport lines it is optimal to ship the devices.
  - In static sensor deployments, the dynamic adjustment of the sampling rate can be performed so that those who remain in low interest areas remain off most of the time and achieve greater energy savings.
- One of the objectives of Urb@nEcoLife and CAMoN is to offer services based on data. The deployment of the WSN should be another system service in the integral monitoring and management system. That is, the optimized deployment of the WSN must be another service within the catalog of value added services that are built on the data obtained.
- Other open sources of information such as climate models, traffic information, health alerts, types of industries, among others, must be incorporated into the optimization model. This information would be complementary to that of crowdsourcing sources and should contribute to obtain better results.
- Optimization of the monitoring device: The selection of the sensors can be done based on crowdsourcing or information from open sources. That is, it is possible that certain environmental parameters are not relevant in an area for various reasons. Reducing the number of sensors allows to build devices at a lower cost and with longer lifetimes.

Acknowledgements. This research has been supported by projects: CAMoN (ref: Organicity Project –ID 645198– Open Call 2), funded by OrganiCity; Urb@nEcoLife (code DGI-COCEIN-No. 613-621116-D41); and AIM, (ref. TEC2016- 76465-C2-1-R, AEI/FEDER, UE).

References

1. Akyildiz, I., Su, W., Sankarasubramaniam, Y., Cayirci, E.: A survey on sensor networks. IEEE Commun. Mag. **40**(8), 102–114 (2002). https://doi.org/10.1109/MCOM.2002.102442
2. Alliance, L.: What is LoRa? (2018). https://www.lora-alliance.org/what-is-lora. Accessed 01 May 2018

3. Bai, X., Kumar, S., Xuan, D., Yun, Z., Lai, T.H.: Deploying wireless sensors to achieve both coverage and connectivity. In: Proceedings of the 7th ACM International Symposium on Mobile Ad Hoc Networking and Computing, MobiHoc 2006, pp. 131–142. ACM, New York (2006). https://doi.org/10.1145/1132905.1132921. http://doi.acm.org/10.1145/1132905.1132921

4. Guo, B., et al.: Mobile crowd sensing and computing: the review of an emerging human-powered sensing paradigm. ACM Comput. Surv. **48**(1), 7:1–7:31 (2015). https://doi.org/10.1145/2794400. http://doi.acm.org/10.1145/2794400

5. He, T., Huang, C., Blum, B.M., Stankovic, J.A., Abdelzaher, T.: Range-free localization schemes for large scale sensor networks. In: Proceedings of the 9th Annual International Conference on Mobile Computing and Networking, MobiCom 2003, pp. 81–95. ACM, New York (2003). https://doi.org/10.1145/938985.938995. http://doi.acm.org/10.1145/938985.938995

6. Zúñiga Cañón, C., Asorey Cacheda, R., Largo Ortiz, J., Sinisterra González, A.: Work in progress: compilation of environmental data through portable low-cost sensors with delay-tolerant mobile ad-hoc networks. In: 2017 IEEE 13th International Conference on Wireless and Mobile Computing, Networking and Communications (WiMob), pp. 212–217 (2017). https://doi.org/10.1109/WiMOB.2017.8115842

Analysis and Characterization
of Thermographic Defects
at the PV Module Level

Sara Gallardo-Saavedra[1,2(✉)] ⓘ, Luis Hernández-Callejo[1] ⓘ,
and Óscar Duque-Pérez[2] ⓘ

[1] School of Forestry, Agronomic and Bioenergy Industry Engineering (EIFAB),
Department of Agricultural and Forestry Engineering,
Universidad de Valladolid (UVa), Campus Duques de Soria, 42004 Soria, Spain
{sara.gallardo,luis.hernandez.callejo}@uva.es
[2] Industrial Engineering School, Department of Electrical Engineering,
Universidad de Valladolid (UVa), Paseo del Cauce, 59, 47011 Valladolid, Spain
oscar.duque@eii.uva.es

Abstract. Cities have evolved towards a new paradigm called Smart City (SC),
which must evolve towards new intelligent infrastructures, which will integrate
new sensors and advanced communications. Energy efficiency is key and fundamental in the SC. The transformation of energy systems due to the increased
deployment of renewable energy is occurring mostly in the electricity sector, in
which recent PV numbers show an undeniable landmark in renewable energies.
Being able to detect, to identify and to quantify the severity of defects that
appear within modules is essential to constitute a reliable, efficient and safety
system, avoiding energy losses, mismatches and safety issues, especially in case
of building integrated systems, as overheated anomalies could generate a fire
risk or an electrical hazard. The main objective of this paper is to perform an in-
depth on-site study of 17,142 monocrystalline modules to detect every single
existing defect manually, classifying them in different groups, studying the
variance of the same kind of defect in different modules and the patterns of each
group of thermal defects that can be used to develop a software to automatically
detect if a module has an anomaly and its classification. Attending the results
obtained, all faults detected have been classified in five different thermographic
defects modes: hotspot in a cell, bypass circuit overheated, hotspot in the
junction box, hotspot in the connection of the busbar to the junction box and
whole module overheated, with a percentage of occurrence of 75.35%, 10.79%,
6.93%, 6.84% and 0.09%, respectively.

Keywords: Photovoltaic energy · Photovoltaic efficiency · Thermography ·
Thermal inspection · Module defects

1 Introduction

Cities have advanced towards a new approach known as Smart City (SC), which must
progress towards new intelligent infrastructures, which will integrate new sensors and
advanced communications [1]. These new SCs need to solve existing problems in

© Springer Nature Switzerland AG 2019
S. Nesmachnow and L. Hernández Callejo (Eds.): ICSC-CITIES 2018, CCIS 978, pp. 80–93, 2019.
https://doi.org/10.1007/978-3-030-12804-3_7

transport, energy, energy efficiency, integration of renewables, mobility, citizenship, etc. [2]. The integration of high shares of Variable Renewable Energy (VRE) into energy systems requires the modification of policies, standards, and market and regulatory frameworks to effectively control the benefits that can be derived from renewables, while ensuring system reliability and security of supply [3].

Energy efficiency is key and fundamental in the SC. The population increase in cities means that the demand for energy is soaring, so it is necessary to achieve the same with fewer resources [4]. The improvement of the energy efficiency is fundamental in many areas of the SC, for example: lighting [5], actuators, electric motors of hydraulic pumps, electric motors of the industry, heating, elements of distributed generation, smart metering [6], etc.

The transformation of energy systems due to the increased deployment of renewable energy is occurring mostly in the electricity sector, where many countries have seen significant growth in deployment driven by the rapid decline in solar photovoltaic (PV) and wind power costs [3]. PV numbers during the last years show an undeniable landmark in renewable energies. The world added more capacity from solar PV than from any other type of power generating technology, and more solar PV was installed than the net capacity additions of fossil fuels and nuclear power combined, about 98 GW of solar PV capacity was installed both on and off the grid, accumulating 402 GW worldwide at the end of 2017 [3]. Sunlight based solar generators have been utilized as a part of the small-scale, low voltage levels of standalone systems and also in greatest-power establishments associated into network manner and working at any level of voltage in smart cities [7]. Some examples of building integrated PV systems are presented in Figs. 1 and 2.

Fig. 1. Photovoltaic system in the rooftop of the offices of CEDER in Lubia (Soria, Spain). Image courtesy of: CEDER.

Fig. 2. Photovoltaic system integrated in the rooftop of the parking area of CEDER in Lubia (Soria, Spain). Image courtesy of: CEDER.

However, regarding energy efficiency, the little transformation productivity, which is not more than 20% for crystalline-based solar cell reaching 30% in new exploratory cells, is one of the issues the PV faces [7]. Additionally, PV configurations show non-uniform current versus voltage (I–V), and power versus voltage (P–V) characteristics [8–10], which affects the efficiency of modules and minimize their reliability. Being able to detect, to identify and to quantify the severity of defects that appear within a module or a string is essential to constitute a reliable, efficient and safety system. In this way, it would be possible to avoid energy losses, mismatches and safety issues, especially in case of building integrated systems (in roofs or façades), as overheated anomalies could generate a fire risk [11] or an electrical hazard [12].

Usually, faulty modules or cells within a PV plant have been located by applying electrical tests to the modules like the I-V curve test, manual electroluminescence and/or manual thermography, which are costly and time-consuming techniques. I–V curves allow detecting the occurrence of defects such as cracks in operation, with the limitation of not determining the area and location distribution of cracks. Electroluminescence (EL) provides really valuable information about active and inactive areas within a module but it requires connecting the modules to a power source, which complicates the inspection of a whole site, especially in building integration for the power source logistics. The thermography technique is simpler to implement, but the accuracy of the information is lower than with the EL technique, and does not allow the measurement of broken part areas in solar cells [13]. Furthermore, applying these practices to building integrated PV systems supposes an important risk. For this reason, newer inspection techniques are being developed, with the objectives of reducing human risks, easily implementing it and decreasing examination time in large installations, as aerial thermographic inspections using Unmanned Aerial Vehicles (UAVs) [14]. In these inspections, an enormous amount of thermal images are generated, in contrast to manual inspections in which the thermographer in charge of performing the inspection filters the information taking images only to the defects seen on-site. Therefore, specific programs are being developed during the last months with the objective of automatically post processing the aerial thermal images, based on the knowledge of PV modules failure patterns.

The main objective of this paper is to perform an in-depth on-site study of the modules defects of a PV plant, detecting every single defect manually, classifying them in different groups, studying the variance of the same kind of defect in different modules and the patterns of each group of thermal defects that can be used to develop a software to automatically detect if a module has an anomaly and its classification. The thermographic analysis for the identification of defects in this research is performed manually, as the spatial resolution of the thermographic images is higher than using UAVs [15]. Although new onboard thermographic cameras have first-rate resolution values, the fact is that the distance from the camera to the PV modules during the inspection is higher than during the manual inspection, thus reducing the final images resolution. Additionally, a 3 MW PV plant has been chosen with the aim of gathering larger amount of data and different cases in comparison with the information which would be available in a small installation in the rooftop of a building. However, the results are perfectly extended for their subsequent application in aerial thermographic inspections and in small scale installations in roofs or façades of buildings, as same defects have to be identified in all PV inspections.

The paper is structured in four sections, staring with the introduction to the subject that shows the importance of the integration of reliable PV systems in SC and the objectives of the study, followed by the methodology, in which the tests performed and equipment used are analyzed, afterwards the results and discussion section presents the results obtained from the field inspection and the analysis of each PV module failure mode identified and finalizing with the main conclusions obtained.

2 Methodology

The PV site that has been analyzed is located in Spain, in Castilla y León region and it has a capacity of 3 MW, with 17,142 monocrystalline modules, model STREAM 175 W, and was commissioned in 2008. Each PV table is composed by thirty-two modules, divided electrically in two arrays of sixteen modules, which are connected in parallel in the combiner box. Tables have fixed structure with 30° tilt, as it can be seen in Fig. 3. Each module has 72 cells (12 × 6).

Fig. 3. General image of the 3 MW PV plant in which has been developed the research.

The thermographic inspection has been performed using the traditional manual thermography method, walking all around the PV site inspecting each module with the thermographic camera. The manual camera used was a Testo 870 (Table 1). It is a precalibrated camera, in which a coded calibration data set is stored, but it should be recalibrated (on a yearly basis, as it is usual in this kind of cameras) by the manufacturer due to the possible degradation of the detector [16]. In this case, the camera has been just acquired to the manufacturer previous to the tests, so it was just calibrated. The manual camera used captures visual RGB images simultaneously to thermographic images, allowing certifying the detected failures during the post-processing steps and avoiding false positives. However, the presence of false positives is less significant in case of manual inspection, as specialists performing inspections on site can check the presence of shadows or dirt in modules during the inspection.

It has been an in-depth inspection, performed by two specialists, in which every single failure detected, regardless of its temperature, was identified and reported. The time needed to complete this inspection has been 34 working days and to post process and to analyze the results 26 working days. The defects have been analyzed using the thermographic camera software, IRSoft, in which every single defect detected has been analyzed obtaining the relative temperature of the defect, the mean temperature of the healthy area and the difference between them, which indicated the overheat of the fault.

Table 1. Main features of the handheld thermographic camera used in the inspections.

Main features	Testo 870-2
Infrared Resolution	160×120 pixels
Field of View (FOV)	$34° \times 26°$
Geometric Resolution (iFOV)	3.68 mrad
Thermal Sensitivity (NETD)	<100 mK @ 30 °C
Accuracy	± 2 °C, $\pm 2\%$
Spectral range	7.5 to 14 µm
Image Refresh Rate	9 Hz

3   Results and Discussion

This section presents the results obtained from the field inspection and a review and discussion of each PV module failure mode identified, detailing different possible causes and analyzing each group in detail.

Of the 17,142 modules thermographically inspected, the number of detected modules with some failure has been 1,140, which corresponds to a 6.65%. According to some recent research, 2% of the PV modules are predicted not meet the manufacturer's warranty after 11–12 years of operation [17]. The percentage of failures detected is over this rate because every single anomaly has being reported in this study, independently of the temperature difference between the overheated area and the healthy part. This means that not all the thermographic failures identified in this research will have enough impact not to meet the manufacturer's warranty, but authors have considered relevant to report every single defect as all of them could generate a fire risk or an electrical hazard, and they could derivate in an relevant failure with the degradation and time.

These hot spots can be caused in the cells, but they can also appear in other elements, such as in the bypass diodes [18]. Attending the results obtained, all these faults detected have been classified in five different thermographic defects modes: hotspot in a cell or in a group of cells, bypass circuit overheated, hotspot in the junction box, hotspot in the connection of the busbar to the junction box and whole module overheated. The distribution of defects among these five groups can be observed in Table 2 and Fig. 4.

Table 2. Thermographic defects detected in the field inspection classified by the module affected component.

Affected component	Number of defects detected	Percentage
Hotspot	859	75,35%
Bypass circuit	123	10,79%
Junction box	79	6,93%
Connection	78	6,84%
Module	1	0,09%

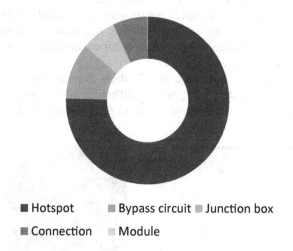

■ Hotspot   ■ Bypass circuit ■ Junction box
■ Connection   ■ Module

Fig. 4. Thermographic defects detected in the field inspection classified by the module affected component represented in a ring chart.

As it can be seen in Table 2, more than three quarters of the affected modules correspond to cell hotspots, presenting one or more cells overheated, followed by the bypass circuit overheated with more than a 10%, the junction box and connection hotspot, with more than a 6% and the whole module overheated, with only one defect of this type identified in the PV plant inspection. This prevailing number of hotspot failures in cells with respect to the rest of failures types is not an isolated case. Statistically, there are a greater amount of cells, 72 cells per module in this case, than of the rest of components, three bypass circuit, one junction box, four bus ribbons connection to the junction box (as it can be observed in Fig. 9) and one module. Additionally, there are a large number of causes responsible of the occurrence of cell hotspots, as cell cracks, snail trails, potential induced degradation (PID) or delamination [17].

Although some of the defects are slightly visible to the human eye, as snail trails, most of them are undetectable without the use of a thermographic camera. The severity of each specific defect, its influence in the production or the risk of fire or electrical hazard danger should be individually analyzed with the objective of determining the action which may be appropriate in each case. In relation with the costs of arrangement of each defect, goes from a diode cost in case there is a broken diode in the junction box to the whole module cost in the rest of cases, as it would be more expensive sending the module to a specialized laboratory to replace some cells or the busbar, considering that the EVA encapsulant and the rest of module layers would have to be removed and replaced. The different defects will be further analyzed in the following paragraphs.

3.1 Cell Hotspots

Hot spots, which are a serious problem in photovoltaic systems, are analyzed along this subsection. The methods of detection of hot spots are very varied, for example in [19], they use I-V techniques for the early detection of hot spots, based on the cell production and climatic information. Other authors [20] use the impedance method for the detection of cell hot spots.

The following images, Figs. 5, 6 and 7, show three examples of the 859 cell hotspots detected during the study, with a difference of temperature between the healthy area and the overheated cell of 71 °C, of 63.5 °C and of 71.2 °C.

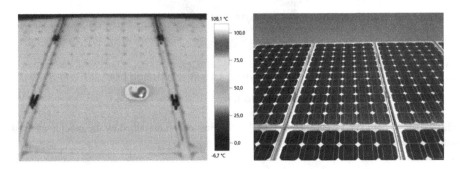

Fig. 5. Thermographic and visual image of a hotspot located in the third string of a module, with a difference of temperature of 71 °C between the healthy area and the overheated cell.

Fig. 6. Thermographic and visual image of two overheated cells within a module, one in the first bypass circuit and the most overheated in the second circuit, with a temperature difference of 63.5 °C between the healthy area and the hotspot. Visual inspection allowed to see those defects.

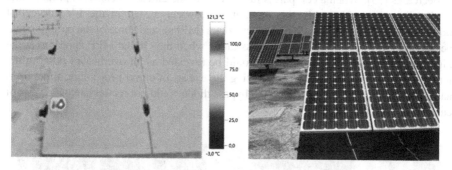

Fig. 7. Thermographic and visual image of one overheated cell in the first bypass circuit next to the module frame, with a temperature difference of 71.2 °C between the healthy area and the hotspot. Visual inspection allowed to see those defects.

Hotspots in cells can appear as a consequence of different failure modes. For example, cell cracks appear in crystalline silicon PV modules during their transportation from the factory to their place of installation, their installation itself, and subsequently to exposure to repeated climatic events such as snow loads, hailstorms or strong wind blows [13], which can derivate on disconnection of some parts of the cell, reducing the output generated and forcing the rest of the cell, being sometimes responsible of the appearance of a cell hotspot. Although the crack part is not totally disconnected, the series resistance across the crack varies as a function of the distance between the cell parts. PV modules may show several cracked cells. A cell crack classification is proposed in [21], grouping the cracks detected in the inspection of 574 PV modules in eight different groups, and the mean frequency of each type of crack proposed in [21] is calculated in [13]: no crack, dendritic crack (2%), several directions (24%), +45° (16%), −45° (16%), parallel to busbar (17%), perpendicular to busbar (5%) and cross crack (20%). In total, in this research it was found that 4.1% of the solar cells in the PV modules show at least one crack [21].

3.2 Bypass Circuit

The possible configuration of cells within the module, and these in the overall photovoltaic generator is critical. The authors in [22] present a simulation work, with alternative solutions, and they demonstrate the improvement of efficiency of some models over others. Usual commercial modules are constituted of three 20-cell double strings connected in series. Each double string is connected in parallel to a bypass diode, which bypasses the current of a severely damaged string. Hence, power output of a module is differently affected if broken cells are located on the same string or on different strings [13]. The thermographic and visual image of one bypass circuit overheated with a temperature difference of 5.7 °C between the healthy area and the overheated bypass is presented in Fig. 8.

In case of a full electrical isolation of a cell part in case of cracks, the current produced by the broken cell, and subsequently by all the cells connected in series with it, decreases [13]. When a cell part is fully isolated, the current decrease is proportional to the disconnected area. In this case, it will appear a step in the I-V curve that originates two different Maximum Power Points (MPPs), and some of the current could be derived through the sub-string bypass diode when the Global MPP appeared at the high current step of the curve, which could be revealed as an overheated point in the junction box if this is forced or conducting the excess of current for a long time, or as an overheated bypass circuit in case the bypass diode could not recirculate the excess of current, as it can be seen in Fig. 8.

Fig. 8. Thermographic and visual image of one bypass circuit overheated with a temperature difference of 5.7 °C between the healthy area and the overheated bypass.

3.3 Junction Box

The PV junction box is an enclosure on the module where the PV strings are electrically connected, housing all the electric bits on a solar panel and protecting them from the environment. Wires connect to diodes inside, providing an easy way to link panels together. Figure 9 shows an open module junction box in which the three bypass diodes are visible.

Fig. 9. Module junction box open, showing the conducting strips which connect the bus ribbon to the bypass diode terminal, three bypass diodes and the terminals for the connection for the PV terminals.

A junction box has bypass diodes that keep power flowing in one direction and prevent it from feeding back to the panels when there's no sunshine, avoiding the effects caused by hot spots and shading, which can adversely affect the performance of PV modules. In a situation close to the short circuit, it would cause the shaded cell to dissipate a high power equal to that generated by the rest of cells, heating and producing the phenomenon of the hot spot. In order to avoid a power dissipation that could raise the temperature to the point of deterioration of the cell, it is necessary to insert the diodes bypass in parallel with a branch of cells connected in series. In case of using bypass diodes, the less resistance to the flow of current in case of hot spot of shading is offered by the diode and not the cell which is a polarized diode inversely.

Two examples of defects detected in the junction boxes are showed in Figs. 10 and 11. As it can be seen in the images, the defect is more marked in the back image than in the front, as the junction box is in the back and the difference measured in the front is only due to the heat transfer from conduction from the junction box. Therefore, to detect this kind of defects, it would be recommendable performing the inspection to the back of the modules; however, it is more complicated due to the PV tables inclination.

A PV junction box is attached to the back of the solar panel with silicon adhesive. It wires the four connectors together and is the output interface of the solar panel.

There are two different junction box production techniques—soldering/potting and clamping. With the soldering and potting method, foils coming out of the solar panel are soldered to the diodes in the junction box. The junction box then has to be potted or filled with a type of sticky material to allow thermal transfer of heat, keep the solder joint in place and prevent it from failing. With clamping production, a simple clamping mechanism attaches the foil to the wires. There are no fumes or major cleanup as with the soldering/potting method.

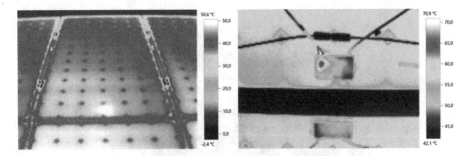

Fig. 10. Thermographic image of the front site of a module with a bypass diode overheated and of the junction box at the back of the module. The difference of temperature between the healthy and the overheated area measured with the thermographic camera is 6.7 °C and 22.6 °C respectively.

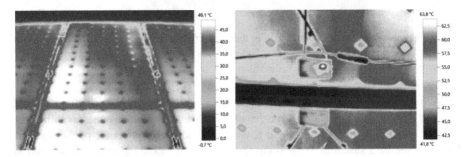

Fig. 11. Thermographic image of the front site of a module with a bypass diode overheated and of the junction box at the back of the module. The difference of temperature between the healthy and the overheated area measured with the thermographic camera is 9.3 °C and 17.2 °C respectively.

3.4   Connection

Another large field of research is the one concerning the design and topology of the connection between cells and connection box. The authors in [23] show the latest advances in simulation and implementation in this subject.

A busbar is a strip of platted copper that conducts electricity within a module. The size of the busbar determines the maximum amount of current that can be safely carried. Busbars can have a cross-sectional area of as little 0.8 mm^2 approximately in PV modules. The thicker bus ribbon is soldered so that it connects to the tabbing ribbon (fingers or cell interconnect ribbons) of each solar cell cluster. The tabbing ribbon collects electric current within its cluster of solar cells and delivers it to the bus ribbon (or bus wires or string interconnect ribbon) and then the bus ribbon conducts the cumulative electric power from all of the solar cell clusters to a junction box for final output. Bus ribbon is larger in cross-section because it has more electrical power to carry. The width range of these ribbons goes from 3 to 6 mm, with a thickness range from 0.1 to 0.4 mm [24].

The influence of structural defects on ribbons has been studied from long ago. By 1981, the influence of defects in laser crystallized silicon ribbons was analyzed [25], categorizing defects into two groups, surface defects associate with turbulence effects and bulk defects as dislocations and stacking faults.

An example of an overheated connection found during the analysis is introduced in Fig. 12. As it can be seen, the overheated area is not in the junction box, but in the connection between bus ribbon or bus wires and the box.

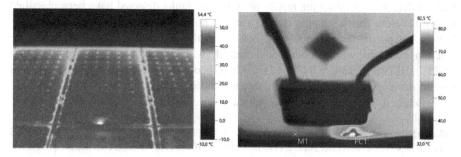

Fig. 12. Thermographic images of one overheated connection between the bus ribbon or bus wires and the junction box with a temperature difference of 11.7 °C and 35.8 °C, at the front and back side respectively.

3.5 Module

The interconnection of photovoltaic modules for the shaping of the photovoltaic generator is of great interest. For example, the authors in [26] show that the serial or parallel configuration directly affects the loss of efficiency in photovoltaic production.

Differences in temperature between a module and the rest of modules of the same row or string could be due to an erroneous connection between them, mismatching or to internal defects of the module affecting all the bypass-circuits. Figure 13 shows the only defect in the whole module detected during the site inspection.

Fig. 13. Thermographic and visual images of one overheated module with a temperature difference of 10.5 °C between the adjacent modules and the overheated area.

4   Conclusions

The paper presents an on-site manual thermal analysis of 17,142 monocrystalline modules, in which every single existing defect has been detected and characterized, calculating the difference of temperature between the defect and the healthy area. All detected anomalies have been analyzed and five different groups of thermographic anomalies have been defined to classify the 1,140 defects found, studying the variance of the same kind of defect in different modules and the patterns of each group of thermal defects. Attending the results obtained, all faults detected have been classified in five different thermographic defects modes: hotspot in a cell, bypass circuit overheated, hotspot in the junction box, hotspot in the connection of the busbar to the junction box and whole module overheated, with a percentage of occurrence of 75.35%, 10.79%, 6.93%, 6.84% and 0.09%, respectively. This study could be used as a base to develop the patterns of the different kind of defects in a software to automatically detect if a module has an anomaly and its classification.

Acknowledgment. The authors thank the CYTED Thematic Network "CIUDADES INTELIGENTES TOTALMENTE INTEGRALES, EFICIENTES Y SOSTENIBLES (CITIES)" nº 518RT0558.

References

1. Pellicer, S., Santa, G., Bleda, A.L., Maestre, R., Jara, A.J., Gómez, A.: A global perspective of smart cities: a survey. In: Seventh International Conference on Innovation Mobile and Internet Services in Ubiquitous Computing, Taichung, Taiwan (China), 3–5 July 2013
2. Batty, M., et al.: Smart cities of the future. Eur. Phy. J. Spec. Top. **214**(1), 481–518 (2012)
3. Renewable Energy Policy Network for the 21st Century (REN21): Renewables 2018, Global Status Report
4. Kling, W.L., Myrzik, J.: Energy efficiency in smart cities. In: IEEE Power & Energy Society General Meeting, Vancouver (Canada), 21–25 July 2013
5. Castro, M., Jara, A.J., Skarmeta, A.F.G.: Smart lighting solutions for smart cities. In: 27th International Conference on Advanced Information Networking and Applications Workshops, Barcelona (Spain), 25–28 March 2013
6. Anda, M., Temmen, J.: Smart metering for residential energy efficiency: the use of community based social marketing for behavioural change and smart grid introduction. Renewable Energy **67**(July), 119–127 (2014)
7. Barsana, J., Blasingh, M.: IOT based augmented perturb-and-observe soft switching boost converters for photovoltaic power systems in smart cities. Wireless Pers. Commun. **108**(4), 1–23 (2018)
8. George, C.K., Antonio, T.A.: Non-linear voltage regulator design for DC/DC boost converters used in photovoltaic applications: analysis and experimental results. IET Renew. Power Gener. **7**(3), 296–308 (2013)
9. Ishaque, K., Salam, Z., Syafaruddin.: A comprehensive MATLAB simulink PV system simulator with partial shading capability based on the two-diode model. Solar Energy **85**(9), 2217–2227 (2011)
10. Gallardo-Saavedra, S., Karlsson, B.: Simulation, validation and analysis of shading effects on a PV system. Sol. Energy **170**, 828–839 (2018)

11. Cancelliere, P., Liciotti, C.: Fire behaviour and performance of photovoltaic module backsheets. Fire Technol. **52**, 333–348 (2016)
12. Mathew, J.K., Kuitche, J., TamizhMani, G.: Test-to-failure of PV modules: hotspot testing. In: 35th IEEE Photovoltaic Specialists Conference, pp. 2839–2843. IEEE, Honolulu (2010)
13. Morlier, A., Haase, F., Kontges, M.: Impact of cracks in multicrystalline silicon solar cells on PV module power - A simulation study based on field data. IEEE J. Photovoltaics **5**(6), 1735–1741 (2015)
14. Gallardo-Saavedra, S., Hernández-Callejo, L., Duque-Perez, O.: Technological review of the instrumentation used in aerial thermographic inspection of photovoltaic plants. Renew. Sustain. Energy Rev. **93**, 566–579 (2018)
15. Gallardo-Saavedra, S., Hernández-Callejo, L., Duque-Perez, O.: Image resolution influence in aerial thermographic inspections of photovoltaic plants. IEEE Trans. Ind. Inform. **14**(12), 1–9 (2018). https://doi.org/10.1109/tii.2018.2865403
16. Schacht, R., Gerner, C., Nowak, T., May, D., Wunderle, B., Michel, B.: Miniaturized black body radiator for IR-detector calibration — design and development. In: 16th International Workshop on Thermal Investigations of ICs and Systems (THERMINIC), pp. 1–5, Barcelona, 6–8 October 2010
17. International Energy Agency: Review of failures of photovoltaic modules. Rep. IEA-PVPS T13-01:2014, ISBN 978-3-906042-16-9 (2014)
18. Kim, K.A., Krein, P.T.: Reexamination of photovoltaic hot spotting to show inadequacy of the bypass diode. IEEE J. Photovoltaics **5**(5), 1435–1441 (2015)
19. Dhimish, M., Holmes, V., Mehrdadi, B., Dales, M., Mather, P.: Output-power enhancement fot hot spotted polycrystalline photovoltaics solar cells. IEEE Trans. Device Mater. Reliab. **18**(1), 37–45 (2018)
20. Ghanbari, T.: Hot spot detection and prevention using a simple method in photovoltaic panels. IET Gener. Transm. Distrib. **11**(4), 883–890 (2017)
21. Kontges, M., Kajari-Schröder, S., Kunze, I.: Crack statistic for wafer-based silicon solar cell modules in the field measured by UV fluorescence. IEEE J. Photovoltaics **3**(1), 95–101 (2013)
22. Giordano, F., Petrolati, E., Brown, T.M., Reale, A., Di Carlo, A.: Series-connection designs for dye solar cell modules. IEEE Trans. Electron Devices **58**(8), 2759–2764 (2011)
23. Romero-Cadaval, E., Spagnuolo, G., García, L., Ramos-Paja, C.A., Suntio, T., Xiao, W.M.: Grid-connected photovoltaic generation plants: components and operation. IEEE Ind. Electron. Mag. **7**(3), 6–20 (2013)
24. PV Busbar. http://www.thepvconnect.com/photo-voltaic-busbar/. Accessed 12 July 2018
25. Sopori, B.L.: Structural defects in laser crystallized silicon ribbons and their influence on photovoltaic behavior. J. Electron. Mater. **10**(3), 517–539 (1981)
26. Mäki, A., Valkealahti, S.: Power losses in long string and parallel-connected short strings of series-connected silicon-based photovoltaic modules due to partial shading conditions. IEEE Trans. Energy Convers. **27**(1), 173–183 (2012)

The Impact of Transmission Technologies on the Evolution of the Electrical Grid

Luis Hernández-Callejo[1](✉) ⓘ, Amaia Arrinda[2] ⓘ,
David de la Vega[2] ⓘ, Igor Fernández[2] ⓘ, and Itziar Angulo[2] ⓘ

[1] University of Valladolid, Campus Universitario Duques de Soria, Soria, Spain
luis.hernandez.callejo@uva.es
[2] Department of Communications Engineering,
University of the Basque Country (UPV/EHU),
Alda Urquijo s/n, 4803 Bilbao, Spain
{amaia.arrinda,david.delavega,igor.fernandez,
itziar.angulo}@ehu.eus

Abstract. The paper describes the use of the communications technologies in the electrical network in the last decades and it provides a quick look at the significant role of these technologies in the development of new functionalities. Hence, the great evolution of the requirements of the electrical networks is summarized, from the first stages of the remote automation to a new scenario where Smart Grids and demand response will generate a different relation between utilities and final users. Then, a compilation of the main network architectures and communication protocols used in the electrical networks is outlined. Moreover, an evaluation of the benefits and drawbacks of the communication technologies, when they are applied to the last mile connectivity in electrical grids, is described. The paper concludes with a selection of the most relevant challenges of the electrical networks where the communication technologies may ne determinant as an enabling technology. In summary, the paper shows the parallel evolution of the communication technologies and the electrical grid, as a basic aspect for the development of new functionalities and services for all the agents involved in the power generation-transmission-distribution system.

Keywords: Electrical grid · Communication technologies ·
Wireless communications · Grid automation

1 Introduction

The current electrical model is evolving from a strongly centralized architecture, both in power generation and in management and based on a radial transmission and distribution scheme, to a decentralized structure where new actors arise to develop new or complementary functionalities. Hence, the scheme of a unidirectional generation-transmission-distribution chain will be replaced by a distributed system.

Concepts such as Smart Grids and demand response will generate a different relation between power generation agents, utilities and final users. The user is expected

© Springer Nature Switzerland AG 2019
S. Nesmachnow and L. Hernández Callejo (Eds.): ICSC-CITIES 2018, CCIS 978, pp. 94–101, 2019.
https://doi.org/10.1007/978-3-030-12804-3_8

to play an active role to become a prosumer due to the promotion of local power generation. The increasing introduction of distributed power generation systems and the active role of a growing number of prosumers will lead to the accomplishment of a real-time demand response. To achieve this goal, more flexible and complex management systems that allow a rapid, efficient and robust control of the electrical network will be required.

This scenario would not be possible without the use of advanced communications system that provide all the high-demanding requirements described in the previous sentences.

2   Automation and Control of the Electrical Grid: Historical Evolution

The proper performance of the electrical infrastructure is a critical factor, because power cuts cause serious economic, social and technical consequences [2]. Due to the expected radical changes in social, economic and demographic areas, the infrastructures of the cities require a radical change [1]. Due to the higher dependence on the electricity, and considering the new functionalities that are being proposed for the city of the future (*Smart City, SC*), the electric network infrastructure is a substantial and fundamental part of this process.

The modernization of the electrical infrastructure has not happened overnight. In the 1950s, analog communications were employed to collect real-time data of power outputs from power plants, and tie-line flows to power companies. To achieve this, operators used analog computers to conduct *Load Frequency Control* (*LFC*) and *Economic Dispatch* (*ED*) [3]. *LFC* was used to control generation in order to maintain frequency and interchange schedules between control areas, and *ED* adjusts power outputs of generators at equal incremental cost.

It is from 1960, with the advent of digital computing, when developing the *Remote Terminal Units* (*RTUs*), which were designed to collect voltage measurements, active and reactive power, and states of protection devices in substations. To make this measure possible, the use of dedicated transmission channels was necessary to interconnect the final devices with the computational center. As a consequence of the blackout of 1965 in the USA, a more extensive use of digital computers was highly recommended, in order to improve the real-time operations of the interconnected power systems. The use of computers and digital systems was considerably increased from 1970, with the introduction of the concept of system security, covering both generation and transmission systems [4].

The first control centers were based on dedicated computers, but in the subsequent years, they were gradually replaced by general-purpose computers. It is already from 1980 when the microcomputers were replaced by UNIX workstations, interconnected by means of *Local Area Networks* (*LAN*) [5]. These first networks of interconnected computers allowed a more rapid and efficient data exchange between different parts of the electrical grid.

The real revolution in the electrical system took place in the second half of 1990s, when the electrical industry launched the reorganization of the system. Since then, services ceased to be vertical and the generation, the transport and the distribution of the energy were separated. In addition, monopolies were replaced by competitive markets [6]. The combination of these both aspects marked a turning point in the evolution of the electrical system.

In this new scenario, three clearly differentiated segments were created in the electrical system: *Energy Management System (EMS)*, *Business Management System (BMS)* and *Market*. The above-mentioned segments and the interaction between then are shown in the Fig. 1.

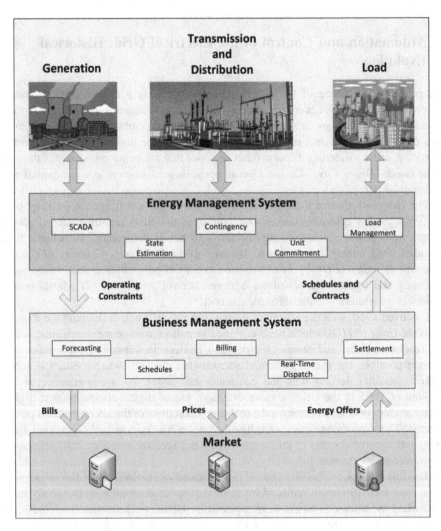

Fig. 1. Segments of the electrical system and interaction between them.

3   The Role of the Communications in the Development of the Smart Grids

3.1   Evolution of the Communication Systems in the Electrical Infrastructure

One of the aspects that enable and foster the great evolution of the electrical system described in the previous section was the development of a robust communications layer. The communication systems used in the electrical infrastructure have also undergone great changes, in order to provide new functionalities adapted to both the evolution of the grid and to the new requirements of the companies in charge of the transmission and distribution services.

Regarding Power Line Communications (the communication technologies based on the use of the electrical cable), the electrical grid was not initially developed as a communication medium, and therefore, the high number of interferences and noise sources, together with the high variability with time and frequency, represent a great challenge for the proper performance of the data transmission.

The strong points for the use of wireless communications have been the higher flexibility, the better conditions of the propagation medium and the potential use of transmission technologies already tested. On the weak side, the difficulties to provide a complete coverage and the need of deploying the complete transmission-reception chain for each link. Nevertheless, these drawbacks were recently overcome by the use of advanced cellular technologies, such as *GPRS* (*General Packet Radio Service*) and *LTE* (*Long Term Evolution* or *4G*), which provide good rates of coverage, availability, data rate and latency. Future Smart Grids functionalities and applications rely on the better performance of wireless technologies, mainly LTE and 5G.

The historical evolution of the wired and wireless communications in the electricity grid is shown in Table 1 [7, 8].

3.2   The Communication Systems in the Structure of the Electrical Grid

The performance of the a communication technology may vary depending on the conditions of the grid, such as the grid topology, the density of communication devices (users, data concentrators or substations) to be connected, the distance between them and the requirements of the communications (data rate, robustness, priority levels) and the presence of interfering electrical noise sources. For example, high-speed communications can be used for the connection of electrical substations in urban areas; however, this solution may not be feasible in other areas, such as rural environments or remote devices.

Table 1. Evolution of the communication systems in the electrical infrastructure.

Year	Achievement	Network architecture	Communication protocols and standards	Communication media
Before 1985	Without standardization	Isolated substations Hierarchical tree Single master	Conitel 2020 ModBus SEL WISP	RS232 RS485 Power-line carrier Dial Up Trunked Radio Speed below 1,200 bps
1985–1995	Standardization begins	Redundant links Hierarchical tree Multiple master	TASE 2 IEC 60870 DNP3 Serial	Packet Radio Leased lines Speed between 9,600 and 19,200 bps
1995–2000	Local Area Network (LAN) and Wide Area Network (WAN)	Substations with peer-to-peer communications Interconnected substations via WAN	TCP-IP Telnet HTTP FTP DNP3 WAN/LAN	Ethernet Spread Spectrum Radio Frame Relay Megabit Data Rates
2000 to present	Integration within the business	Use of Internet Utility connection with business network Extension of network to customer premises	TCP-IP IEC 61850 XML Power Line Communication (PLC)	Digital Cellular IP Radios Wireless Ethernet Gigabit backbones

Accordingly, the network infrastructure can be separated into two zones [9]:

- Last mile connectivity: it can be understood as the high-speed communications between the substations and the control center. There are wired communications (*PLC* and fiber optic) and wireless communications (via satellite and wireless in general).
- High speed communication core network: this network can be private or public. A high-speed network for the automation of substations is Internet based on Virtual Private Network.

Although everything is important, perhaps the last mile communications are crucial for the operation of the electric network. In this sense, one type of communications or others will bring advantages or disadvantages, as can be seen in Table 2.

Table 2. Advantages and disadvantages of possible communication technologies for last mile connectivity.

Communication technology	Advantages	Disadvantages
PLC	• Wide coverage, due to the existence of already deployed power lines (distribution and transport) • Investment in infrastructure is more economical	• Electric cables conduct noise and interferences, which degrade communications [10, 11] • As the power line is a shared medium, the data rate per user is lower than the nominal capacity, depending on the number of users simultaneously transmitting • The switches, inverters and other protection devices degrade the quality of PLC, [8] • The impedance varies with time, network topology and devices connected at each moment, which causes that the attenuation and distortion of the signal are high and changing • Power cables are not twisted and use no shielding, which may cause significant *Electro Magnetic Interference* (*EMI*)
Satellite communication	• Satellite communication has wide coverage, which allows communication between remote substations without additional infrastructure [12]	• The latency in the communications is quite large due to the long distance between satellite and devices on the ground • Protocols such as TCP/IP are not suitable for satellite communication, because the TCP/IP speed settings can cause a lot of delay [13] • The use of satellite communication for remote substations may be justified, but its use for the entire electrical infrastructure can be excessively expensive
Optical fiber communication	• It provides high bandwidth, required by applications such as electrical automation • There is no EMC problem • Immune to interferences from external sources	• The cost of devices and installation is more expensive
Wireless communication	• Wireless communication is quick to install • In case of cellular network, the cost of infrastructure is low, since the existing infrastructure can be used	• IEEE 802.11b presents the limitation of coverage (100 m), although other technologies such as WiMAX do not have this limitation • However, technologies such as WiMAX can have the drawback of the absence of infrastructure in remote areas

3.3 A Representative Example: Wireless Communications Applied to Automation Tasks

The *Wireless Sensor Networks* (*WSN*) can be used in automation tasks [14]. Specifically, *WSN* is used in *Wireless Automatic Meter Reading* (*WAMR*) systems, for reading consumption/generation in *Smart Meters* (*SM*). *WSN* presents some benefits in automation, namely:

- The sensors used in *WSN* are reliable, self-configurable, robust and are not affected by climatic conditions (pressure, temperature, etc.).
- The coverage of a sensor is low, but the entire network of sensors converts the network into an extensive communications network.
- The *WSN* is a redundant network, due to the intervention of all the sensors.
- The sensors perform a pre-filtering, so that the network presents an efficient data processing.
- The *WSN* presents self-configuration and automatic organization of the devices.
- The *WSN* has low installation and maintenance costs.

4 Conclusions

An essential feature in the evolution of the Smart Grids is the use of information and communications technology to gather different types of data from a distributed network of sensors and take fast decisions according to the analysis of this information. The final purpose is the improvement of the efficiency, reliability, economics, and sustainability of the production, transmission, and distribution of electricity.

The conversion of the user from a consumer to a prosumer, together with the new generated distribution systems, will change completely the architecture and the procedures to manage the electrical grid. This will lead to employ two-way communication systems in the smart grid.

In parallel, the recent developments on the wireless technologies, mainly in cellular systems, providing higher data rates, much lower latency values and the possibility to provide simultaneous service to a high number of devices, will open the door to innovative services for the users and the rest of the agents related to the electrical grid.

Acknowledgements. The authors thank the CYTED Thematic Network "CIUDADES INTELIGENTES TOTALMENTE INTEGRALES, EFICIENTES Y SOSTENIBLES (CITIES)" nº 518RT0558.

References

1. Lugaric, L., Krajcar, S., Simic, Z.: Smart city—Platform for emergent phenomena power system testbed simulator. In: 2010 IEEE PES Innovative Smart Grid Technologies Conference Europe (ISGT Europe), Gothenberg, Sweden, 11–13 October 2010
2. Clinton, W.J.: Executive order 13010-critical infrastructure protection. Fed. Reg. **61**(138), 37347–37350 (1996)

3. Dy-Liacco, T.E.: Control centers are here to stay. IEEE Comput. App. Power **15**(4), 18–23 (2002)
4. Wu, F.F.: Real-time network security monitoring, assessment and optimization. Elect. Power Energy Syst. **10**, 88–100 (1988)
5. Dy-Liacco, T.E.: Modern control centers and computer networking. IEEE Comput. App. Power **7**, 17–22 (1994)
6. Joskow, P.: Restructuring, competition and regulatory reform in the U.S. electricity sector. J. Econ. Perspect. **11**(3), 119–138 (1997)
7. Gungor, V.C., Lambert, F.C.: A survey on communication networks for electric system automation. Comput. Netw. **50**, 877–897 (2006)
8. McGranaghan, M., Goodman, F.: Technical and system requirements for advanced distribution automation. In: 18th International Conference and Exhibition on Electricity Distribution, 2005, CIRED 2005, Turin, Italy, 6–9 June 2005
9. Tan, N.K.: Building VPNs: With IPSec and MPLS. McGraw-Hill Networking (2003)
10. Uribe-Perez, N., Angulo, I., Hernández-Callejo, L., Arzuaga, T., De La Vega, D., Arrinda, A.: Study of unwanted emissions in the CENELEC-A band generated by distributed energy resources and their influence over narrow band power line communications. Energies **9**(12), 1–24 (2016)
11. Angulo, I., Arrinda, A., Fernandez, I., Uribe-Perez, N., Arechalde, I., Hernandez, L.: A review on measurement techniques for non-intentional emissions above 2 kHz. In: 2016 IEEE International Energy Conference, ENERGYCON 2016, Leuven, Belgium, 4–8 April 2016
12. Tisot, A.: Rio grande electric monitors remote energy assets via satellite. Util. Autom. Eng. T&D **9**(4), 58–60 (2004)
13. Hu, Y., Li, V.O.K.: Satellite-based Internet: a tutorial. IEEE Commun. Mag. **39**(3), 154–162 (2001)
14. Akyildiz, I.F., Su, W., Sankarasubramaniam, Y., Cayirci, E.: Wireless sensors networks: a survey. Comput. Netw. **38**(4), 393–422 (2002)

Municipal Solid Waste Management in Smart Cities: Facility Location of Community Bins

Diego Gabriel Rossit[1], Sergio Nesmachnow[2], and Jamal Toutouh[3(✉)]

[1] DI, Universidad Nacional del Sur and CONICET, Bahía Blanca, Argentina
diego.rossit@uns.edu.ar
[2] Universidad de la República, Montevideo, Uruguay
sergion@fing.edu.uy
[3] Universidad de Málaga, Málaga, Spain
jamal@lcc.uma.es

Abstract. Residential garbage collection is an important urban issue to address in modern cities, being a key activity that explains a large proportion of budget expenses for local governments. Under the smart cities paradigm, specific solutions can be developed to plan a better garbage collection system, improving the quality of service provided to citizens and reducing costs. This article addresses the problem of selecting locations for community bins in a medium size Argentinian city, that stills uses a door-to-door system. An integer programming model is presented to locate community bins that minimize the installment cost while also maximize the days between two consecutive visit of the collection vehicle. Results demonstrate that the proposed model and the proposed resolution algorithm were able to provide a set of suitable solutions that can be used as a starting point for migrating from the current door-to-door system to a community bins system.

Keywords: Smart cities · Municipal solid waste ·
Multiobjetive optimization

1 Introduction

Urbanization has increased the pressure over governments to find intelligent and efficient solutions to provide high quality services to citizens. In this sense, Information and Communication Technologies (ICT) is a valid tool for the authorities to enhance the living conditions under the new paradigm of *smart cities*. Therefore, several urban services have been improved with the aid of ICTs. Recent examples have been reported for public transportation [22,27], health services [33] and energy management [26], but also in other non-traditional fields, such as education [16]. ICTs have also been effectively applied to mitigate the environmental and economic problems in Municipal Solid Waste (MSW) management [19,25,34].

© Springer Nature Switzerland AG 2019
S. Nesmachnow and L. Hernández Callejo (Eds.): ICSC-CITIES 2018, CCIS 978, pp. 102–115, 2019.
https://doi.org/10.1007/978-3-030-12804-3_9

This article studies the problem of selecting the proper location of garbage community bins for a city with the aim of migrating from a door-to-door collection to a community bins system that is expected to be more efficient in terms of logistic costs [2]. Particularly, a case of study of the city of Bahía Blanca, which is an important medium size city in the South of Argentina, is addressed in this work. The objective of migrating from the current door-to-door collection system to a community bin based one, where the citizens have to carry their waste to certain bins, is usually among the plans of the local authorities for reducing the collection complexity. Solutions that contribute to reduce logistics cost are of particular interest for Argentinian cities since they are extremely high in this country [4]. As stated, using a community bins system has certain advantages over the door-to-door system. However, the location of bins in an urban area is not a trivial problem if it is supposed to be efficient [34]. This is mainly due to the characteristic of the underlying optimization problem, which is a variation of the Capacitated Facility Location Problem (CFLP). CFLP has been proven to be NP-hard through a reduction to a *3-dimensional matching problem* (3DM) [6]. Besides, finding the ubity of garbage accumulation points have an extra difficulty associated with the conflicting relationships between the several criteria that are expected to be taken into account during the process. For example, containers should not be very far from the generators since this would provoke its misuse. On the other hand, a proper scheduling of collection vehicles should be established to avoid bins overflowing. Moreover, the frequency of garbage collection will have an impact on the necessary bin capacity.

The article is structured as follows. In Sect. 2, the mathematical formulation of the target problem and the main related work is presented. Section 3 describes the solution approach used for solving the proposed model. Then, in Sect. 4 the scenarios in which the model was applied and the analysis of the main results are presented. Finally, Sect. 5 outlines the main conclusions and formulates the lines for future work.

2   Problem Description

This section describes the model for the problem addressed in this article, the proposed mathematical formulation and a review of relevant works from the related literature.

2.1   Problem Model

The problem consists in locating garbage accumulation points (GAP) while optimizing two different criteria. The first criteria is to minimize the total investment cost, i.e., the cost of installing each individual bin. The second criteria is to enhance the 'autonomy' of the GAPs. Autonomy is related to the number of days that a GAP can wait between two consecutive visits of the collection vehicle (to empty the bins). Naturally, the larger number of bins a GAP has, the larger is the storage capacity and the larger is the period of autonomy. However, having many bins implies large investment to purchase the bins.

2.2   Mathematical Formulation

The problem can be modeled as a an Integer Programming (IP) model by considering the following elements:

- A set $I = \{i_1, \ldots, i_{|I|}\}$ of potential GAPs for bins. Each GAP i has an available space Es_i for installing bins.
- A set $P = \{p_1, \ldots, p_{|P|}\}$ of generators. Following a usual approach in the related literature, nearby generators are grouped in clusters, assuming a similar behavior between elements in each cluster. The amount of waste produced by generator p (in volumetric units) is b_p. The distance from generator p to GAP i is d_{pi}, and the maximum distance between any generator in P and its assigned GAP (in meters) is D.
- A set $J = \{j_1, \ldots, j_{|J|}\}$ of bin types. Each type has a given purchase price cin_j, capacity C_j, and required space for its installation e_j. The maximum number of bins of type j that is available is MB_j.
- A set $Y = \{y_1, \ldots, y_{|Y|}\}$ of collection frequencies profiles. These profiles are defined by parameter a_y that indicates the number of days among two consecutive visits of the collection vehicle.

The model is described in Eqs. 1–11, using the following variables:

- t_{ji} is the number of bins of type j installed in GAP i.
- x_{pi} is 1 if dwelling p is assigned to GAP i and 0 otherwise
- f_{iy} is 1 if frequency profile y (defined by parameter a_y) is used for GAP i and 0 otherwise.

$$\min \sum_{\substack{j \in J \\ i \in I}} (t_{ji}\, cin_j) \tag{1}$$

$$\min \frac{\sum_{\substack{i \in I \\ y \in Y}} \left(\frac{f_{iy}}{a_y}\right)}{|I|} \tag{2}$$

Subject to

$$\sum_{i \in I} (x_{pi}) = 1, \ \forall\, p \in P \tag{3}$$

$$\sum_{j \in J} (t_{ji} e_j) \leq Es_i, \ \forall\, i \in I \tag{4}$$

$$\sum_{\substack{p \in P \\ y \in Y}} (b_p x_{pi} f_{iy} a_y) \leq \sum_{j \in J} (cap_j t_{ji}), \ \forall\, i \in I \tag{5}$$

$$\sum_{y \in Y} f_{iy} \leq 1, \ \forall\, i \in I \tag{6}$$

$$|P| \sum_{y \in Y} f_{iy} \geq \sum_{y \in Y} x_{pi}, \ \forall\, i \in I \tag{7}$$

$$d_{pi}x_{pi} \leq D, \ \forall \ p \in P, \ i \in I \tag{8}$$

$$x_{pi} \in \{0,1\}, \forall \ p \in P, \ i \in I \tag{9}$$

$$f_{iy} \in \{0,1\}, \forall \ i \in I, y \in Y \tag{10}$$

$$t_{ji} \in \mathbb{Z}_0^+, \forall \ j \in J, \ i \in I \tag{11}$$

There are two objective functions. Equation (1) is the cost of the installed community bins and Eq. (2) is the average collection frequency of the set of GAPs (hereafter Obj_c and Obj_f, respectively). Regarding constraints, Eq. (3) establishes that each dwelling should be assigned to a GAP. Equation (4) ensures that the occupied space by the bins is not larger than the available space in a GAP. Equation (5) limits the garbage assign to a GAP to the capacity of the installed bins in that GAP. Equation (6) forces that only one frequency profile is chosen for a GAP. Equation (7) establishes that if a dwelling is assigned to a GAP, that GAP has a collection frequency profile. Equation (8) restricts the maximum distance between a dwelling and the assigned GAP to a certain threshold distance. Equations (9) and (10) define the binary nature of the variables x_{pi} and f_{iy}. Equation (11) defines that t_{ji} is a non-negative integer variable.

The proposed model formulation is not linear due to the presence of Eq. (5). Although linearization is a common practice to handle nonlinear problems, the benefits of using linear equivalent forms can be offset if the transformation increases the number of integer variables since this is generally an indicator of the difficulty of the problem [14]. Therefore, the linearization technique proposed by Glover [14,15], which does not increase the number of integer variables, is applied and Eq. (5) is replaced with Eqs. (12)–(16) through the definition of the continuous variable u_{piy}. Finally, the linear equivalent formulation of the model is composed by Eqs. (1)–(4) and (6)–(16).

$$\sum_{\substack{p \in P \\ y \in Y}} [b_p a_y (u_{piy} + f_{iy} - 1 + x_{pi})] \leq \sum_{j \in J} (cap_j t_{ji}), \ \forall \ i \in I \tag{12}$$

$$u_{piy} \geq 1 - x_{pi} - f_{iy}, \ \forall \ p \in P, \ i \in I, \ y \in Y \tag{13}$$

$$u_{piy} \leq 1 - f_{iy}, \ \forall \ p \in P, \ i \in I, \ y \in Y \tag{14}$$

$$u_{piy} \leq 1 - x_{pi}, \ \forall \ p \in P, \ i \in I, \ y \in Y \tag{15}$$

$$u_{piy} \geq 0, \ \forall \ p \in P, \ i \in I, \ y \in Y \tag{16}$$

2.3   Related Work

Few articles have addressed the GAPs location problem using exact methods. Tralhao et al. [35] solved the problem of locating bins in the city of Coimbra, Portugal, considering four different objectives to minimize: the total cost of the system, the average distance between a generator and its assigned container, and the number of generators within the "push" and "pull" thresholds distances of an open candidate site. These lasts are related to the semi-obnoxiousness of the GAPs since citizens do not want them very near to reduce inconvenient environmental costs but neither very far to reduce the transportation costs.

The authors used the goal programming and the weighted sum to obtain a set of multiobjective solutions. A similar problem was solved by Coutinho et al. [7], applying the ε-constraint method but only considering two objectives: the total investment cost and a novel "dissatisfaction function" that takes into account the semi-obnoxiousness of the waste bins. Kao and Lin [20] presented three different monobjective models to solve the GAPs location problem in Hsinchu, Taiwan. These models are compared according to the average distance between generators and assigned containers. Hemmelmayr et al. [18] solved the GAP location problem with the aim of minimizing the installment costs using CPLEX inside a more generic model that also considers the routing scheduling of collection vehicle. Similarly, in Lin et al. [21] the problem of locating GAPs was solved with CPLEX in a general framework that also defines the routing plan. Ghiani et al. [12] presented an integer model that minimizes the total number of opened GAP in different scenarios of the city of Nardò, Italy. A modified version of this model, that prevents an opened GAP from having incompatible bins (i.e., bins that require a different vehicle to be emptied), was applied by Ghiani et al. [13]. This modification simplifies the posterior collection logistics since no GAP has to be visited by more than one type of vehicle.

Since facility location problems are know to be NP-hard, several authors have addressed them heuristically [30]. For example, our previous work [34] proposed a set of PageRank heuristics and metaheuristics to solve the GAP location problem in some scenarios of the city of Montevideo considering the objectives of minimizing the investment cost and maximizing the collected garbage. Di Felice [8] presented a two-phase heuristic that firstly locates the GAP in the urban network and, then, determines the size of the containers that are going to be assigned to those GAPs. Chang and Wei [5] proposed a fuzzy multi-objective genetic algorithm to solve the recycling drop-off sites allocation and routing collection in Kaohsiung, Taiwan.

In Argentina, some works have proposed improving the routing collection plans in MSW management [2,3] but few applications of ICTs have been proposed for bins location. Our previous works [31,32] applied a weighted sum approach and AUGMECON, considering the cost of the system and minimizing the average distance to the generators. Therefore, there is still room to improve collection network in Argentina through the application of ICTs.

The research reported in this article contributes with a mathematical formulation for solving the problem of locating GAPs while considering the objective of maximizing the autonomy of the GAPs, through the frequency objective as a way of bounding the posterior collection costs. Moreover, this objective is considered jointly with the objective of minimizing the installment cost. Although the visit frequency of the GAPs has been considered in previous integral approaches [18] for location-routing problems, the assignment of generators to GAPs has not been taking into account. Furthermore, in this article a real case considering the scenario from the Argentinian city of Bahía Blanca is solved.

3   Solution Approach: An Adaptation of the Augmented ε-Constraint Method

The proposed solution approach is based on the augmented ϵ-constraint method (AUGMECON). AUGMECON was first presented by Mavrotas in 2009 [23] and later improved by Mavrotas and Florios [24], in order to addressed some of the drawbacks of the traditional ϵ-constraint approach, originally developed by Haimes et al. [17]. One of the main highlights of AUGMECON is that it successfully reduces the required computing time to solve complex problems, through the avoidance of weakly efficient or repeated solutions.

AUGMECON requires as input the efficient range of the objective functions, i.e., the *nadir* and *ideal* values that each objective assumes within the Pareto front. For the problem studied in this article, since there are only two objectives involved, a single objective optimization approach can be used to find the nadir and ideal value of each objective, as proposed by Ehrgott and Ryan [10]. However, in bicriteria optimization problems, the ranges obtained using single objective optimization are the efficient ranges of each objective only if there are no alternative solutions [1]. Mavrotas proposed computing the nadir and ideal values of the objectives over the efficient set using lexicographic optimization [23]. Nonetheless, lexicographic optimization evidenced highly time consuming for the problem addressed in this paper. This approach roughly consists in optimizing the set of criteria sequentially providing that the already optimized criteria in the previous runs do not get a worse value in the subsequent runs. In a bicriteria problem, as is the case of this paper, basically this implies solving a plain single objective optimization for one of the objectives and, then, solving a second problem to optimize the second criteria subjected to not deteriorating the first criteria, which is added as a constraint to the second model. This second problem is a more constrained problem than directly optimizing the second criteria in a single objective fashion and, therefore, can only be equally (if not more) difficult to solve than the single objective model.

To overcome that efficiency problem, this article proposes a less computational expensive procedure to approximate the efficient range of the objectives, using weighted sum to 'filter' the single objective optimization results. In a second stage, a largely unbalanced vector of weights is used: the function is strongly biased towards the criteria that is optimized but the second criteria still has a small positive weight in order to avoid weakly efficient solutions. Therefore, conversely to lexicographic optimization, this approach does not increase the original set of constraints of the problem. Moreover, differently to the previous proposal by Tralhao et al. [35], the values of the criteria in the weighted sum are normalized with the results of the single objective optimization in order to make this bias significant since criteria have different measure units and, thus, their ranges may have different absolute values. Next section evaluates the three studied approaches to estimate the efficient ranges of the criteria: single objective optimization, biased weighted sum, and lexicographic optimization.

4   Experimental Analysis

This section describes the experimental analysis of the proposed approach for GAP location. Section 4.1 presents the development and execution platform. The real scenario and different problem instances considered in the experiments are described in Sect. 4.2. Finally, Sect. 4.3 reports the numerical results and their analysis.

4.1   Development and Execution Platform

The experimental analysis was performed on a Core i7 processor, with 16 GB of RAM memory, in a Windows 10 environment. The problem was modeled in C++ and the resolution was performed with the parallel mode of CPLEX 12.7.1. as the IP solver through the use of Concert Technology to link Visual Studio C++ and CPLEX.

4.2   Scenarios: The City of Bahía Blanca

The scenario is based on a real location, "Barrio Universitario", a densely populated neighborhood of Bahía Blanca, shown in Fig. 1. As regard to the input data for the model presented in Sect. 2.2, the garbage generation rate (b_p) is retrieved from a report that considered the particular characteristics of this city [29]. The density of garbage, which is required to estimate the capacity of the bins in kilograms of waste, was taken from a recent study carried out in Argentina [28].

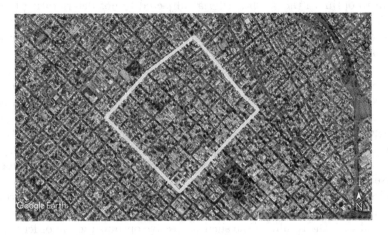

Fig. 1. Studied area ("Barrio Universitario") in Bahía Blanca. Base image: Google Earth Pro 7.3.1

The population density (per square block) was obtained by analyzing the information of the Argentinian national census [9]. This study was carried out in collaboration with the local government. The set of frequency profiles is composed by three alternatives. If a GAP is opened, it can be emptied either every day ($a_y = 1$), every two days ($a_y = 2$) or every three days ($a_y = 3$). Regarding to the bins types, three different classes of bins are considered (j_1, j_2, and j_3, respectively). The associated parameters of these three classes are: capacity (cap_j) of 1, 2, and $3\,m^3$; required space (e_j) of 1, 2, and $3\,m^2$; and installation cost (cin_j) of 100, 180, and 250 monetary units. The available space in a GAP to install containers (Es_i) is equal to $5\,m^2$. The generators in the area of study were clustered in eighty-eight groups (Fig. 2).

The spatial information was organized using QGIS 2.18.6 and the urban walking distances (d_{pi}) were calculated through an adapted version of the *osmar* package of R developed by Eugster and Schlesinger [11]. This package retrieves information directly from OpenStreetMap (https://www.openstreetmap.org/).

Three different scenarios were considered in our experiments: the *normal demand scenario*, with the waste generation rate estimated by the authorities [29], the *demanding scenario*, and the *undemanding scenario*, with generation rates 20% larger and 20% smaller than the one defined in the *normal demand scenario*, respectively. These 20% of increment and reduction in the normal waste generation rate are in line with the variations along the year presented in the surveys provided by the practitioners.

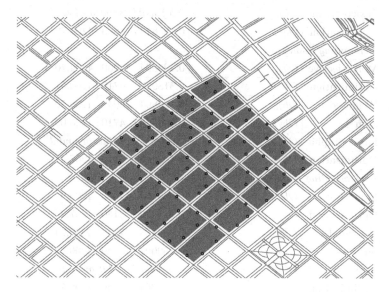

Fig. 2. Location of potential GAPs in the studied area ("Barrio Universitario" in Bahía Blanca)

4.3   Numerical Results

Table 1 reports the results of calculating the objectives ranges with monobjective optimization, biased weighted sum, and lexicographic optimization for the three studied scenarios. The table presents the method used, the optimized objective, the obtained values of both objectives, and the CPU time for each execution. The optimized objective in the biased weighted sum refers to the objective with the largest weight, while in lexicographic optimization refers to the criteria taken into account in the first place during the optimization. The biased weighted sum was able to improve the lower bounds of the nadir values of the monobjective optimization for the three evaluated scenarios.

Table 1. Payoff solutions.

Method	Optimized objective	Obj_c	Obj_f	CPU time (s)
Normal scenario				
Monobjective	Obj_c	0.104167	44000	4205.94
Optimization	Obj_f	0.687500	3880	4267.95
Weighted	Obj_c	0.104167	5710	4202.16
Sum	Obj_f	0.181818	4060	4202.16
Lexicographic	Obj_c	*No feasible solution found*		
Optimization	Obj_f	0.181818	3880	4209.72
Demanding scenario				
Monobjective	Obj_c	0.126894	44000	4204.70
Optimization	Obj_f	0.518939	4710	4260.51
Weighted	Obj_c	0.126894	8040	4206.59
Sum	Obj_f	0.204545	4710	4206.09
Lexicographic	Obj_c	*No feasible solution found*		
Optimization	Obj_f	0.193182	4710	4207.41
Undemanding scenario				
Monobjective	Obj_c	0.083333	44000	4205.94
Optimization	Obj_f	0.318182	3140	4267.95
Weighted	Obj_c	0.083333	7230	4230.24
Sum	Obj_f	0.159091	3140	4200.72
Lexicographic	Obj_c	*No feasible solution found*		
Optimization	Obj_f	0.106061	3140	4209.72

According to the results in Table 1, lexicographic optimization was not able to find a feasible solution for the scenarios when the order of the optimized objectives was first Obj_c and then Obj_f within the time limit. The main reason for this might be based on the aforementioned characteristics of lexicographic approach, which is able to solve more constrained models. In this case, the monobjective problem of minimizing Obj_f plus an additional constraint prevents the deterioration of Obj_c. Therefore, for the proposed scenarios, this enlarged problem seems to be harder to be solved than the straightforward monobjective optimization one of Obj_f, which was already a NP-hard CFLP. Thus, the efficiency of the solver to obtain feasible solutions is reduced. Furthermore, this ordering of objectives is more challenging for the solver than when Obj_f is the first stage, since in this last case, CPLEX do find a feasible solution within the time limit.

AUGMECON uses an input parameter that sets the maximum number of solutions to be search in the solution space, known as *gridpoints* [23, 24]. This is an upper bound because during the execution AUGMECON can consider convenient to bypass some of these gridpoints if one of the two following situations arise. AUGMECON considers that the next run will obtain the same solution and, therefore, will only waste computing time to find repeated information. Or,

Table 2. Multiobjective solutions for the scenarios of the city of Bahía Blanca.

Solution id	Obj_c	Obj_f	CPU time (s)	Dominance
Normal scenario				
1	0.128788	4800	4207.63	Non-D
2	0.111742	4900	4204.45	Non-D
3	0.107955	5080	4202.89	Non-D
4	0.106061	5230	4203.36	Non-D
5	0.106061	5360	4206.07	D
6	0.104167	5510	4203.56	Non-D
Demanding scenario				
3	0.130682	5700	4208.45	Non-D
4	0.125	6020	4204.72	Non-D
4	0.126894	7120	4207.63	D
5	0.126894	7400	4205.05	D
6	0.128788	7830	4210.22	D
7	0.128788	8190	4207.14	D
8	0.125	9320	4208.45	D
Undemanding scenario				
1	0.102273	3500	4200.50	Non-D
2	0.104167	3630	4204.91	D
3	0.092803	3690	4210.39	Non-D
4	0.090909	3790	4203.47	Non-D
5	0.100379	3850	4208.70	D
6	0.089015	3890	4229.86	Non-D
7	0.085227	4190	4206.56	Non-D

since a previous trial could not find a feasible solution, AUGMECON considers that the following trials will be also unsuccessful to find a feasible solution. This last situation is related to structure of the AUGMECON algorithm, in which the trials are performed in an increasing grade of complexity (the bound of the constrained objective becomes tighter in each trial).

For the three scenarios the gridpoints were set to 20. In the case of the *demanding scenario*, AUGMECON bypasses 11 gridpoints to avoid repeated solutions. Moreover, 3 trials were avoided since the solver was not able to find a feasible solution within the time limit. In the *normal scenario*, the bypasses to avoid repetition were 4 and the unperformed trials because not been able to find a feasible solution were 9. Finally in the *undemanding scenario*, these numbers were 3 and 10, respectively. Table 2 summarizes the solutions obtained with AUGMECON: the values of the objectives, the computing times and whether these solutions are dominated by another solution (D) or not (Non-D). A solution is dominated by another solution when this last one has a better value in at least one of the optimization criteria and not a worse value in any of the other optimization criteria. The AUGMECON guarantees obtaining a non-dominated solution if and only if the problem is solved to optimality. As it can be seen from the Table 2 none of the solutions were solved to optimality since they were aborted due to time limit, which is again probably related with the complexity of the underlying facility location problem.

5   Conclusions and Future Work

Urban waste management is a complex issue for local governments that usually struggle with high logistic costs. The research reported in this article focused on the initial stage of the reverse logistic chain of municipal solid waste.

Particularly, a mathematical formulation for defining the location of garbage accumulation points in a densely populated urban area while considering the minimization of both installment cost and the required frequency of visits of the collection vehicle to empty the bins is proposed. This model is solved for real scenarios of the Argentinian city of Bahía Blanca, where the government is interested in migrating from a door-to-door system to a community bins based one to simplify the collection logistic.

A set of multiobjective solutions for the problem were obtained applying the augmented ε-constraint method (AUGMECON). Moreover, a novel variation for finding the efficient range of the objectives (which is an input of the AUGMECON) is presented in order to deal with this computationally challenging facility location problem. Another important conclusion is that this work was mainly performed with free software to obtain and process geographic information (OpenStreetMap, R packages and QGIS) This represents an asset for local authorities of developing countries that generally have a short budget to incorporate ICTs in public services, as is the case of the Argentinian city of Bahía Blanca. Only the optimizer solver, CPLEX, requires a paid license.

The main lines for future work are focused on addressing more complex scenarios of the city of Bahía Blanca, either by analyzing larger urban sectors of the city or by considering the installment of different containers for different types of waste to allow source classification and facilitate posterior recycling. These larger scenarios may require the application of heuristic algorithms and the exact algorithm that is proposed in this paper can be used for validating the heuristic approaches. Since one of the main characteristics of this work it is that it has been done mostly with free software, tests performance on CBC free solver from the COIN-OR project can be performed to analyze the replacement of CPLEX. Another relevant line to research is to continue experimenting different approaches for finding the efficient ranges of the objectives in computationally complex problems.

References

1. Beeson, R.M.: Optimization with respect to multiple criteria. Ph.D. thesis, University of Southern California, United States of America, June 1972
2. Bonomo, F., Durán, G., Larumbe, F., Marenco, J.: A method for optimizing waste collection using mathematical programming: a Buenos Aires case study. Waste Manag. Res. **30**(3), 311–324 (2012)
3. Braier, G., Durán, G., Marenco, J., Wesner, F.: An integer programming approach to a real-world recyclable waste collection problem in Argentina. Waste Manag. Res. **35**(5), 525–533 (2017)
4. Broz, D., Rossit, D., Cavallin, C.: The Argentinian forest sector: opportunities and challenges in supply chain management. Uncertain Supply Chain. Manag. **6**(4), 375–392 (2018)
5. Chang, N.B., Wei, Y.: Siting recycling drop-off stations in urban area by genetic algorithm-based fuzzy multiobjective nonlinear integer programming modeling. Fuzzy Sets Syst. **114**(1), 133–149 (2000)
6. Cornuéjols, G., Sridharan, R., Thizy, J.M.: A comparison of heuristics and relaxations for the Capacitated Plant Location Problem. Eur. J. Oper. Res. **50**(3), 280–297 (1991)
7. Coutinho-Rodrigues, J., Tralhão, L., Alçada-Almeida, L.: A bi-objective modeling approach applied to an urban semi-desirable facility location problem. Eur. J. Oper. Res. **223**(1), 203–213 (2012)
8. Di Felice, P.: Integration of spatial and descriptive information to solve the urban waste accumulation problem. Procedia Soc. Behav. Sci. **147**, 182–188 (2014)
9. Dirección Provincial de Estadística de la Provincia de Buenos Aires, Argentina: Censo 2010 Provincia de Buenos Aires Resultados Definitivos por Partido (2010)
10. Ehrgott, M., Ryan, D.M.: Constructing robust crew schedules with bicriteria optimization. J. Multi-Criteria Decis. Anal. **11**(3), 139–150 (2002)
11. Eugster, M.J.A., Schlesinger, T.: osmar: OpenStreetMap and R. R J. **5**(1), 53–63 (2013)
12. Ghiani, G., Laganà, D., Manni, E., Triki, C.: Capacitated location of collection sites in an urban waste management system. Waste Manag. **32**(7), 1291–1296 (2012)
13. Ghiani, G., Manni, A., Manni, E., Toraldo, M.: The impact of an efficient collection sites location on the zoning phase in municipal solid waste management. Waste Manag. **34**(11), 1949–1956 (2014)
14. Glover, F.: Improved linear integer programming formulations of nonlinear integer problems. Manag. Sci. **22**(4), 455–460 (1975)

15. Glover, F.: An improved MIP formulation for products of discrete and continuous variables. J. Inf. Optim. Sci. **5**(1), 69–71 (1984)
16. Gómez, J., Huete, J.F., Hoyos, O., Perez, L., Grigori, D.: Interaction system based on internet of things as support for education. Procedia Comput. Sci. **21**, 132–139 (2013)
17. Haimes, Y.Y., Lasdon, L.S., Wismer, D.A.: On a bicriterion formulation of the problems of integrated system identification and system optimization. IEEE Trans. Syst. Man Cybern. **1**(3), 296–297 (1971)
18. Hemmelmayr, V.C., Doerner, K.F., Hartl, R.F., Vigo, D.: Models and algorithms for the integrated planning of bin allocation and vehicle routing in solid waste management. Transp. Sci. **48**(1), 103–120 (2013)
19. Hoornweg, D., Bhada-Tata, P.: What a waste: a Global Review of Solid Waste Management. Urban Development Series Knowledge Papers 15, World Bank, Washington, United States (2012)
20. Kao, J.J., Lin, T.I.: Shortest service location model for planning waste pickup locations. J. Air Waste Manag. Assoc. **52**(5), 585–592 (2002)
21. Lin, H.Y., Tsai, Z.P., Chen, G.H., Kao, J.J.: A model for the implementation of a two-shift municipal solid waste and recyclable material collection plan that offers greater convenience to residents. J. Air Waste Manag. Assoc. **61**(1), 55–62 (2011)
22. Massobrio, R., Toutouh, J., Nesmachnow, S., Alba, E.: Infrastructure deployment in vehicular communication networks using a parallel multiobjective evolutionary algorithm. Int. J. Intell. Syst. **32**(8), 801–829 (2017)
23. Mavrotas, G.: Effective implementation of the ε-constraint method in multi-objective mathematical programming problems. Appl. Math. Comput. **213**(2), 455–465 (2009)
24. Mavrotas, G., Florios, K.: An improved version of the augmented ε-constraint method (AUGMECON2) for finding the exact pareto set in multi-objective integer programming problems. Appl. Math. Comput. **219**(18), 9652–9669 (2013)
25. Nesmachnow, S., Rossit, D., Toutouh, J.: Comparison of multiobjective evolutionary algorithms for prioritized urban waste collection in Montevideo, Uruguay. Electron. Notes Discret. Math. **69**, 89–96 (2018)
26. Orsi, E., Nesmachnow, S.: Smart home energy planning using IoT and the cloud. In: URUCON IEEE, pp. 1–4, October 2017
27. Peña, D., et al.: Operating cost and quality of service optimization for multi-vehicle-type timetabling for urban bus systems. J. Parallel Distrib. Comput. (2018). https://urldefense.proofpoint.com/v2/url?u=https-3A__doi.org_10.1016_j.jpdc. 2018.01.009&d=DwIDaQ&c=vh6FgFnduejNhPPD0fl_yRaSfZy8CWbWnIf4XJhS qx8&r=UyK1_569d50MjVlUSODJYRW2epEY0RveVNq0YCmePcDz4DQHW-Ck WcttrwneZ0md&m=jk_RFgHjMeaRBt3cXArfDVv0_FhuSxjH3iA1Fn3M_M&s= DOIIQ7WWSBeVPqom2Grp3KZdldqBap6VSqlOgXXyq3Y&e=
28. Pettigiani, E., Muzlera, A., Antonini, S.: Caracterización de residuos sólidos urbanos domiciliarios en Unquillo, Córdoba. In: III Jornadas Nacionales GIRSU 2013, pp. 5–17. Instituto Nacional de Tecnología Industrial, Rawson, Argentina (2013)
29. Planta Piloto de Ingeniería Química UNS-CONICET: Análisis estadístico de los residuos sólidos domiciliarios de Bahía Blanca, February 2013
30. Purkayastha, D., Majumder, M., Chakrabarti, S.: Collection and recycle bin location-allocation problem in solid waste management: a review. Pollution **1**(2), 175–191 (2015)

31. Rossit, D., Tohmé, F., Frutos, M., Broz, D.: An application of the augmented ε-constraint method to design a municipal sorted waste collection system. Decision Sci. Lett. **6**(4), 323–336 (2017)
32. Rossit, D.G., Broz, D., Rossit, D.A., Frutos, M., Tohmé, F.: Una herramienta logística para la localización de contenedores de residuos separados en origen. In: Mazzeo, N.M., Muzlera Klappenbach, A.M.M. (eds.) Avances en Gestión Integral de Residuos Sólidos Urbanos 2014–15, pp. 50–69. Instituto Nacional de Tecnología Industrial, Buenos Aires, Argentina (2015)
33. Solanas, A., et al.: Smart health: a context-aware health paradigm within smart cities. IEEE Commun. Mag. **52**(8), 74–81 (2014)
34. Toutouh, J., Rossit, D., Nesmachnow, S.: Computational intelligence for locating garbage accumulation points in urban scenarios. In: Battiti, R., Brunato, M., Kotsireas, I., Pardalos, P.M. (eds.) LION 12 2018. LNCS, vol. 11353, pp. 411–426. Springer, Cham (2019). https://doi.org/10.1007/978-3-030-05348-2_34
35. Tralhão, L., Coutinho-Rodrigues, J., Alçada-Almeida, L.: A multiobjective modeling approach to locate multi-compartment containers for urban-sorted waste. Waste Manag. **30**(12), 2418–2429 (2010)

Cloud Computing for Smart Energy Management (CC-SEM Project)

Emmanuel Luján[1(✉)], Alejandro Otero[1,2(✉)], Sebastián Valenzuela[3(✉)],
Esteban Mocskos[1,4(✉)], Luiz Angelo Steffenel[5(✉)], and Sergio Nesmachnow[3(✉)]

[1] CSC-CONICET, Godoy Cruz 2390, Ciudad Autónoma de Buenos Aires, Argentina
{elujan,aotero}@csc.conicet.gov.ar
[2] Facultad de Ingeniería, Universidad de Buenos Aires, Intendente Giraldes 2160 -
Ciudad Universitaria, Ciudad Autónoma de Buenos Aires, Argentina
[3] Universidad de la República, Julio Herrera y Reissig 565, Montevideo, Uruguay
{svalenzuela,sergion}@fing.edu.uy
[4] Facultad de Ciencias Exactas y Naturales, Universidad de Buenos Aires,
Buenos Aires, Argentina
emocskos@dc.uba.ar
[5] Université de Reims-Champagne Ardenne, 9 Boulevard de la Paix,
51100 Reims, France
angelo.steffenel@univ-reims.fr

Abstract. This paper describes the Cloud Computing for Smart Energy
Management (CC-SEM) project, a research effort focused on building
an integrated platform for smart monitoring, controlling, and planning
energy consumption and generation in urban scenarios. The project integrates cutting-edge technologies (Big Data analysis, computational intelligence, Internet of Things, High Performance Computing and Cloud
Computing), specific hardware for energy monitoring/controlling built
within the project and explores their communication. The proposed platform considers the point of view of both citizens and administrators,
providing a set of tools for controlling home devices (for end users),
planning/simulating scenarios of energy generation (for energy companies and administrators), and shows some advances in communication
infrastructure for transmitting the generated data.

Keywords: Smart cities · Cloud computing · Energy efficiency

1 Introduction

Energy management is a crucial issue in modern society. Many strategies have
been proposed to guarantee an increased access to the energy resources at affordable costs for citizens, while ensuring the conservation of the resources and the
protection of the environment [1].

For the implementation of effective energy management policies, innovative
technologies must be integrated in an easy-to-use and efficient system to include

© Springer Nature Switzerland AG 2019
S. Nesmachnow and L. Hernández Callejo (Eds.): ICSC-CITIES 2018, CCIS 978, pp. 116–131, 2019.
https://doi.org/10.1007/978-3-030-12804-3_10

the capabilities of performing realistic simulations, controlling and planning the electricity market (to be applied by the energy companies), and end user applications to monitor and manage the energy consumption at home level. The capabilities of monitoring/controlling/managing the energy consumption and generation are key issues when implementing the smart city paradigm, especially when considering the emphasis on citizen engagement, environment protection, and economic considerations [2].

This article describes the Cloud Computing for Smart Energy Management (CC-SEM) project, developed by researchers from Argentina (Consejo Nacional de Investigaciones Científicas y Tecnológicas (CONICET) and Universidad de Buenos Aires (UBA)), Uruguay (Universidad de la República (UdelaR)) and France (Université de Reims-Champagne Ardenne (Reims)), and presents preliminary results. CC-SEM proposes developing an integrated platform for smart monitoring and controlling the energy consumption in urban scenarios, by integrating Big Data analysis, computational intelligence, Internet of Things (IoT), High Performance and Cloud Computing. In our Latinamerican region, there have been some limited developments towards building some specific components for energy management, but no global solutions have been explored or made available to the public. As a consequence, the CC-SEM project proposes a useful system with real application and social relevance.

Integrating renewable energy is a relevant interest nowadays, as part of a global effort to reduce the effect of the CO_2 emissions [3,4]. However, this integration poses a big challenge for the operation of the energy grid, due to the unpredictable nature of some of the renewable energy sources, such as wind and solar. Instability on renewable energy affects the electric grid, causing voltage fluctuations, changes on current and frequency, etc. In this scenario, the utilization of specific techniques for smart grid management is mandatory. Conceiving an automatic management strategy that works correctly on macro scenarios (energy grid management and energy distribution) and micro scenarios (guaranteeing appropriate quality of service for users) is not an easy task. One viable alternative is using mathematical models and computational intelligence techniques for planning and operating the energy distribution and utilization in real time. In order to apply intelligent management systems, specific hardware is needed to evaluate and control the energy consumption by using sensors, data communications, and control devices. These devices must be able to communicate between them and with central servers to integrate all the logic of the system and determine quick responses to different dynamic situations (sudden increase in energy consumption, reduction in energy generation, increase on the energy generation costs). Recently, new smart consumption monitors were made available to be installed. For example, the Linky smart meter [5] by Électricité de France (EDF) that is being widely deployed, allowing not the collection of consumption but also some remote actions. Other projects such as ElectriSense [6] can even identify the families of devices consuming energy. None of these systems are open-source and their capabilities are often restricted to data acquisition and basic automation.

Having sensors to generate data consumption measures is not enough. Strategies to transmit and use this information should be developed and adopted by users and companies. Understanding and applying computational intelligence algorithms is one of the possible paths to analyze this data, determining routines and patterns of energy utilization by individual users. Another option is planning strategies to optimize the energy consumption, by deciding when to power on and off each device from the home, building or neighborhood. The planning strategies will have into account the user restrictions and support real time actions from the user without having a critical impact to the planning. According to the capabilities of the devices, this planning can be fully automatized using IoT actuators or manually, by suggesting actions to the user via the smartphone interface [7–9].

CC-SEM project addresses the aforementioned issues, by proposing a research effort focused on building an integrated platform for smart monitoring, controlling, and planning energy consumption and generation in urban scenarios.

This article is organized as follows. Section 2 presents an overall description of the project. The main activities within the project are described in Sect. 3. Preliminary results are reported in Sect. 4. Finally, some conclusions about the ongoing work and the main lines for future work are formulated in Sect. 5.

2   Project Description

This section describes the main features of the CC-SEM project.

2.1   Project Goals and Motivation

The main goal of the project is to design a platform that allows the integration of fundamental concepts and tools for energy management in smart cities, using cloud computing, computational intelligence for big data analysis, and software for simulation and optimization of the energy generation and distribution. The aim is providing both users and administrators of the electrical grid a useful set of tools for intelligent planning and organization of the electricity consumption and generation in nowadays and future smart cities. From the point of view of the users, the project proposes the design and management of a smart home controller for electric devices applying IoT related software, and the application of Big Data processing techniques for the analysis of domestic energy consumption and smart planning. From the point of view of the electric grid administrators, novel tools are presented to monitor the state of network and the overall quality of services, and the use of novel simulation tools is proposed to analyze and foresee the energy demand. This approach is planned to be adopted by electric market regulators in Argentina and Uruguay.

Energy optimization and planning is in the agenda of many countries, but there are few solutions that integrate hardware, software, and communications, to implement an easy-to-use platform to be used by both end users and energy companies. Actually, energy providers has few (or even no) knowledge about the electricity utilization in homes. With the current electrical infrastructure, it is not possible for the provider to determine if the energy is well-used or wasted. Having a hardware infrastructure that allows obtaining useful information about utilization is the first stage in a global system to optimize energy at homes, with the main goals of reducing the costs of energy consumption and generation, and improve the quality of service offered to the users.

Another important motivation of the project is to conceive a generic set of tools to allow both users and administrators to extract useful information from the raw data measured by the home controller by applying computational intelligence/machine learning techniques. The system will be controlled by communications applying the IoT paradigm to guarantee ubiquitous access to the system, everywhere, everytime, and using a wide range of communication devices (smartphones, tablets, web interface, other management systems, etc.). The applications that integrate the proposed system are conceived as a part of a global monitoring/planning system to be used in real time in modern smart cities.

2.2 Methodology

The proposed methodology, in line with the project goals, is two-fold. On one hand, the methodology is based on missions that help the project members to consolidate a collaboration network. The partners institutions have been in contact in the past: research groups at UdelaR and Reims have collaborated in research activities related to distributed computing and cloud computing, and research groups at UdelaR and UBA have collaborated in research activities related to high performance/distributed computing and applications. However, CC-SEM is the first initiative to set a common project between the three institutions. On the other hand, the research subject is realistic and represents a real need, as observed in recent contacts with Academia, Industry, and social actors related to energy management and the real implementation of the smart cities paradigm.

Due to the interdisciplinary nature of the project, and the fact that several actors (e.g., users, companies, agencies) are interested in the project outcomes, all results achieved during the project are being rapidly made available to the community via the project website, public repositories, and on seminaries, meetings, and conferences.

3 Activities

To organize our work, we decided to concentrate efforts on three major axis, covering both end user and electrical grid operator issues.

Axis 1: Automatic energy management for home devices. One of the challenges with smart metering is how to obtain consumption data. Therefore, this first research axis aimed at designing a hardware platform for monitoring and controlling domestic consumption. This platform must follow an open architecture approach, allowing future expansions without the risk of loosing compatibility or accessibility. Indeed, the IoT paradigm drives this development as it support communication between components, guaranteeing ubiquitous access to the proposed controller and software tools to be developed within the project. The development of smart metering devices has several issues that require attention: power consumption measuring, data transmission, privacy concerns, etc.

Axis 2: Big Data analytics for domestic energy consumption and smart planning. When using nowadays electric systems, a lot of data is generated minute-by-minute about the energy utilization on homes for powering domestic appliances. This data contains useful information to be taken into account when planning the energy utilization (by end users) and generation (by energy companies). In spite of this, the information is seldom used in an integrated methodology for energy optimization in city-scale scenarios. This axis focus on developing integrated methodologies and techniques for extracting useful information from the raw energy consumption data, to be used in smart energy management and optimization in urban scenarios. Because of the environmental and structural challenges in the countries covered by this project, the main focus is on energy utilization, estimation of the economic cost, and maintaining of a good acceptance and quality of service from the user perspective. Hence, this means that the user will not be forced to perform drastic changes in his daily routine but will be guided with the plans towards a more rational and comfortable usage of electricity. Also, the feedback from users consumption may help identifying situations and usages that can be improved, favoring both the utilization of electrical energy and a better life quality. Finally, data visualization both in the frontend (e.g., a smartphone application for the user) and at the backend (a dashboard with the production and consumption charts, consumption estimation, planning schedules, etc.) is also part of our objectives. All these developments will be backed with techniques from Big Data processing, computational intelligence, and cloud computing, in order to guarantee the scalability of the system.

Axis 3: Tools and algorithms for electrical network simulation. Next generation advanced power networks, the so called *smart-grids*, will have distinctive characteristics: they will be composed by a power network similar to the present ones with the addition of a communication network. One defining characteristic of smart grids is that both power and information flow in both senses, from and to the consumers, who will take a more active role. In this context, with an increasing number of devices, effective data communication strategies are needed. Some devices can communicate directly to the home user gateway and to the Internet, but many of them cannot [10]. Thus, ad-hoc networks must be established [11]. In addition, modeling real world scenarios for estimating the energy demands for a whole national power system or in big cities like Montevideo or Buenos Aires is not an easy task. The phenomena occurring in both networks working in a coupled manner, characterized by a wide range of time scales, and the level of description needed to get a detailed representation preclude the use of common simulation tools presently used by the industry. The goal of this axis is to build a unified computational framework to simulate smart grids with the capability of analyze a national-wide power network under typical situations of interest for the different actors of the power sector: generators, carriers, utilities, consumers, planners, developers, decision-makers, etc. Future smart grids will also characterize for an increasing share of intermittent renewable energy generation (mainly wind and photo-voltaic) which are dependent on the weather. Linking numerical climate modeling with load and generation models will create a novel predictive capacity, not available in nowadays simulation tools. Models relating weather and network loads and generation will be obtained from the studies in the other research axis previously stated. The model testing and validation will be done jointly with the partnering facility operators (i.e., ADEERA in Argentina and ADME in Uruguay) by identifying the key situations to be simulated. This axis ultimately proposes integrating all the previous information and tools and build a large computing facility to ease the execution of large simulations.

4   Preliminary Results

This section reports partial results obtained in the main activities of the project.

4.1   Low Cost Energy Consumption Monitor and Controller

A prototype for smart metering system was designed and built according to the general specification from our project. The proposed system integrates three components: (i) a specific module and protocol (Energy EFficiency, EFEN), which allows defining/storing user actions and preferences, and compute plannings; (ii) the monitor/controller itself, and an interface for communication with the home controllers, based on Khimo framework. These components are implemented in independent modules that allow monitoring, operating, and controlling home devices according to specific rules.

EFEN is meant to define home devices, store power consumption data, provide and interface for device control, and also compute ad-hoc planning taking into account user preferences. In EFEN, electric devices are grouped in homes, but larger aggregations are also supported: homes can be grouped in buildings and buildings can be grouped in neighborhoods. This categorization allows performing energy planning at different levels, according to the preferences of single users/community users, and/or the needs of electric companies.

EFEN also provides an Application Programming Interface (API) meant to implement the integration of computational intelligence algorithms for big data analysis/pattern recognition and energy planning, to be designed in WP 4. EFEN also includes a feasibility check for defined agendas, a tool to simulate historical power consumption time series (useful for verification purposes), energy and cost evaluation, and user satisfaction estimation algorithms.

The controller is based on a Single Board Computer (raspberry Pi, providing a flexible and portable solution) that controls other two modules: (i) a power meter STPM01/10, integrated using the steval-ipe016v1 board, which performs the measurements using the SPI protocol, and (*ii*) a relay for power supply control. The controller communicates with the central system (Khimo) via Internet. The system is controlled by the Khimo module, which allows performing communications via the IoT paradigm [12] to guarantee ubiquitous access (everywhere, everytime), and using multiple communication devices (e.g., smartphones, tablets, web interfaces, etc.). Khimo allows remote monitoring and controlling of several devices in real time.

A specific protocol (EFEN_PROTO) was developed to guarantee efficiency in the communications between Khimo and EFEN, and also to enable different functionalities for device control. Using a bidirectional communication channel, enabling event subscription, and avoiding intermittent queries (i.e., *polling*) to each controlled device, EFEN_PROTO provides efficiency for gathering power consumption and other information from devices, and also to define actions to perform regarding the state of home appliances. Action grouping is applied to deliver messages of the same type. By grouping home appliances according to the actions to perform over them, EFEN_PROTO avoids redundancy, thus improving the communication efficiency.

A greedy algorithm was proposed as a first step to design computational intelligence methods for home energy planning. The greedy algorithm focuses on minimizing power consumption and maximizing user satisfaction, by taking local decisions to build a global agenda and considering the maximum power available is a hard restriction.

The main details about the design of the controller were published in [13] and the application of IoT-based information for designing simple heuristics for smart home energy planning were described in [14]. Further details can be found in the website https://www.fing.edu.uy/inco/grupos/cecal/hpc/EFEHO.

4.2   Characterization of Domestic Energy Consumption

The massive expansion of smart meters created the opportunity to gather costumers data and use big data algorithms to extracting useful information to be used by machine learning and planning tools.

On the literature we mostly found methodologies to estimate the electric load at the system level. Indeed [15,16], the electrical consumption at the system scale often follows seasonal variations at macro and micro scale (seasons, weekdays, hour of the day), and the aggregation of several customers profile produces a smooth profile with consistent patterns that favor the forecasting accuracy. Unlike the system-level load, the individual residential consumption depends on the daily routine and users lifestyle but also on other elements that are harder to predict. For instance, while it is easy to forecast the consumption of a programmable water heater, it is much harder to estimate the consumption of other devices that may be activated alone or at the same time (does one always turn on the oven and the dishwasher at the same time?). Some external elements such as the air temperature and the external weather can help to improve the predictions, but they also have a limited impact and correlation,

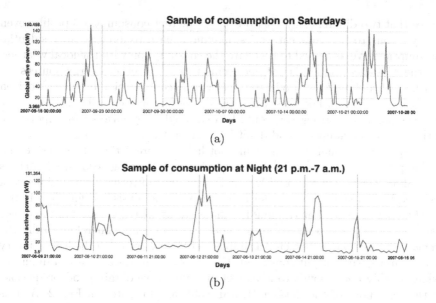

Fig. 1. Example of individual consumption classified by day of the week (a) or by time of the day (b)

depending on the residential characteristics (solar exposure, gas or electric heating), the thermal inertia of the buildings and the psychological resiliency of the inhabitants.

Due to the objectives of our project, our goal is less to predict the exact consumption for each user but rather to identify potential peaks that, combined with the consumption from other users, may lead to disturbances in the local distribution grid (in a building or in the neighborhood). Hence, we try to predict situations that may stress the grid and trigger passive (warning the users) or active (automatic shutdown of devices) measures to avoid the overload.

Several datasets for energy disaggregation can be found on the literature[1]. We chose to start by analyzing the *Individual household electric power consumption dataset* from Hebrail and Berard [17] as this dataset covers more than three years of consumption of a house located at the south of Paris, France. It presents the overall consumption and the detail of specific sets of devices, with a resolution of one minute between measures. Furthermore, weather data for that location can be easily obtained from MeteoFrance[2].

Our first analysis involved the attempt to extract consumption patterns, like for example the profile for each weekday or for parts of the day (dawn, morning, afternoon, night), which are reputed to present similar behaviors. Neither of the categories we tested leaded to conclusive results, as illustrated in Fig. 1. Indeed,

---

[1] http://wiki.nilm.eu/datasets.html.
[2] https://donneespubliques.meteofrance.fr/?fond=produit&id_produit=90&id_rubrique=32.

we see that two different days/periods have different consumptions profiles even if they belong to the same categories, making it hard to forecast the residential consumption. We also tried to correlate the consumption with the local weather, but the residence from this dataset seems to rely on other energy sources for heating and cooking (gas or oil), so the electrical consumption profile was driven mostly by less powerful devices that depend a lot on the users habits. While a few patterns pointed by Hong [18] could be extracted, they have small importance in the overall consumption and don't help forecasting.

As specific seasonal patterns could not help the prediction of the residential consumption, our next approach was to use deep learning techniques such as Long-Short Term Memory (LSTM). LSTM is a type of recurrent neural network designed for sequence problems such as time-series analysis and forecast. In our specific case, we aimed at training the model to predict the consumption of the residence based on a sequence of previous measurements. Therefore, using the previous dataset, we constructed a simple LSTM network using the Keras library and a non-negative output constraint. Using 30% of the dataset as a training set (what roughly corresponds to a year of measures), we obtain good predictions on the remainder of the dataset (RMSE=35), as illustrated in Fig. 2. At this point of our work, we didn't tried to optimize the parameters or develop more elaborated LSTM networks.

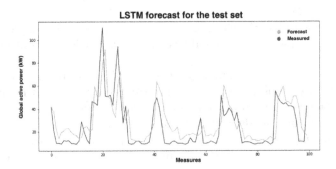

Fig. 2. Sample of LSTM forecast for the reference dataset

One inconvenient of applying deep learning techniques to the consumption of each residential user is that we need sufficient data to train the model. Indeed, a good training requires at least a few months of readings, which would delay the start of operations for new costumers. As a consequence, we decided to circumvent this drawback by applying an existing model (from another residence) and verifying its effectiveness.

Therefore, we applied the LSTM model trained with the previous dataset over an independent dataset, obtained from a real user through the Linky smart meter [5]. Contrarily to the reference dataset, this second residence fully relies on electricity for heating and cooking, which can raises different consumption profiles. Three different intervals were compared as input history for the LSTM model: 1 day, 1 week and 4 weeks (roughly a month), as illustrated in Fig. 3. Forecasts using only 24 h of history tend towards the "persistence" of the previous state, evidencing the lack of data. Forecasts with a month of history are better but tend to smooth the consumption and raise the expectation for the lower values. Finally, the forecasts made with a week of history seem to offer the better trade-off between accuracy and the history length.

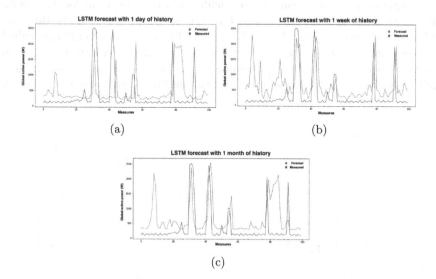

(a)   (b)

(c)

Fig. 3. LSTM forecasts with different history lengths: (a) 1 day, (b) 1 week and (c) 1 month.

While prediction errors still occur (mostly "false positive" forecasts, like for example on the mark 1–20 on the samples), these estimations are good enough to help a recommendation system or to help detecting potential overloads (summing up the expected consumption from several residences). As expected, the RMSE is quite important (300 or more) but at least we have a baseline model that can be quickly deployed. As soon as a sufficient number of measurements is collected, individual models can be created by incrementally training the model. Also, specific parameter optimizations can be performed to improve the accuracy.

The scalability and portability of the developed solution can be ensured by relying on basic ETL (Extraction, Transformation, Load) using MapReduce, while more advanced operations can be conducted with high-level tools (e.g., Pig or Apache Spark and Tensorflow/Keras). Storage and access to the data can be made using NoSQL databases, which are especially adapted to store data series from sensors and other data sources (e.g., power generation, historical consumption charts, weather forecast) [19].

4.3   Renewable Energy Generation Forecast

Although there are some options to produce energy from wind and other sources, photovoltaic (PV) systems are the more likely way to generate renewable energy in an urban setting in a massive scale. The challenges for adopting higher shares of this type of energy are posed by its intermittence, inherited from solar radiation dependency on local climatology, mainly the cloud cover. In order to be able to forecast PV generation for a particular system in a specific location, both consideration about the resource and the system should be taken. To this end, in this project we combined the WRF[3] model with a PV modeling library called `pvlib-python` [20,21]. The `pvlib-python` library comes with some functions to retrieve weather forecast data from some particular web services, thus through minimal modifications it was adapted to read data produced by our installation of the WRF model.

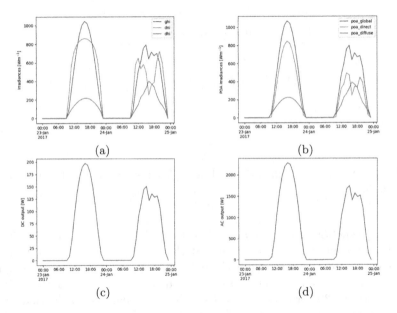

Fig. 4. Example output of the pipeline of PV generation forecast for two sample days with different solar resource characteristics.

In this setting, the pipeline to get generation data from weather prediction models for a particular PV system is as follow:

1. WRF provides forecast for irradiances: global horizontal (*ghi*), diffuse horizontal (*dhi*), and direct normal (*dni*); and other variables which affect the PV system working condition like temperature and wind speed (see Fig. 4a).

---

[3] https://www.mmm.ucar.edu/weather-research-and-forecasting-model.

2. Irradiance data is processed through `pvlib-python` to obtain irradiance components projected on the PV modules plane-of-array (POA): global (*poa_global*), direct (*poa_direct*), and diffuse (*poa_diffuse*) (see Fig. 4b).
3. Considering the configuration (number of series and parallel connected) and model of PV modules, the `pvlib-python` is used to forecast the DC power production (Fig. 4c shows the individual generation of each module).
4. Regarding the information about the PV inverter of the system, the AC power is forecasted (Fig. 4d shows the aggregated system AC power).

The proposed methodology allows forecasting the generation of individual PV systems. Although Fig. 4 shows data in an hourly base for convenience, more frequent sampling can be obtained as the actual model time step is much smaller, allowing to capture the dynamics of the possible generation. For modeling multiple systems assigned to the same WRF grid point, for which no difference will be detected in the radiation forecast, equivalent systems could be defined. At the moment, development efforts are focused on model calibration and validation. Several configuration and submodel options could be chosen and a systematic error quantification study is under way.

4.4   NB-IoT in Smart Cities: Optimizing Bandwidth Usage

To assess the state of smart cities [22], smart sensors are deployed to monitor the grid, those devices inform magnitudes that can be used to derive information about the whole urban scenario. Thus, the supporting communication network plays a fundamental role to ensure collecting state information. While wired networks entail high economic costs, wireless networks are positioned as a competitive alternative [23]. In particular, the exponential growth of cellular wireless networks establish a powerful infrastructure for the new communication technologies. In recent years, a narrow band radio technology (<200 kHz) has been developed: Narrow Band Internet of the Things (`NB-IoT`) [24]. It is designed to satisfy requirements of low-bitrate applications, with special emphasis in coverage enhancement, ultra-low power consumption and massive terminal access. Another characteristic of this technology is non-latency-sensitivity, despite this, high channel occupation scenarios occur, thus, increasing latency levels over tolerable thresholds (up to 10 s). These scenarios generate a negative impact in user equipment such as smart alarms, where successful message deliver is a must. A proper distribution of radio resources offer a useful tool to overcome this challenge. Here we present preliminary results of an `NB-IoT` priority-based uplink scheduling algorithm, with the goal of mitigating latency issues over prioritized smart devices.

In an `NB-IoT` communication cell, during the uplink process, the base station (`BS`) determines the modulation and coding scheme (`MCS`), and the number of repetitions (`NR`) that will be used for the user equipment (`UE`), i.e. the smart device. These parameters determine the number of resource units (`RUs`) of the encoded transmission block that has to be send, as well as they determine the block error rate (*BLER*). Thus, the `BS` can adjust the number of block losses of each device, with a correlated `RU` cost.

In our general proposal, framed in uplink unacknowledged transmission scenarios, the BS schedules priority devices first, but with one important addition: the definition of different tolerable block error rates ($BLER_{tol}$) to each device according to its priority. In extreme coverage scenarios, zero $BLER_{tol}$ can not be guaranteed to every device, hence we reserve this value for maximum priority devices. Surely, low $BLER_{tol}$ has associated an RU cost drawback, but in exchange it ensures message successful arriving.

BS actual algorithms conform proprietary software of each manufacturer, however there are currently methods available in literature [25]. In this preliminary development stage, we propose an straightforward BS strategy Algorithm 1 for calculating (MCS,NR) tuple, based on mentioned previous work. Successive iterations approximate $BLER$ to $BLER_{tol}$. This algorithm allows to estimate the RU cost associated to a particular $BLER_{tol}$, which is a fundamental piece of the general scheduler.

Currently there are no FLOSS software tools for running and testing this kind of algorithms. To accomplish this task, we developed a reduced NB-IoT uplink simulator which depicts the uplink iterative sub-process, where the BS determines the MCS and NR and sends this information to the smart device.

```
1: repeat
2:     Estimate BLER
3:     if BLER > BLER_tol then
4:         if MCS > MCS_min then
5:             MCS ← MCS - 1
6:         else if NR < NR_max then
7:             NR ← NR * 2
8:         else if  then
9:             Bad channel quality.
10:            Target BLER can't be achieved.
11:        end if
12:    else if BLER < BLER_tol then
13:        if MCS < MCS_max then
14:            MCS ← MCS + 1
15:        else if NR > NR_min then
16:            NR ← NR/2
17:        else if  then
18:            Good channel quality.
19:            RU consumption can't be decreased.
20:        end if
21:    else if  then
22:        BLER is in range.
23:    end if
24: until BLER = BLER_tol {re-scheduling is not needed}
```

Algorithm 1. MCS-NR

Figure 5 reports preliminary results. The experiment consists in 500 realizations of a UE transmitting to the BS 20 blocks of 256 bits, i.e, the magnitude of a possible alarm message. The RU cost of possible target $BLER_{tol}$ was estimated considering three characteristic coverage scenarios, represented by different signal-to-noise (SNR) values: –16, –7 and 2 dB.

Figure 5 also shows a reasonable trade-off between radio resource consumption, associated with transmission costs: bandwidth, latency and channels occupancy; and block losses, associated with $BLER$. Obtained results points out that

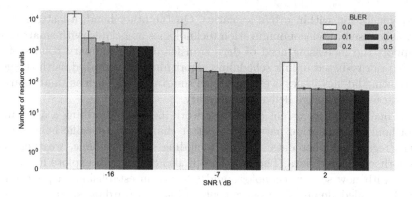

Fig. 5. Estimated RU cost for each target *BLER*.

an adequate *BLER* threshold is between 0 and 0.1 (0 and 10% of block losses), which is the transition with highest RU gradient.

It is expected that the outcome of the whole scheduling strategy be relevant in the design and implementation of future BS software, mitigating transmission cost issues over prioritized smart devices, improving communication quality.

5   Conclusions and Future Work

This article presented an overall description of the CC-SEM project in conjunction with preliminary results. In this project it is proposed to build an integrated platform for smart monitoring, controlling, and planning energy consumption and generation in urban scenarios. In particular three main activities were specified.

Regarding *axis 1*, where the defined goal was to automatically manage energy for home devices, main contribution consisted in the development of a low cost IoT device capable of monitoring, operating, and controlling home appliances according to predefined rules.

With respect to *axis 2*, in which it was proposed to utilize Big Data techniques for analyzing domestic energy consumption and smart planning; the contribution was based on the analysis of domestic consumption patterns to help predicting home consumption through a sequence of previous measurements. The obtained estimations were good enough to help a recommendation system or to help detecting potential network overloads.

In the last activity, *axis 3*, the objective was to simulate an electrical network (which includes three stages: generation, transmission and distribution) with the addition of a communication network. Following two main contributions were presented: on the one hand, a new methodology to forecast the generation of individual PV systems was proposed. A WRF model was combined with a PV modeling library called `pvlib-python`. This approach results of utterly importance due to PV systems represent a major technology for massive renewable energy generation within urban scenarios. On the other hand, a last contribution was focused in telecommunication technologies associated with smart cities to support the increasing need of data transference. Preliminary results of an NB-IoT priority-based uplink scheduling algorithm were reported, with the goal of mitigating latency issues over prioritized smart devices, such as smart alarms, where successful message deliver is necessary.

The main lines for current and future work include performing a deep analysis of home consumption patterns to better characterize specific behaviors of citizens regarding other data sources, including socio-economic, weather, and neighborhood-related data. The project will also continue to explore IoT development with new sensor technology and advance in establishing a program of controlled scaled domestic measurements. Finally, regarding smart grid, new communications standards will be analyzed and their impact on protocols and infrastructure will be analyzed focusing on creating a new communication layer on top of electric network.

Acknowledgment. CC-SEM project is supported by the STIC-AmSud regional program (France–South America).

References

1. Turner, W., Doty, S.: Energy Management Handbook. The Fairmont Press, Lilburn (2007)
2. Towsend, A.: Smart Cities: Big Data, Civic Hackers, and the Quest for a New Utopia. Ww Norton & Co (2013)
3. Soares, A., Antunes, C., Oliveira, C., Gomes, A.: A multi-objective genetic approach to domestic load scheduling in an energy management system. Energy **77**, 144–152 (2014)
4. Zakariazadeh, A., Jadid, S., Siano, P.: Economic-environmental energy and reserve scheduling of smart distribution systems: a multiobjective mathematical programming approach. Energy Convers. Manage. **78**, 151–164 (2014)
5. Wahyuddin, Y.: To What extent the grand lyon metropole can harness the smart meter project towards the governance of territorial climate energy plan (PCET) study case: smart electric lyon project initiated by EDF [French Electric Utility Company]. In: International Conference on Public Policy (2017)
6. Gupta, S., Reynolds, M., Patel, S.: Electrisense: single-point sensing using EMI for electrical event detection and classification in the home. In: Proceedings of the 12th ACM International Conference on Ubiquitous Computing, pp. 139–148 (2010)
7. Spagnolli, A., et al.: Eco-feedback on the go: motivating energy awareness. Computer **44**(5), 38–45 (2011)
8. Gamberini, L., et al.: Tailoring feedback to users' actions in a persuasive game for household electricity conservation. In: Bang, M., Ragnemalm, E.L. (eds.) PERSUASIVE 2012. LNCS, vol. 7284, pp. 100–111. Springer, Heidelberg (2012). https://doi.org/10.1007/978-3-642-31037-9_9
9. Costanza, E., Ramchurn, S., Jennings, N.: Understanding domestic energy consumption through interactive visualisation: a field study. In: Proceedings of the 2012 ACM Conference on Ubiquitous Computing, pp. 216–225 (2012)

10. Rabaey, J., Ammer, M., da Silva, J., Patel, D., Roundy, S.: Picoradio supports ad hoc ultra-low power wireless networking. Computer **33**(7), 42–48 (2000)
11. Niyato, D., Xiao, L., Wang, P.: Machine-to-machine communications for home energy management system in smart grid. IEEE Commun. Mag. **49**(4), 53–59 (2011)
12. Karnouskos, S.: The cooperative Internet of Things enabled smart grid. In: 14th IEEE International Symposium on Consumer Electronics, pp. 7–10 (2010)
13. Orsi, E., Nesmachnow, S.: Iot for smart home energy planning. In: XXIII Congreso Argentino de Ciencias de la Computación (2017)
14. Orsi, E., Nesmachnow, S.: Smart home energy planning using IoT and the cloud. In: 2017 IEEE URUCON. IEEE (2017)
15. Kong, W., Dong, Z., Jia, Y., Hill, D., Xu, Y., Zhang, Y.: Short-term residential load forecasting based on lstm recurrent neural network. In: IEEE Transactions on Smart Grid Early Access (2017)
16. Amarasinghe, K., Marino, D., Manic, M.: Deep neural networks for energy load forecasting. In: IEEE 26th International Symposium on Industrial Electronics, pp. 1483–1488 (2017)
17. Dheeru, D., Karra Taniskidou, E.: UCI machine learning repository, May 2018
18. Hong, S.: Individual household electric power consumption, May 2018
19. Zhou, K., Yang, S.: Understanding household energy consumption behavior: the contribution of energy big data analytics. Renew. Sustain. Energy Rev. **56**, 810–819 (2016)
20. Holmgren, W., Andrews, R., Lorenzo, A., Stein, J.: PVLIB Python 2015. In: 2015 IEEE 42nd Photovoltaic Specialist Conference, pp. 1–5 (2015)
21. Holmgren, W., Groenendyk, D.: An open source solar power forecasting tool using PVLIB-python. In: 2016 IEEE 43rd Photovoltaic Specialists Conference, pp. 0972–0975 (2016)
22. IEEE: "Smart cities." https://smartcities.ieee.org/. Accessed 02 Feb 2019
23. Ramírez, C.A., Barragán, R.C., García-Torales, G., Larios, V.M.: Low-power device for wireless sensor network for smart cities. In: 2016 IEEE MTT-S Latin America Microwave Conference (LAMC), pp. 1–3, December 2016
24. Wang, Y.E., et al.: A primer on 3G pp narrowband internet of things. IEEE Commun. Mag. **55**, 117–123 (2017)
25. Yu, C., Yu, L., Wu, Y., He, Y., Lu, Q.: Uplink scheduling and link adaptation for narrowband internet of things systems. IEEE Access **5**, 1724–1734 (2017)

Using Smart-Grids Capabilities as a Natural Hedge Against Novel Risks Coming from Non-conventional Renewable Electricity Generation

Claudio Risso[✉]

Facultad de Ingeniería, UdelaR, Montevideo, Uruguay
crisso@fing.edu.uy

Abstract. Whether due to economic pressure or environmental concerns, the penetration rate of renewable energies has been increasing over recent years. Uruguay is a leader country in the usage of renewable energies, getting 98% of its electricity from such sources. Its lack of fossil energy resources has historically pushed this country to rely on hydro-energy. Recently, in a scenario where most natural hydro-resources have been deployed, Uruguay has moved to non-conventional renewable energies, to biomass and wind power mostly, although nowadays solar sources are rapidly increasing. As clean and financially stable as they are, non-conventional energies have weaknesses. Unlike thermic and most hydro-sources, wind and solar energies are not controllable, are intermittent and uncertain some hours ahead, complicating the short-term operation and maintenance of electrical systems. This work explores how to use smart-grids capabilities to adjust electricity demand as a natural hedge against novel short-position risks in the Uruguayan electricity market.

Keywords: Renewable energies · Smart-grids ·
Short-term power dispatch scheduling · Combinatorial optimization

1 Introduction

The absence of fossil energy sources, such as oil, coal or gas, spurred decades ago to Uruguayan authorities to invest in hydroelectric dams as its main source of electricity. Unlike fossil resources, the country accounted important hydraulic assets. Hence, Uruguay historically figured among top countries regarding the percentage of electricity coming from renewable sources. The national electric power matrix was complemented with conventional oil-fired thermal generation plants. Later on, the interconnection with its border neighbors (Argentina and Brazil) supplied and additional level of resilience and robustness to the system. As demand grew, the frequency at which thermal generation plants were used increased as well, so did the energy costs. Similar conditions were taking place in Argentina and Brazil, so importing electricity was as expensive as importing

© Springer Nature Switzerland AG 2019
S. Nesmachnow and L. Hernández Callejo (Eds.): ICSC-CITIES 2018, CCIS 978, pp. 132–147, 2019.
https://doi.org/10.1007/978-3-030-12804-3_11

oil to keep thermal plants running. By 2007, the situation became critical and the national authorities started a process of diversification of the power sources, which aimed on biomass and wind power at early stages. Today, Uruguay is a world leader in the usage of renewable energies, serving 98% of its own demand of electricity from renewable sources (see [8]).

Table 1. Installed power plant by type of energy source [ADME: 2017]

Energy by type of source	Number of units	Installed power plant (MW)	Relative subtotal	Produced energy total 2017 (GWh)	Relative subtotal
Biomass	12	200	4.4%	900	7.1%
Wind-power	37	1.437	31.5%	4.400	34.9%
Solar	17	230	5%	200	1.6%
Hydroelectric	4	1.534	33.7%	6.200	49.2%
Combined Cycle	1	550	12.1%	100	0.9%
Other Thermal Units	4	604	13.3%	800	6.3%

Table 1 presents the main details regarding the Uruguayan power plant by late 2017. The source is ADME (Administración Del Mercado Eléctrico) and it is available at http://adme.com.uy. The extremely low dependence upon fossil energies isolates the Uruguayan electricity market from commodities volatility. On the other hand, and as it counts in Table 1, over one third of the total energy consumed comes from wind-power, which is highly volatile in the short-term. Variable renewable energies (VRE) have a negative impact in the operation costs of the system. Real-world examples (UK and Germany) of such problems are described in [2]. Managing the electric grid of a country is a challenging task that must be carried out carefully and optimally. In order to accomplish that, multiple problems are to be solved, spanning different scales of time and components. Main objects are: generating plants, the transmission and distribution networks. Long-term planning usually applies to assess the return of investments over those objects along many years ahead. Medium-term planning usually refers to the valuation of intangible resources, such as the height of the lake in an electric dam accounted as an economic asset. Short-term planning consists in crafting optimal dispatch schedules some days ahead, in order to efficiently coordinate the usage of available resources. Beyond that time scale, there are almost real-time models to keep the physical variables of the system (e.g. frequency, active and reactive power) under control. This work aims on the short-term power dispatch of the grid, whose results set the prices of energy in the electricity market. Due to its short scale of time (a few days ahead), such models can assume many sources of uncertainty as deterministic. For instance, oil prices can be considered as fixed along some days to follow, and although sudden/unexpected rains could arise, they hardly change the level of water reservoirs to a significant point.

The former premisses are actually quite realistic when applied to conventional and some non-conventional energy sources (e.g. biomass). Regarding wind and solar power however, those hypotheses become erroneous. The intrinsic stochastic nature of wind and solar power turns out the short-term dispatch of the grid into a much harder challenge, which is object of academic and industrial interest (see [3,6]). In its economical dimension that volatility indicates that wind-energy constitutes a risk position. Under steady conditions (energy prices, weather conditions, date of a year) demand is highly predictable, so given a particular date of the year and an accurate weather forecast, the demand over the grid is among those variables that could be considered as known. This is due to low deviations associated with a large number of users under a stationary behaviour. As a consequence, legacy short-term optimal schedules models are deterministic, or deal with narrow variance in the variables. In addition, traditional instruments to modulate demand with economic measures go by setting different prices between hours on a day, intending to move a fraction of energy consumption from the demand's peak hour towards demand valleys (night-valley filling). Such instruments are based on the premisse that energy is scarce, while the truth is that non-conventional energies, especially wind-power, can be either lower or higher than forecasted. Smart-grid technologies are a cornerstone for Smart-cities paradigm. Smart-grids allow to coordinate important portions of the demand, which could now be directed in opposite direction to wind-power variations and accounted as a hedge instruments against generation risks (demand response). There are many ways to get benefits from demand control. For instance, works [4,5,7] are inspired in a free-market environment, with a kind of underlying stock exchange where energy offers are traded. Sometimes this is not possible due to regulatory or scalability issues. Besides, wind and solar power fluctuate so rapidly, that implementing classical financial contracts (e.g. forwards or swaps) is not always optimal, even a-day-ahead. Using batteries is another instrument to compensate power variations in the offer with demands. This document explores the benefits of using smart-grid technologies and residential energy storage, to coordinate part of the residential demand with the uncertain offer of energy in the system. The application case is based on the particulars of the Uruguayan market, where only large-scale energy consumers are allowed to trade in the electricity market, while residential users only can get electricity from the state-owned company. In this wholesale electricity market, the price is not set by pairing bids and offers. Instead, their production parameters of generators (e.g. minimum and maximum power, fixed and variable costs) are public, and up from them, the authorities that operate the system dictate when and how much energy is going to be produced by each unit. Production decisions are driven by a short-term reference optimization model, whose objective function aims on minimizing the total cost of generation. Such premisses are ideal for the approach presented in this work, which is stated from a short-term point of view optimization. These results show how the existence of smart-grid technologies allow to improve the efficiency of the system, not the return of the investments necessary to achieve such smart-grid grade. Problem instances are based on real data of the Uruguayan market, chosen to be representative of different scenarios. The remaining of this document is organized as follows: Sect. 2 shows the shot-term volatility of wind power and the techniques used to master it; Sect. 3 describes the main characteristics of the optimization models used to estimate the benefits of counting with smart-grid technologies; Sect. 4 presents the set of test scenarios used as instances of the previous models; while Sect. 5 summarizes the main conclusions of this work and lines of future work.

2   Dealing with Wind Power Uncertainty

This section shows how variable wind-power is, when described as a stochastic process, and it briefly presents some of the techniques used to likely fence its realizations. The historical of wind-power data in Uruguay has a few years, and along this period the installed power plant was firmly growing, so instead of expressing power in term of MW we use the Plant Load Factor (PLF), which corresponds to the actual power generated at each time, divided by the sum of the installed power capacity of each wind turbine in the system at each moment. So, $0 \leq \text{PLF} \leq 1$ for each hour. Hence, information is normalized, and we can disregard of changes in the installed capacity during the period of analysis.

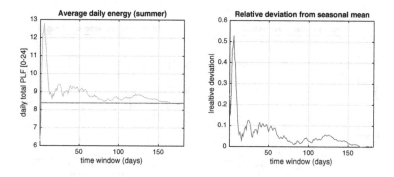

Fig. 1. Time window average for daily wind energy on summer days

Figure 1 shows the daily cumulated PLF (the sum of hour PLFs, which then ranges from 0 to 24) along two consecutive years of summer days. We have selected days of one season to avoid deviations coming from seasonal behaviour. The figure shows how after a week or two the process goes inside the 10% error band, respect to the expected value for that season.

Therefore, wind-power is fairly regular when used in medium-term planning. For shorter periods of the time, the situation is quite the opposite. The leftmost of Fig. 2 sketches the distribution of daily cumulated PLFs, while the rightmost part plots actual daily realizations of the process (blue curves) along one and a half years and the average PLF at each hour (black asterisks). Complementarily, there are approaches for short-term wind power forecasting based on

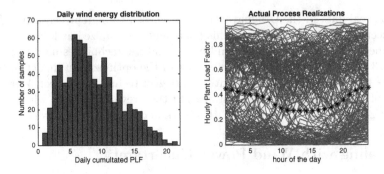

Fig. 2. Histogram of daily wind energy samples [leftmost] and 30% most atypical realizations for Uruguayan wind-power [rightmost] (Color figure online)

numerical simulations of atmosphere's wind flows. For a day ahead period, or even larger time windows, numerical simulations are usually more accurate than purely statistical models. Figure 3 presents 72 h ahead forecasts (blue curves) and actual power series (red curve) for two samples within the actual data-set. These and other historical series are available at: http://www.ute.com.uy/SgePublico/ConsPrevGeneracioEolica.aspx.

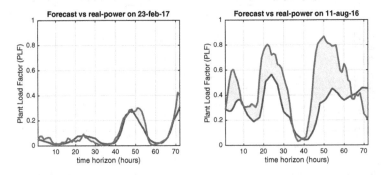

Fig. 3. Examples of 72 h forecasts (blue) and the actual power registered (red) (Color figure online)

Although numerical simulations perform better than purely statistical methods to follow the process whereabouts at early stages, they are far from being trustworthy in what respects to the construction of likely scenarios at larger times. On the rightmost of Fig. 3 there is an example where the difference of energy between forecast and actual processes (i.e. the grey area), accounts 57% of the average PLF for the period.

Besides assessing potential savings coming from using smart-grids, this work benchmarks the performance of deterministic and stochastic optimization models over the same test scenarios. Therefore, confidence bands were used to fence

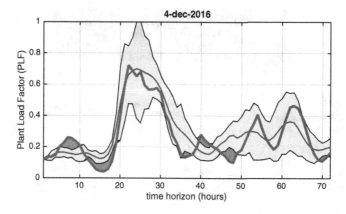

Fig. 4. A confidence band (grey) crafted after forecast and the actual process (red) (Color figure online)

wind-power process with a high degree of certainty. Those bands were crafted up from the combination of three independent sets of forecasts and the correspondent actual power series. As an example, Fig. 4 shows the confidence band for a particular day within the test-set. Bands were calibrated seeking for the average off-band energy (i.e. green areas in the figure) to be below 10% of the average PLF. Besides, bands are adjusted so less than 10% of the days violate the previous condition. The calibration whose average band width is minimal while fulfills the previous conditions, has an average width deviation respect to the centroid (i.e. blue curve) slightly above 10% of the average energy demand (the fact this final figure replicates the previous is just a coincide). The details of the technique used to craft these bands are documented in [9].

3   Optimal Short-Term Optimization Model

This section describes the main entities of the Uruguayan electricity market and examples about how some of them are modeled, and how their instances are combined into a single optimization model.

Over the upmost part of Fig. 5 is represented the power offer of the system. Renewable (green) energies comprise: wind and solar power (non-cumulative renewable/NCR), Hydroelectricity (HYD) and the Biomass, whose units are basically thermal generation plants (TER). The installed power plant is completed with fossil thermal generation units. Upon the rightmost-bottom of Fig. 5 non-manageable demands are represented. They are typically associated (though not limited) to some residential appliances. Such inelastic appliances (IAP) are considered hourly predictable demands over the time horizon to optimize, which is 72 h ahead in this work (i.e. the time horizon of wind-power forecasts). In other words, inelastic appliances impose a power requirement to the system. Variants of the basic model introduce: elastic applications (EAP) or active applications

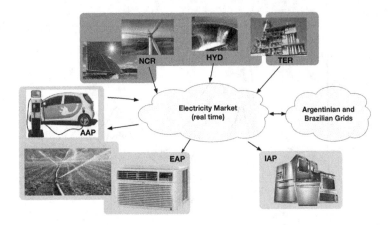

Fig. 5. Entities of the wholesale electricity market

(AAP). Elastic applications are those where requirements are better expressed in terms of energy rather than power. A fraction of what they need could be expressed as a power constraint, but the idea is that substantial portions of the required energy within certain time windows could be either deferred or advanced into that window. Finally, in addition to being elastic, active applications can return power to the network when necessary. In all the models explored in this work, elastic and active applications are at the service of the system (i.e. social-welfare). We assume they can be remotely controlled, so as long as basic power requirements are fulfilled, the gaps of energy to complete those demands constitute control variables just as those of the installed power plant, and they are also used to get the most of the optimization.

3.1   Thermal Units

Each entity has a reference mixed-integer optimization sub-model or block. All these blocks combined and instantiated for a particular data-set define the whole optimization problem for that instance and variant. For example, Eq. 1 is the framework to model simple thermal plants, labeled as *Other Thermal Units* in Table 1.

$$
\begin{cases}
\min_{x_t^g, w_t^g} a \sum_{t \in T} x_t^g + b \sum_{t \in T} w_t^g + \alpha \sum_{t \in T} y_t^g \\
m_{GT} \cdot x_t^g \leq w_t^g, & t \in T & (i) \\
w_t^g \leq M_{GT} \cdot x_t^g, & t \in T & (ii) \\
y_t^g \geq x_t^g - x_{t-1}^g, & t \in T & (iii) \\
2x_t^g - 2x_{t+1}^g + x_{t+2}^g + x_{t+3}^g \geq 0, & t = 1, \ldots, T_m - 3 & (iv) \\
2x_t^g - 2x_{t+1}^g + x_{t+2}^g + x_{t+3}^g \leq 2, & t = 1, \ldots, T_m - 3 & (v) \\
x_t^g, y_t^g \in \{0, 1\}
\end{cases}
\tag{1}
$$

Boolean variables x_t^g indicate whether the unit g is active or not at the time moment t. The period of activation of a small thermal unit is bellow 10 min, so it can be considered instantaneous for a time slot of one hour. Whenever active $(x_t^g = 1)$ the power generated by each unit must be between technical minimum (m_{GT}) and maximum (M_{GT}) values. This is imposed with constraints (i) and (ii). Boolean variables y_t^g identify the instants of time t at which a unit g is activated, which is forced by constraint (iii). The terms in the objective function respectively correspond to: the hourly fixed cost of operation when the unit is active; the variable cost incurred by the level of power generated; and the operational costs incurred in by activating the unit, i.e., fuel expenditures for warming up the unit plus a maintenance share per operation cycles. Besides of being costly in terms of maintenance, the process of frequently activating thermal units is not operationally friendly. Therefore, we added constraints to guarantee that once started, a unit should be active (for instance) at least 3 h (constraints (iv)), and also to force it to be inactive for at least 3 h after stopped (constraints (v)). The last sets of constraints should be complemented with boundary constraints when the initial or final activity states are inherited as part of the instance. Table 2 shows a possible set of parameters for those simple thermal units, for a particular oil price during 2016. We could not find public data to valuate parameters a.

Table 2. Parameters for simple thermal units

Name of each thermal unit	Number of power subunits	Power min (MW) max		a USD	$b \ \frac{USD}{MWh}$
Central Batlle (Motores)	6	6	60	0	82
Punta del Tigre: 1 to 6	6	90	288	7423	86
Punta del Tigre: 7 and 8	2	0.6	48	1619	88
Central Térmica Respaldo	2	40	208	6819	103

Unlike simple thermal units, the *Combined Cycle Plant* (or CCC) has slow time commitments, of around four hours till full operation, so its start-up details should be integrated into the model. To model such type of unit we used four types of variables and over twenty types of constraints. Elaborating into those details would deviate the focus of this document, so they were intentionally left outside of the scope. Reference parameters are: $m_{GT} = 58$ MW, $M_{GT} = 550$ MW, $a = 5240$ USD (hourly fixed cost), $b = 63$ USD/MW (variable cost) and $\alpha = 5500$ USD. Along the four hours it takes the CCC to attain its full operation, the plant gradually increases the output power following a predetermine ramp. During that ramp-up, the efficiency is lower, so b is 35% higher. Once in full operation condition, the CCC should not be stopped until four hours later (i.e. eight hours since started), and once stopped there should be a period of at least 6 h until start it up again. The CCC is the most efficient among the thermal units. However, it is not always chosen by the optimization process because of its complex commitment times, which sometimes does not fit system needs.

3.2   Hydroelectric

A third of the installed power plant and a half of the energy produced in Uruguay still come from hydroelectricity. Hydroelectric dams are geographically distributed over the mid-north of the country, as sketched in Fig. 6. Three of them are in tandem over an internal river (Río Negro), while the fourth, placed over the Uruguay River, is a binational joint project with Argentina. The main state variable of a hydroelectric dam is the volume of water in its storage lake. That volume determines the *head* (i.e., the height difference between the surface of the reservoir and the turbines). Control variables regard with how much water flows through the turbines, and how much is spilled. The higher the head, the most energy obtained by volume of water turbinated. Actually, this also depends on the level the river after the dam, which in Uruguayan low steep river courses is highly dependent on the total flow itself (i.e. turbinated and spilled), so the production function is far from being linear. Natural influxes into the reservoir increase the volume of water in it, while turbinated water decreases it. Intuition suggests that production efficiency passes by keeping the head as high as possible, while waters flow turbines downwards. However, whenever the head surpasses a security threshold, water must be spilled. Spilling not only wastes the resource, but, as mentioned before, increases the level downstream, what reduces the efficiency for the fraction of water really passing through the turbines.

Table 3. Parameters of the hydroelectric Uruguayan power plants

Hydroelectric power plant	Power	Empty	Influxes
Rincón del Bonete	148 MW	20 weeks	Río Negro
Baygorria	108 MW	1 day	Bonete's outflux 6 h earlier
Palmar	333 MW	2 weeks	Yí river and Baygorria 10 h earlier
Salto Grande	1/2 1890 MW	2 weeks	Uruguay river

As it counts in Table 3 and can be observed in Fig. 6, the sequence of dams over the Río Negro binds influxes of some dams with the outflux of the previous.

Table 3 also shows the emptying time when the unit is used at its maximum power. Within an optimization horizon of three days, control decisions hardly affect the efficiency (head or spilling) in Bonete, Palmar or Salto. Baygorria on the other hand must be finely tuned.

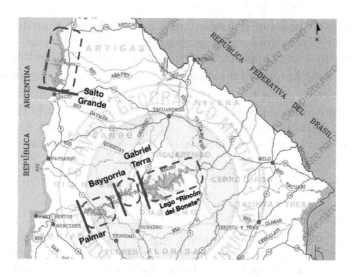

Fig. 6. Geographical distribution of hydroelectric dams in Uruguay

3.3 Storage Batteries

Units of energy storage are modeled without an objective function, i.e., without a direct profit. So they are at the service of the system.

$$
\begin{cases}
b_t = b_0 + \delta \sum_{\tau=1}^{\tau=t} r_\tau^c - \sum_{\tau=1}^{\tau=t} r_\tau^d & (i) \\
0 \le r_t^c \le \overline{r_c} & (ii) \\
0 \le r_t^d \le \overline{r_d} & (iii) \\
0 \le b_t \le \overline{b} & (iv)
\end{cases}
\tag{2}
$$

The state variable b_t indicates the level of charge of the battery, i.e., the energy cumulated in it at time t. Control variables r_t^c and r_t^d indicate how much power is used at time t to respectively charge or discharge the battery. In the first case the power is taken from the grid (as a demand), while in the second is returned (as generation). There are upper limits for control and state variables. The parameter $\delta < 1$ represents the inefficiency (loss of power) of charge/discharge cycles. There are no storage units in the Uruguayan grid, so as a reference, we used parameters as in a real-world project ("Neoen & Tesla Motors" in Australia). They are: $\overline{r_c} = 35\,\mathrm{MW}$, $\overline{r_d} = 100\,\mathrm{MW}$, $\overline{b} = 140\,\mathrm{MWh}$ y $\delta = 0.9$.

3.4 Demands

Demands are the entities that bind all sub-problems into one. When demands are hourly determined, they form part of the data-set of the instance and are integrated into problem as set of T constraints: $\sum_{g \in G} w_t^g \ge d_t$, $t \in T$. Being T the number of hours along which we are optimizing, d_t the expected demand at the hour t, G the set of generation units and w_t^g the power produced by the unit g at time t (plus storage's uncharging). In more general terms, consider an application j in a set of applications J, and A^j a set of c_j disjoint time intervals $A^j = \{A_1^j, \ldots, A_{c_j}^j\}$ proper of that application. Let D_p^j be the energy requirement of the application j along the pth interval ($1 \leq p \leq c_j$), and consider the control variable z_t^j, the power supplied by the grid to fulfill demand j at hour t. Besides, let $\underline{z}_t^j$ and $\overline{z}_t^j$ respectively be the lower and upper power bounds. Expressed so, an elastic demand is satisfied whenever constraints in Eq. 3 are satisfied.

$$\begin{cases} \sum_{t \in A_p^j} z_t^j \geq D_p^j, & 1 \leq p \leq c_j, j \in J \quad (i) \\ \underline{z}_t^j \leq z_t^j \leq \overline{z}_t^j & \forall t \end{cases} \qquad (3)$$

The new power balance condition is $\sum_{g \in G} w_t^g \geq \sum_{j \in J} z_t^j$, for every $t \in T$. Observe that traditional (hourly fixed) demands can be easily expressed using $A = \{1, \cdots, T\}$ and setting $D_t = d_t$. In this document we derive two flavors from this general model for demands. One of them is the traditional, where there is only one kind of demand, whose hourly requirements are known. In the other, we assume that 30% of the residential demand is elastic within each day. Almost 52% of the total energy in Uruguay is dispatched for residential use. So, power demand is first disaggregated between residential (d_t^R) and large scale energy consumers (d_t^L). Next, we set $\underline{z}_t = 0.7 d_t^R + d_t^L$, $\overline{z}_t = \infty$, $A = \{A_1, A_2, A_3\}$ where $A_1 = \{1, \ldots, 24\}$, $A_2 = \{25, \ldots, 48\}$ and $A_3 = \{49, \ldots, 72\}$. Finally, we assign $D_1 = \sum_{t=1}^{24} 0.3 d_t^R$, $D_2 = \sum_{t=25}^{48} 0.3 d_t^R$ and $D_3 = \sum_{t=49}^{72} 0.3 d_t^R$.

4   Experimental Results

In addition to opening models by demand elasticity, we branch them by using deterministic or stochastic versions of the problem. So the number of versions totalizes four. Since solar power was incipient by the time this work was being developed, we only consider uncertainties coming from wind-power. In every case, confidence bands (see Fig. 4) are used to bound process realizations. Deterministic versions assume the wind power will be as the centroid of the band (blue curve in Fig. 4). Stochastic versions use the classic stochastic programming framework (see [6]) with four stages. Time intervals (in hours) for each stage are: [1, 6], [7, 24], [25, 48] and [49, 72]. Assuming a power assimilation preprocessing, forecasts are proven accurate during the first six hours (see [1]), so we can model stage-1 as deterministic. For the rest of the stages, trajectories are built to explore the confidence bands in order to reproduce different realizations. For stochastic programming versions of the problems we used 27 trajectories. In summary, for each representative scenario four versions of the problem are solved. They are defined by combining "inelastic" or "elastic+inelastic" demands, in their deterministic or stochastic versions. Historical data about actual dispatch is not available (they are considered confidential by authorities). However, since the historical information for the actual wind-power is available, we tested the convenience of the optimal schedule crafted, by comparing it with results of simulations of the real cost the system would have incurred in by using that plan as a guide. We remark that no algorithm was developed to tackle down these problem instances, since all of them were solved using a generic comercial MIP optimizer: *IBM(R) ILOG(R) CPLEX(R) Interactive Optimizer 12.6.3.0*, on an *HP ProLiant DL385 G7* server with *24 AMD Opteron(tm) 6172* processors, 72 GB of DDR3 RAM and running *CentOS 6.10* Linux operating system.

4.1   Problem Instances

Instances were defined up from scenarios particularly interesting to analyze sensibility against some key aspect the problem. Due to the importance of hydro-electric energy for the country, the availability of hydraulic resources is one the dimensions to explore. We defined five hydro-scenarios to test, they are as follows. *HB1* is the historically typical scenario, with a good head of water in the reservoirs and high expectations of new influxes the next weeks to come. *SH1* assumes a drought condition, with medium resources in the reservoirs and poor expectations about the new influxes. *SH2* is a worse drought condition than in SH1, since now the head level in reservoirs is critical. *EHT1* is an intermediate situation to HB1 and SH1. Resources are good but important new influxes are unlikely, so the valuation of the water (that comes from mid-term planning models) pushes prices towards those of fossil fuels. The valuation gives lowest prices for those reservoirs over Río Negro. *EHT2* is similar to EHT1, but now Salto Grande reservoir has lower prices than those of Río Negro. Although not representative regarding the typical volume of rains in a year, SH1, SH2, EHT1 and EHT2 are important to stress the model. The second dimension for scenarios is defined by the second power source by importance: the power-wind. We selected four "forecasts+actual power" among the set of historical series.

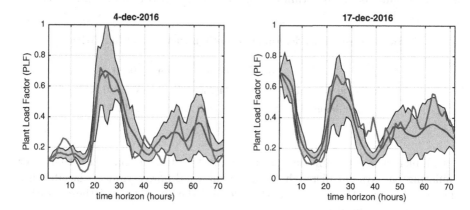

Fig. 7. Representative wind-power samples

Days in Fig. 7 were chosen because they are typical, i.e., they are close to the medians of: off-band error, effective wind-power produced, and width of their confidence band. Days in Fig. 8 on the other hand were chosen to stress the model. The leftmost sample for having the confidence band with the larger width, and the rightmost one for being among the samples with the higher off-band energy, i.e., for being among those bands with the poorest performance.

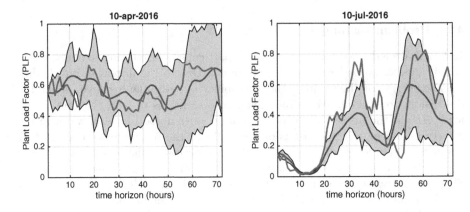

Fig. 8. Stressing samples regarding forecast and wind-power series

In addition, the last sample has a particularity regarding power. Observe that in the period between the hour 51 and 54 rises almost 70% of the PLF, which rounds 1GW, close to the average power consumption of the country.

Therefore, 80 problems were solved to explore those scenarios over different models (4 models × 5 hydro-scenarios × 4 wind-scenarios). In the first place, we show the results for the deterministic models over all hydro and wind scenarios.

Table 4. Cost [USD] deterministic optimization 72 h ahead. [HB1]

	4-dec	17-dec	10-apr	10-jul
Inelastic demand	348,930	334,760	241,230	359,730
Elastic demand	327,200	311,240	239,350	344,780

Complementing the information in Tables 4 and 5, we must add that after simulating the system dispatch using actual wind-power values, the absolute difference between the projected schedule and the simulation of the operation was between 3% and 6%.

Instances for hydro-scenario HB1 do not require the usage of thermal generation. This fact explains the low production costs. Conversely, several thermal units are to be activated in hydro-deficient scenarios EHT1, EHT2, SH1 and SH2,

Table 5. Cost [thousands of USD] deterministic optimization 72 h ahead

	EHT1				EHT2			
	4-dec	17-dec	10-apr	10-jul	4-dec	17-dec	10-apr	10-jul
Inelastic demand	5,389	5,120	3,737	5,448	4,091	3,869	2,850	4,126
Elastic demand	5,281	5,026	3,660	5,338	3,951	3,761	2,667	3,958
	SH1				SH2			
	4-dec	17-dec	10-apr	10-jul	4-dec	17-dec	10-apr	10-jul
Inelastic demand	5,696	5,419	3,857	5,731	5,706	5,428	3,857	5,742
Elastic demand	5,602	5,316	3,735	5,630	5,621	5,337	3,735	5,646

Table 6. Relative deviation stochastic vs deterministic models [HB1]

	4-dec	17-dec	10-apr	10-jul
Inelastic demand	−0.01%	−0.24%	−0.12%	−0.09%
Elastic demand	0.18%	−0.01%	−1.00%	−0.21%

Table 7. Relative deviation stochastic vs deterministic models

	EHT1				EHT2			
	4-dec	17-dec	10-apr	10-jul	4-dec	17-dec	10-apr	10-jul
Inelastic demand	−0.28%	−0.29%	−0.19%	−0.13%	−0.45%	−0.21%	−1.41%	−0.30%
Elastic demand	−0.42%	−0.41%	−0.36%	−0.10%	−0.44%	−0.34%	−0.25%	−0.14%
	SH1				SH2			
	4-dec	17-dec	10-apr	10-jul	4-dec	17-dec	10-apr	10-jul
Inelastic demand	−0.34%	−0.33%	−0.04%	−0.09%	−0.33%	−0.34%	0.00%	−0.10%
Elastic demand	−0.51%	−0.45%	0.05%	−0.02%	−0.50%	−0.47%	0.09%	−0.01%

then costs increase over the order of magnitude. Observe that although costs and other conditions are similar, the system manages much more efficiently hydro-scenarios ETH2 than their homologous in EHT1, whose figures are similar to those of SH1 and SH2.

Regardless of the hydro-scenario or demand elasticity, Apr/10/2016 always gets the lowest cost, with reductions in the order of 30%. That date corresponds with three windy days in a row and evinces how sensible the system cost is to the power coming from wind farms.

Focusing now on the expected cost for stochastic versions, the values are quite similar to the corresponding deterministic instance, so Tables 6 and 7 present the relative difference with respect to figures in Tables 4 and 5.

Observe that in 36 out of 40 instances, the stochastic version gets schedules with lower expected values than those of the deterministic version. This fact by itself is not relevant, however, a-posteriori simulations run to assess models' robustness, show that differences between projected schedules and simulations are always under 3.5% for the stochastic version. Thus, the stochastic version is not only better in quality but in confidence, so we use its figures as a reference to valuate the benefits of having smart-grids capabilities to control up to 30% of the residential demand of energy. Those figures show that having such control allows to reduce costs in all the hydro-scenarios: 4.7% (HB1), 3% (EHT1,2) y 2.1% (SH1,2). Saving are relative higher in the hydro standard HB1 scenario, but in absolute terms are much higher in those of drought. If all those savings were transferred to elastic demands, reductions of price could round 25%.

5   Conclusions and Future Work

This document presents how classical optimization models were used to quantify the benefits of having smart-grids technologies, a fundamental component of smart-cities. Such benefits were computed upon a real-world scenario, the Uruguayan electricity market, a world leader in the usage of renewable energies, which is facing the challenge of getting over 35% of its electricity from windpower, a volatile source of energy. Experimentation was realized assuming that 30% of the residential demand can be controlled, showing that if billed differentially, discounts could round 25%. Large scale energy consumers can trade in the wholesale electricity market according on their needs. Residential users however, must contract with the public owned company (UTE), so a centralized mechanism as that described in this document is viable in Uruguay.

Regarding the particulars of the dispatch schedules, their results show that smart-grids not only allow to reduce production costs, but also softness the stress to operate the grid. A secondary but highly desirable consequence of controlling demands to reduce costs, is that the set of components necessary to provide power to the grid, is lower than in regular conditions. In addition, there are fewer cycles of activation/deactivation of components. As a consequence, spot prices are also more regular for smart-grid based dispatch schedules, turning the wholesale market less volatile for all of the users.

Experiments realized so far are punctual, and simulate specific days taking its parameters from historical data sets. A promising line of work consists in expanding the software components developed so far, to run instances along larger periods of time. Hence, historical information could be used to evaluate results over months or years. The analysis of the solutions shows that most of the savings are consequence of a better use of hydraulic resources. Therefore, it is probable that the sustained application of such controls makes the system more immune against falling in drought conditions, in which costs are much higher. Another line of future work is the integration of solar-power among the sources of uncertainty.

Acknowledgements. This work was partially supported by PEDECIBA-Informática (Uruguay), by the STIC-AMSUD project 15STIC-07 DAT (joint project Chile-France-Uruguay), and by ANII (Agencia Nacional de Investigación e Innovación, Uruguay).

References

1. de Mello, S., Cazes, G., Gutiérrez, A.: Operational wind energy forecast with power assimilation. In: 14th International Conference on Wind Engineering (2014)
2. Joos, M., Staffell, I.: Short-term integration costs of variable renewable energy: wind curtailment and balancing in britain and germany. Renew. Sustain. Energy Rev. **86**, 45–65 (2018)
3. Karki, R., Billinton, R.: Cost-effective wind energy utilization for reliable power supply. IEEE Trans. Energy Convers. **19**(2), 435–440 (2004)
4. Li, N., Chen, L., Low, S.H.: Optimal demand response based on utility maximization in power networks. In: 2011 IEEE Power and Energy Society General Meeting, pp. 1–8, July 2011
5. Mohsenian-Rad, A.H., Leon-Garcia, A.: Optimal residential load control with price prediction in real-time electricity pricing environments. IEEE Trans. Smart Grid **1**(2), 120–133 (2010)
6. Morales, J.M., Conejo, A.J., Madsen, H., Pinson, P., Zugno, M.: Integrating Renewables in Electricity Markets, vol. 205, No. 1. Springer, Boston (2014). https://doi.org/10.1007/978-1-4614-9411-9
7. Paganini, F., Belzarena, P., Monzón, P.: Decision making in forward power markets with supply and demand uncertainty. In: 2014 48th Annual Conference on Information Sciences and Systems (CISS), pp. 1–6, March 2014
8. REN21. Renewables 2018 global status report. Technical report, REN21 Secretariat, Paris (2018)
9. Risso, C., Guerberoff, G.: Nonparametric optimization of short-term confidence bands for wind power generation. ArXiv e-prints, May 2018

Computational Intelligence for Detecting Pedestrian Movement Patterns

Juan P. Chavat$^{(\boxtimes)}$ (iD) and Sergio Nesmachnow (iD)

Universidad de la República, Montevideo, Uruguay
{juan.pablo.chavat,sergion}@fing.edu.uy

Abstract. This article presents a system that uses computational intelligence to detect pedestrian movement patterns by applying image processing and pattern detection. The system is capable of processing in real time multiple image/video sources and it is based on a pipes and filters architecture that makes it easy to evaluate different computational intelligence techniques. The system counts with two main stages: the first stage extracts the relevant features of images and the second stage is responsible for the detection of patterns. The experimental analysis performed over more than 1450 problem instances covers the two main stages of the system. The system was evaluated using PETS09-S2L1 videos and the results were compared with part of the MOTChallenge benchmark results. Results suggest that the proposed system is competitive, yet simpler, than other similar software methods.

Keywords: Computational intelligence · Image processing ·
Pedestrian movement patterns · Surveillance cameras

1 Introduction

Nowadays, there is a growing trend in the installation of security and surveillance cameras, with the main argument of increasing the level of security in public spaces and private businesses. Traditional security cameras do not include real time systems for detecting incidences without an operational center to process the images and take actions on certain events. Nowadays, the kind of operational center needed to process security cameras images are populated by persons with the role of visualizing agents. The visualizing agents constantly observe an amount of image sources (security cameras) and generate alerts in case an event of interest is detected [1].

Because of the high costs of the personnel, most operational centers assign to each visualizing agent several image sources, which exceeds their capacity. As a consequence, there is either a degradation of the level of global attention or the visualizing agent is forced to pay attention just to a reduced number of image sources at a time, ignoring events from the rest of the sources. In addition, due to the monotony of the task, the visualizing agents experience boredom and/or fatigue, causing poorer results.

© Springer Nature Switzerland AG 2019
S. Nesmachnow and L. Hernández Callejo (Eds.): ICSC-CITIES 2018, CCIS 978, pp. 148–163, 2019.
https://doi.org/10.1007/978-3-030-12804-3_12

This article presents an approach applying computational intelligence to overcome the attentional problem of human visualizing agents that works in operational centers. A system capable of processing in real time multiple image/video sources is proposed to help human visualizing agents in the process of detecting pedestrian movement patterns. It is based on a filter and pipe architecture that makes it easy to exchange and evaluate different computational intelligence techniques in each stage of the process. The system is comprised of two main stages. In the first stage, filtering is applied to images from multiple sources, extracting relevant features of images and discarding not interesting images, according to pre-loaded rules. This stage allows visualizing agents to focus their attention efficiently. The second stage is responsible for the detection of patterns, taking into account typical situations arising in surveillance that are worth identifying (*e.g.*, people running, agglomerations, prowling, etc.). The system architecture and design allow extending its capabilities without significant effort, as it is easily adaptable for detection of different types of events of interest.

The article is structured as follows. Section 2 contains a brief theoretical introduction to image processing and pattern detection. A review of related work on recognition and pattern detection/tracking on surveillance systems in presented in Sect. 3. Section 4 presents the general architecture and design of the system. The main implementation details of the proposed system are described in Sect. 5. Sample results from the evaluation are presented in Sect. 6. Finally, Sect. 7 presents the conclusions and the main lines for future work.

2   Image Processing and Pattern Detection

Image processing is defined as the process of applying techniques to modify, improve, or obtain information from images [2]. A standard image processing flow includes five steps (the output of each phase is the input of the next):

1. *capture* consists in acquiring raw images from a source (*e.g.* surveillance cameras). Depending on the device used, noise and other type of degradations such as blurring, high contrast of the scene, etc. are added to the image [3];
2. *pre-proceessing* applies methods to remove or reduce the information in the image that is not of interest for solving the problem. Pre-processing tries to improve those characteristics of the image that are important for solving the problem (*e.g.*, contour and shine), by using mathematical tools.
3. *segmentation* splits an image into regions that represents different objects or background, based on its contour, connectivity, or in pixel based characteristics (*e.g.*, shades of gray, textures, gradient magnitude, etc.). Some authors recognizes that segmentation algorithms focus in two properties: discontinuity and similarity, while others adds a third property: connectivity. The output of this step is a binary representation of the original image.
4. *features extraction* consists in finding, selecting, and extracting relevant features of an image, which allow identifying objects of interest for the problem.
5. *object identification* categorizes the set of features extracted in the previous step, by using different decision models, such as supervised classifiers.

Pattern detection is the study of how computer programs can observe a context, learn, and classify patterns of interest, allowing to take intelligent decisions [4]. A pattern detection system partitions the universe of classes and assigns elements to classes depending on a set of characteristics of each element (the characteristics pattern). When patterns are unknown a priori, the process is called *pattern recognition*; when the patterns are known, the process is called *pattern matching*. The pattern detection process usually consists of three stages:

1. *segmentation*, similar to image processing, the goal of this stage is to simplify the input, resulting in information that is easier to process.
2. *feature extraction* is applied to extract relevant information about specific objects, remove redundant/irrelevant information in order to reduce the problem. Quantitative (*e.g.*: speed, distance, etc.) or qualitative (*e.g.*, occupation, sex, etc.) features are used to build a vector of features. The goal is to select a subset of features (from the original set) in order to optimize a predefined target function. Feature selection can be done by statistical techniques and usually requires a deep knowledge of the problem. Selection features methods consist of three components: at least one evaluation criterion, a procedure or search algorithm and a stop criterion.
3. *classification* assigns features to specific classes. The performance of classifiers depends on the quality and number of extracted features. There are two main groups of classifiers: *supervised*, and *unsupervised* [5]. Supervised classifiers are based on a set of elements (*training data*) whose class is previously known by the classifier. Some typical supervised methods are Bayesian, Support Vector Machine, k-nearest neighbors (k-NN) and neural networks, among others [6]. Unsupervised classifiers tries to discover the classes of a given problem from a set of elements whose classes are unknown. The number of classes to be discover can be fixed or left free, depending exclusively on the datasets. Some typical unsupervised methods are Simple Link, ISODATA and k-means, among others [6].

The proposed system applies in a first step image processing techniques to extract a set of features from the scene and detect objects of interest. In a second step, the system applies pattern detection techniques over objects of interest detected in the previous step.

3   Related Works

Valera and Velastin [7] identified important issues in intelligent surveillance systems, including: object recognition, detection and tracking of movement patterns, and behavior analysis. Systems were classified in three generations: (1) analog systems that are not easy to distribute; (2) automatic systems using computer vision, increasing the surveillance efficiency by event detection; and (3) distributed automatic systems combining sensors, robust tracking algorithms, and optimized big data management. The system proposed in our research is within the third generation, as complex pattern detection methods are included.

Piccardi [8] described the main features of seven background subtraction methods and analyzed their performance (processing speed, memory utilization and precision). Results showed that Running Gaussian Average obtained the best processing speed and the lower memory utilization, while Mixture of Gaussians and Kernel Density Estimation were the best methods regarding precision.

Lopez [9] proposed detecting apparent movement on images (caused by camera movements) using global alignment methods. The system obtains an aligned image without apparent movement and both original and aligned images are sent to a segmentation module that applies background subtraction, labeling, and grouping. The output of segmentation is a set of *blobs* of interest. Blobs are sent to the tracking module that applies filters to detect movement. Results close to 90% were achieved without tracking and almost 100% using tracking.

The counting system by Lefloch [10] applied background subtraction to determine which pixels belong to the bottom and to the front of the area that has movement. Then, morphological operations (*e.g.*, erosion, dilatation, opening, and closure) were applied to eliminate noise and also small, isolated areas that exhibit minimal movement. The resulting image was sent to a stage that detects contiguous pixels and calculates its bounding box. Bounding boxes that potentially contained people were identified.

Rodriguez et al. [11] proposed detecting and tracking people in very dense crowds, where occlusion and change of location pose big challenges. An object detector, trained to detect human heads, and density estimation algorithms, which provide information about the number of persons within a region, were applied. The detector generated a map that contains scores that indicate the possible presence of people. The map of scores was combined with data obtained by the density estimation algorithms to obtain accurate detection results.

Leach et al. [12] studied the detection of subtle behavior anomalies, by processing social signals, based on that two individuals who share trajectories have similarities and a 'social dependency'. Experiments were performed on PETS 2007 and Oxford datasets, improving over methods that do not take into account the social context. These results suggest that inferring social connections between people helps improving decision making.

Cho and Kang [13] detected abnormal behavior by studying group interaction. Static agents (to calculate speed and direction of background objects), and dynamic agents (to calculate social interaction between neighbors using a Social interaction Force Magnitude (SFM)) were used. The proposed system outperformed the SFM method over PETS 2009 and UCSD datasets.

Zhu et al. [14] proposed detecting anomalies using low- or medium-level visual information from surrounding regions. Local context information and a feature descriptor was used to describe the movement information and extract dense trajectories, preferably with noise screening. The system was evaluated on UCSD Ped1, Ped2, and Subway datasets, obtaining better results than previously developed methods, mainly due to proper use of context information.

The analysis of related works showed that there is still room to contribute regarding efficient systems for detecting pedestrian movement patterns.

4   The Proposed Detection System

This section describes the proposed pedestrian patterns detection system.

4.1   Architecture and Design

The proposed must be able to collect images from different data sources. In turn, the architecture must be flexible enough to allow replacing or adding new algorithms without significant effort. To assure efficiency, the concurrent processing of multiple data sources must be supported. Taking into account the review of related works, an architecture based on *pipes* and *filters* [15] is proposed. The processes applied on the images are independent of each other and they adapt correctly to a chain pattern [7,10].

The system consists of two main modules. The *recognition and tracking* module is responsible for detecting and monitoring pedestrians (objects of interest); the *pattern detection* module analyzes the results of the first module to detect patterns based on (recent) historical information. Both modules support multiple concurrent executions using multithreading. The pattern detection module supports multiple sources of data. The system also includes three auxiliary modules: *control panel, instance launcher* and *events generator*. The system modules and the exchanged information are described in Fig. 1.

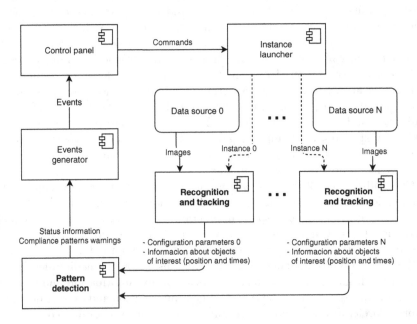

Fig. 1. Diagram of the architecture of the proposed system

Advanced Message Queuing Protocol (AMQP) protocol is used for communications between modules. AMQP is an open and secure protocol that guarantees delivery on time (or the consequent expiration), uniqueness, and correct ordering of messages, and also data integrity. The following subsections describe each module of the system.

4.2   Recognition and Tracking Module

The recognition and tracking module consists of four stages, arranged in pipes and filters. The first filter receives raw images and applies background subtraction, resulting in a binary image. The second filter takes binary images, detects blobs (set of adjacent pixels that belongs to the front of the image) and transfers the set of blobs to the blobs filter, which discards those blobs that do not contain objects of interest and adds spatial information to those relevant blobs. The last stage takes the information of the objects of interest in the image space and associates each one of them to the position of previously detected objects; thus, calculating the movement of each object. The different stages that compose the tracking and recognizing module are presented in Fig. 2.

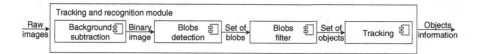

Fig. 2. Diagram of components of the recognition and tracking module

4.3   Pattern Detection Module

The pattern detection module receives information of objects of interest from multiple instances of the recognition and tracking module. Data is stored in a repository that contains the recent history for each object. Periodically, the module process the last entries for each object to identify a set of features, called *primitives*, which represent basic characteristics of the objects, depending on the movement speed, direction, or another attribute(s) of the object. A sequence of primitives plus a set of associated properties' values define a *pattern*.

There are single and multi-target primitives. Single-target primitives takes into account only one object of interest, ignoring the rest of objects in the scene, while multi-target primitives takes into account multiple objects in the scene. For example, single-target primitives can determine if a person is standing, walking, or running, depending only on the speed of movement of that person. On the other hand, a multi-target primitive can detect an agglomeration depending on the position of a group of persons for a period of time.

A specific method for patterns detection, based on the work by van Huis et al. [16] is implemented. Patterns detection takes into account the 'proximity' between an identified sequence of primitives and a set of previously established patterns. Proximity is evaluated using an error function that applies the concept of temporal distance, *i.e.*, the total time of primitives within a sequence that are not included in the reference pattern.

Reference patterns are integrated to the system dynamically. For each primitive that integrates a pattern, a quantifier and a value are defined. For example, a primitive that take into account the movement speed is fulfilled within a pattern if a pedestrian walk with a movement speed greater or equal to (*quantifier*) 5 km per hour (*value*).

4.4   Auxiliary Modules

Three auxiliary modules allow simplifying the operation of the main modules of the system and displaying results.

The *instance launcher* auxiliary module starts instances of the pattern detection, control panel, and events generator modules. After that, it remains waiting for the arrival of command orders (*e.g.*, attend a new source of data, which causes that a new instance of recognition and tracking module is launched). The *control panel* module consist of a web service and a web interface that allow final users to start new processing instances and visualize partial and final results. The *event generator* module stays idle while waiting for results generated by the patterns detector. Generated results, when available, are sent to the event generator. Based on the results received, the event generator generates web events that are sent to all web users using the control panel.

5   Implementation

This section describes the main decisions about technologies and algorithms taken during the implementation of the system.

5.1   Technology Selection

The search of technologies for implementing the system was based on a set of predefined conditions related to the main requirements of a pedestrian movement patterns detection system, including: (*i*) using a cross-platform programming language; (*ii*) develop over a programming language without technical complexities (not to be hardly typed, has an automatic memory handler, etc.) and having a broad and active community; (*iii*) using libraries free of use and preferably open source; (*iv*) achieving good performance on all tasks covered by the system: image processing, pattern detection, message passing and management, etc.

After a literature and technology research and based on the works by Mallick [17] and Coelho [18], a group of configurations were selected for a deeper study: Matlab, OpenCV over C/C++, and OpenCV over Python. Both OpenCV and Python are free and open source. In addition, Python is a dynamically typed language and counts with an automatic memory manager. Python has a wide variety of free and open source scientific libraries and the community is broad and active. Regarding performance, Python is also an efficient option. The study allowed to conclude that the best choice for implementing the system is using OpenCV library (version 3.0.0 was selected) over Python (version 3.4.3).

5.2   Communication Between Modules

The AMQP implementation from RabbitMQ (www.rabbitmq.com) is used for the communication between modules. RabbitMQ was thought to support parallelism and be robust for messages' management. For the connection between Python and the RabbirMQ service, the pika library was used.

In AMQP, *exchange* elements provide the message delivery service, according to instructions about how and where to send them. Exchanges are of four types: direct, topic, fanout, or header. All data in RabbitMQ is in JSON format, a standard, language independent, and simple format for data exchange.

An exchange of type direct was defined between recognition and tracking and pattern detection modules. Each instance of the recognition and tracking module generates messages that are addressed to a unique queue attended by an instance of the pattern detection module. Messages exchanged between the two main modules are of two types: *configuration*, used to attend the instance of recognition and tracking that sends the message; and *data*, which contains precise information about objects of interest.

The pattern detection module sends its results to an exchange of type topic. Each message contains a key that indicates the message type: commands, state information, and matched patterns warnings. The events generator module binds the exchange with a queue to receive the three types of messages, while the instance launcher module binds the exchange to receive just commands messages.

5.3   Recognition and Tracking Module

The main implementation details of the four stages of the recognition and tracking are described next.

Background subtraction. Algorithm 1 presents the steps followed by the component in charge of performing background subtraction.

Algorithm 1. Background subtraction steps

1: frame ← raw image
2: grey image ← BGRToGrey(frame)
3: blurred image ← GaussianBlur(grey image)
4: binary image ← BackgroundSubtractor(blurred image)
5: binary image without noise ← MorphologicalOperations(binary image)
6: output ← binary image without noise

First, background subtraction transforms the raw image to an image in gray scale (line 2 in Algorithm 1). The grayscale image allows processing less information and results in a lower processing time. After that, the gray scale image is blurred (line 3). Blurring is a technique for reducing the noise presented in the image [19]. Blur operations are made by the application of filters. In the proposed system, a Gaussian filter is applied. A Gaussian filters filter applies a convolution in each point of the image using a Gaussian kernel and then returns the summation as the final result. The implementation of the Gaussian filter used in the system is included in the OpenCV library. After blurring the image, the background is subtracted (line 4). Two different methods were integrated to the system for this purpose: Improved Mixture of Gaussians (MOG2) and k-NN. Both methods are included in OpenCV and their use is indicated by a parameter in the configuration of each instance of the recognition and tracking module.

A binary image is obtained after background subtraction. In this image, some elements are detected incomplete or are too close to others, generating a not-desired union of blobs. To mitigate these problems, morphological operations (MO) are applied to study the shape and structure of elements (line 5). *Erosion* allows separating elements that appears together by small contact areas. *Dilatation* allows joining nearby elements by applying edge thickening. *Opening* consists in applying first erosion and then dilatation, while *closing* is the result of applying first dilatation and then erosion. The result obtained after applying MO is an image with less noise and better identified elements. A sample of the results of the processing, step by step, is presented in Fig. 3.

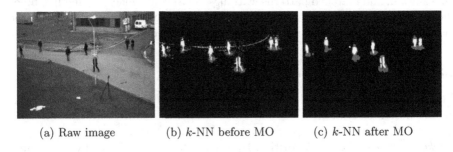

(a) Raw image   (b) k-NN before MO   (c) k-NN after MO

Fig. 3. Background subtraction steps

Blobs Detection. The proposed system includes two methods for processing the binary images for detecting blobs: *simple blob detector* (SBD) and *blob detection based on bounding boxes* (BBBD). SBD is a basic implementation of a blob extractor provided by OpenCV [20] BBBD is a specific method implemented as part of the reported research. It operates in two phases: the first phase consist on detecting the contour of elements and the second phase performs a search of the minimum rectangles that contains the detected contours (the *bounding boxes*). Both methods return a set of rectangles that contains the blobs detected.

Blobs Classification. Blobs classification takes the set of rectangles as input and classifies them into *useful blobs*, *i.e.*, those containing objects of interest, or as *not useful blobs* when not. Not useful blobs are discarded.

Three different techniques are implemented, which can be applied isolated or in combination with each other, to improve the results of the classification:

- *Aspect ratio* (AR) classifies blobs based on the relation (ratio) between their width and height. If the ratio is close to the average value of the objects of interest, AR indicates that the blob contains at least one object of interest. The major benefit of AR its low computational cost. However, it tends to be inaccurate because the reference aspect ratio often varies significantly for different data sources. AR is not useful for discarding blobs (*i.e.*, the fact that a blob fulfills the relation does not mean that it contains an object of interest) and wrongly discards blobs that does not comply with the established aspect ratio criterion due to they contain multiple objects of interest (*e.g.*, objects close enough one of each other that conforms a unique blob).
- *Computational intelligence* uses *default people detector*, a pre-trained learning algorithm included in OpenCV. Dalal and Triggs [21] demonstrated that a combination of Histograms of Oriented Gradients (HOG) for feature extraction, and Support Vector Machine (SVM) for the classification of the feature vectors, allows obtaining accurate detection results. The method is based on moving a gridded window all over the image, extracting the vectors of features (using HOG) and classifying them (using SVM) to decide if the image contains a person. Considering that the proposed system studies the movement of persons, the blob classification technique process just those areas where movement was detected. Thus, the default people detector algorithm is applied just over each detected blob, reducing the computational cost of the processing. This method returns a set of rectangles that contains persons, some of them overlapped. To reduce and unify the number of rectangles, the *Non-Maximum Suppression* algorithm [22] is used.
- *Aspect ratio frequency* filters blobs depending on the frequency that similar blobs were filtered by computational intelligence algorithms. In this way it is possible to simulate a behavior close to the computational intelligence algorithms without the need to execute them in each iteration.

Tracking. This stage determine the one-to-one correspondence between the detected objects of interest in the current and previous frames. A specific variant of the Hungarian algorithm [23] was developed for this purpose. The Hungarian algorithm receives as input a set of blobs, a set of objects of interest, and a cost function, and returns a correspondence between both input sets that optimizes the defined cost function. The original Hungarian algorithm only accepts inputs of the same size, thus the result is always surjective. A modified implementation was developed to allow the system to handle a different number of blobs than the number of objects of interest. This way, it is possible to process those cases where the number of blobs detected is lower than the objects of interest in the previous frame, or vice versa. In addition, the modified version declares invalid all correspondences whose cost is greater than a certain threshold, assuming that the blobs do not correspond to the objects in question.

The cost function used in the proposed system has three components, weighted according to specific parameters in the instance file configuration: (i) the distance between the position of an object in the previous frame and the current position of the blob; (ii) the distance between the predicted position of the object for the current frame and the current position of the blob; and (iii) the difference between the colors of the blob that contained the object in the previous frame and the color of the blob in the current frame.

The position of a blob is not always accurately adjusted to the shape of the objects. As a consequence, the raw trace of an object can suffer zig-zag movements, making it difficult to track the object and detect movement patterns. Kalman filters [24] are applied to avoid the zig-zag effect and to predict the next probable position of each object. The Kalman filters method keeps the state of each object, updating it in each frame based on a prediction and correction model (considering position, speed and acceleration for each person).

Two structures were implemented to store information of different objects and their tracking, and to resolve occlusions: *tracklets*, associated to a unique object, to store and update the relevant tracking information (position, color, frame when it appears, last frame when its object was not occluded, etc.) and *groups*, used to store tracklets and associate blobs to frames. Due to occlusion, some groups may have many tracklets and one or more blobs associated.

Tracklets are updated or removed in each iteration of the tracking algorithm, depending on the groups they belong to, and both the time of permanence in the group and in the system. A tracklet can be removed from the system due to a ghost blob, resulting from noise in the cameras or in previous steps, due to low tracking confidence, not associated to a one-to-one group for a certain time, or because the object disappears from the scene.

Three levels are considered for tracklet information updating: (i) *correction with maximum confidence*, when a tracklet is associated one-to-one to a group, the blob of the group represents the tracked object and the tracklet is updated with the information of position and appearance of the blob; (ii) *correction with minimum confidence*, when an object suffers multiple occlusion for a certain time, the tracklet is not associated one-to-one to a group, the predicted position is no longer trustworthy and the tracklet is updated with the position of the blob that represents the occlusion; and (iii) *prediction only*, when a tracklet was recently associated one-to-one to a group, it is assumed that the predicted position is reliable and no correction is made (*e.g.*, when objects are occluded by a short time or two paths cross each other); this level makes possible keep tracking positions of the objects even when there is no blob assigned in the current iteration.

5.4   Pattern Detection Module

The pattern detection module is capable of processing multiple source of data concurrently. The module consists of two stages:

- The first stage receives messages from multiple instances of the recognition and tracking module and routes them depending on the source identifier.

Two types of messages exist: (i) when processing requests by new instances of recognition and tracking arrive, the pattern detection module creates the structures to handle data from the new data source identified in the message, and configuration values in the message are applies to process data from the respective data source; (ii) when data of detected objects arrive, messages are routed to the structures previously created to handle the data source.

– The second stage receives data of the detected objects and has the patterns definition, the recent history of primitives fulfilled by each detected object, and all the logic needed to check patterns compliance. Patterns are defined as a sequence of primitives, defined by a 'primitive type' (in the implemented system: SPEED, DIRECTION, AGGLOMERATION), an 'event type' for each type of primitive (*e.g.*, for the SPEED primitive, WALKING, RUNNING and STOPPED are possible), 'quantifier' defines how the values of the met primitives are compared with the required by the pattern (LE–lesser or equal, GE–greater or equal, AX–approximate, EQ–equal and NM–irrelevant value).

6 Sample Validation Results

This section presents sample validation results of the proposed system.

6.1 Recognition and Tracking Module

The validation of the recognition and tracking module was performed using the video from scenario S2.L1 of the PETS09 dataset (fixed camera over people's head, at 7 FPS) [25]. During the 1:54 min of the video, 19 people get in and out of scene and walk around, generating multiple occlusions among them and with objects of the scene. A good performance of the module is characterized by an accurate tracking, processed and sent to the pattern detection module in real time (*i.e.*, in less than a second). Thus, the metrics used in the experimental analysis focus on the final result of the module and not in partial filter results.

The average and maximum processing time per frame are computed to evaluated efficiency. The MOTChallenge benchmark, an unified evaluation platform created by Leal-Taixé et al. [26], is used to evaluate the tracking accuracy. MOTChallenge consist of three components: (i) a public dataset including own and well known videos (some of them with ground truth information, like PETS09-S2L1); (ii) a centralized evaluation method that allows the comparison of results; and (iii) an infrastructure that makes it possible the crowdsourcing of new data, new evaluation methods and new notations (*i.e.*, ground truth).

MOTChallenge provides several metrics. Multiple Object Tracking Accuracy (MOTA) is used to evaluate the tracking accuracy. MOTA is a percentage that combines three indicators: false positives, false negatives, and identity changes of the tracked persons. The greater the MOTA value is, the more accurate is the tracking of the persons. In addition, the average and maximum difference between the number of persons in each frame (from the ground truth) and the detected tracklets and blobs in each frame are evaluated.

The system has a set of configuration values that determine how accurate the module performs in a given scene. Thus, experiments were performed to find the best combination of configuration values. Since the module has a pipes and filters architecture, it is assumed that the performance of each filter depends only on its configuration values, so finding the best configuration values for each filter result in the best for the entire module. The 40 parameters were studied in an execution plan composed of four sub-plans (divided into 11 blocks). A total number of 1458 experiments were performed.

For each executed block, three configurations are selected to process the next block, taking into account the following three criteria: (i) higher MOTA value, (ii) lower average difference in the person counting, (iii) from the ones with higher MOTA value, the one with lower average processing time per frame.

When compared with the (manual) configuration used during the development of the system, the three best configurations were able to improve the MOTA value 14.8% and the person counting 34%. In addition, the highest MOTA value obtained by the system (52,7) is higher than the average MOTA value (36,6) obtained by algorithms in the 2D MOT 2015 benchmark [27] for a set of images. The average processing time per frame is similar for all three configurations, between 0,02–0,05 s, being the blobs classification the filter that requires the most processing time. The maximum processing times per frame are in the range of 0,06–0,1 s. For all cases, the average processing time is lower than 0,05 s, which allows processing in real time a 20 FPS data source.

No differences were registered in the count of persons in 533 frames for the best configuration and in 433 frames for the worst configuration (from a total of 795 frames). As for the maximum difference in the counting, a difference of five in one configuration and four in the other two configurations was registered.

6.2   Pattern Detection Module

The validation of the pattern detection module was performed over a recorded video (2:51 min, resolution of 800 × 600 pixels, in natural light). In the video, nine persons walk around and get in and out of the scene occasionally.

Five events occur in the video, which can be detected by the four pre-loaded patterns in the system: two agglomerations, two street robberies and one 90-degree turn. The detection of the first street robbery is shown in Fig. 4.

Experiments were oriented to evaluate the capability of the system to detect pre-defined patterns exactly, at the moment they occur. The closer to the start of the event it is detected, the more accurate the system is. In addition to the timing accuracy of event detection, the number of false positives and false negatives during the processing is taken into account. The accuracy of the detection of true positive cases is evaluated by the difference between the moment that an event is notified and the real starting time of the event. For false positives and false negatives, only the number of occurrences is taken into account.

Fig. 4. Scene where the first street robbery occurs.

Three of the five events were notified during the video processing: three true positives, two false negatives, and no false positive event notifications were recorded. True positives events were notified in a mean time of 8.3 s and a median of 4.0 s.

The first not reported event was the second street robbery. This event was not detected due to an incorrect resolution of an occlusion. The second not reported event corresponded to a 90-degree turn. From the empirical evaluation, it was observed that the detection patterns module has a high sensitivity to small variations of consecutive positions of objects. The fact that the system detects a sequence of small turns instead of a single turn suggests that, in order to detect the event correctly, it is necessary to use a longer history of the last positions of the person who turns.

7 Conclusions and Future Work

This article presented a system for detecting pedestrian movement patterns, based on computational intelligence for image processing and pattern detection.

The proposed system is capable of processing in real time multiple image/video sources. An architecture based on pipes and filters is used to allow an easy evaluation of different computational intelligence techniques in each stage of the processing. Two main stages are identified in the system, focusing on extracting relevant features of the processed images (implemented in the recognition and tracking module) and detecting movement patterns (implemented in the pattern detection module). Several techniques are applied for image processing and pattern detection. The proposed implementation fulfills important requirements for a pedestrian movement patterns detection system: it is cross-platform, open source, and efficient.

The experimental analysis performed over more than 1450 problem instances covers the two main stages of the system. The system was evaluated using PETS09-S2L1 videos and the results were compared with part of the MOTChallenge benchmark results. Results suggest that the proposed system is competitive, yet simpler, than other similar software methods.

Further details about the proposed system are available on the project website https://www.fing.edu.uy/inco/grupos/cecal/hpc/APMP.

Acknowledgments. The research reported in this article was developed on the project 'Algoritmos de inteligencia computacional para detección de patrones de movimiento de personas' by J. Chavat, J. Gómez and I. Silveira (advisor: S. Nesmachnow). The work of S. Nesmachnow is partly supported by ANII and PEDECIBA, Uruguay.

References

1. Kruegle, H.: CCTV Surveillance: Video Practices and Technology, 2nd edn. Butterworth-Heinemann, Newton (2006)
2. Gonzalez, R., Woods, R.: Digital Image Processing. Pearson Education, London (2008)
3. Ramírez, B.: Procesamiento Digital de Imágenes: Fundamentos de la Imagen Digital. Universidad Nacional Autónoma de México (2006). http://verona.fi-p.unam.mx/boris/teachingnotes/Capitulo2.pdf, May 2018
4. Jain, A., Duin, R., Mao, J.: Statistical pattern recognition: a review. IEEE Trans. Pattern Anal. Mach. Intell. **22**(1), 4–37 (2000)
5. Webb, A.: Statistical Pattern Recognition. Wiley, New York (2003)
6. Carrasco, J., Martínez, J.: Reconocimiento de patrones. Komput. Sapiens **2**(3), 5–9 (2011)
7. Valera, M., Velastin, S.: Intelligent distributed surveillance systems: a review. IEE Proc. Vis. Image Signal Process. **152**(2), 192–204 (2005)
8. Piccardi, M.: Background subtraction techniques: a review. In: IEEE International Conference on Systems, Man and Cybernetics, pp. 3099–3104 (2004)
9. López, H.: Detección y seguimiento de objetos con cámaras en movimiento. Engineering Thesis, Universidad Autónoma de Madrid, Spain (2011)
10. Lefloch, D.: Real-time people counting system using video camera. M.Sc. Thesis, Université de Bourgogne, France (2007)
11. Rodriguez, M., Laptev, I., Sivic, J., Audibert, J.: Density-aware person detection and tracking in crowds. In: IEEE International Conference on Computer Vision, pp. 2423–2430 (2011)
12. Leach, M., Sparks, E., Robertson, N.: Contextual anomaly detection in crowded surveillance scenes. Pattern Recognit. Lett. **44**, 71–79 (2014)
13. Cho, S., Kang, H.: Abnormal behavior detection using hybrid agents in crowded scenes. Pattern Recognit. Lett. **44**, 64–70 (2014)
14. Zhu, X., Jin, X., Zhang, X., Li, C., He, F., Wang, L.: Context-aware local abnormality detection in crowded scene. Sci. China Inf. Sci. **58**(5), 1–11 (2015)
15. Buschmann, F., Meunier, R., Rohnert, H., Sommerlad, P., Stal, M.: Pattern-Oriented Software Architecture: A System of Patterns. Wiley Publishing, Hoboken (1996)
16. van Huis, J., et al.: Track-based event recognition in a realistic crowded environment. In: Proceedings of SPIE-The International Society for Optical Engineering, vol. 9253, p. 92530E (2014)
17. Mallick, S.: Learn OpenCV (C++ / Python) (2016). http://www.learnopencv.com/. Accessed May 26 2018
18. Coelho, L.: Why Python is Better than Matlab for Scientific Software. https://metarabbit.wordpress.com/2013/10/18/, May 2018
19. Nixon, M., Aguado, A.: Feature Extraction and Image Processing. Academic Press, Cambridge (2008)
20. OpenCV Developers Team: OpenCV Simple Blob Detector. https://docs.opencv.org/3.4/d0/d7a/classcv_1_1SimpleBlobDetector.html, May 2018

21. Dalal, N., Triggs, B.: Histograms of oriented gradients for human detection. In: IEEE Conference on Computer Vision and Pattern Recognition, pp. 886–893 (2005)
22. Rosebrock, A.: Non-Maximum Suppression for Object Detection in Python (2014). http://www.pyimagesearch.com/2014/11/17. Accessed May 26 2018
23. Kuhn, H.: The Hungarian method for the assignment problem. Nav. Res. Logist. Q. **2**(1–2), 83–97 (1955)
24. Kalman, R.: A new approach to linear filtering and prediction problems. J. Basic Eng. **82**(1), 35–45 (1960)
25. University of Reading: Performance Evaluation of Tracking and Surveillance. http://www.cvg.reading.ac.uk/PETS2009, May 2018
26. Leal-Taixé, L., Milan, A., Reid, I., Roth, S., Schindler, K.: MOTChallenge: Multiple Object Tracking Benchmark. https://motchallenge.net/, May 2018
27. Leal-Taixé, L., Milan, A., Reid, I., Roth, S., Schindler, K.: MOTChallenge results 2D. https://motchallenge.net/results/2D_MOT_2015/, May 2018

An IoT Group-Based Protocol for Smart City Interconnection

Jaime Lloret[1], Sandra Sendra[1,2(✉)], Pedro Luis González[3],
and Lorena Parra[1]

[1] Instituto de Investigación para la Gestión Integrada de zonas Costeras,
Universitat Politècnica de València, Carretera Nazaret-Oliva s/n, 46730 Valencia,
Grao de Gandia, Spain
jlloret@dcom.upv.es, loparbo@doctor.upv.es
[2] Departamento de Teoría de la Señal, Telemática y Comunicaciones (TSTC),
Universidad de Granada, Calle Periodista Daniel Saucedo Aranda s/n,
18071 Granada, Spain
ssendra@ugr.es
[3] Departamento de electrónica, Universidad Central,
Cra 5 No. 21-38, Bogotá, Colombia
pgonzalezrl@ucentral.edu.co

Abstract. The evolution of the information and communication technologies
(ICT) and the need to solve and improve some services in large cities such as
environmental monitoring, health, traffic, etc., day by day, new sensors capable
of taking parameters of the environment are developed. These sensors must be
integrated into larger networks and, in turn, these networks must be integrated
into a bigger network so that these sensors together can improve the efficiency
and sustainability of cities. These cities equipped with sensors are known as
Smart cities. This paper presents an architecture and communication protocol for
interconnecting all these sensors and networks. The proposal is group-based
architecture able to connect the different infrastructures that provide services to
the smart cities. The proposed system is scalable and fault-tolerant. The paper
also provides the mathematical model for this interconnection system. Finally,
the system is simulated in different topologies to see its operation and performance. The results show that although the size of network increases the amount
of generated traffic remains quite stable.

Keywords: Smart City · Internet of Things (IoT) · Protocols ·
Group-based topology · Sustainability · Wireless Sensor Networks (WSNs)

1 Introduction

The paradigm of the Internet of Things (IoT) is a new concept based on the interconnection of objects of everyday life which surround us. These devices are composed
by digital systems, microcontrollers, sensors and a communications interface that will
allow them to communicate with each other and with the users, being integral elements
of the Internet [1]. Therefore, IoT tries to extend the networks and the Internet to give
access to devices such as appliances, surveillance cameras, monitoring sensors,

© Springer Nature Switzerland AG 2019
S. Nesmachnow and L. Hernández Callejo (Eds.): ICSC-CITIES 2018, CCIS 978, pp. 164–178, 2019.
https://doi.org/10.1007/978-3-030-12804-3_13

actuators, screens, vehicles, etc. IoT networks and wireless sensor networks currently serve a wide range of applications such as home automation, industrial processes, medicine, remote healthcare, Ambient Assisted Living (AAL) [2], intelligent energy resource management, automotive, waste management traffic and many others [3]. Each one of these applications can be understood as an improvement tool in the current cities. This is known as Smart Cities.

A Smart City [4] can be understood as a complex scenario composed by networks and heterogeneous technologies that generate a huge amount and variety of data with the aim of improving the welfare of its inhabitants and providing new services to citizens, businesses and public administrations. There are many application areas where new technologies are applied in a Smart City [5]. The most current ones are:

- Environment
- Education
- Mobility and Traffic
- Economy
- Government
- Security
- Health
- Tourism
- Industry
- Home

The implementation of Smart City and ICT solutions such as Big Data and IoT promote a new way of understanding the relationships of citizens and their urban environment and promote these benefits in our environment. In smart cities, the quality of life of its citizens increases. A Smart City is committed to improving the quality of public services that become more efficient. The smart city reduces CO_2 emissions and reduces the impact on the environment, thus reducing the problems that the greenhouse effect is causing in today's society.

One of the most important factors for the development of the Smart City is the correct interconnection and the design of the architecture that unites the different infrastructures [6]. There are different architectures and network protocols that can be easily adapted to this type of networks. However, many of them do not provide the efficiency we require when large amounts of data are sent. One of the most interesting architectural proposals is the group-based networks [7]. There are several architectures and protocols usually used for WSN that could be used for connecting Smart Cities. However, group-based topologies and networks improve the performance and the efficiency of the whole network [8]. Group-based topologies permit a more flexible and efficient sensors operation. This also implies lower energy consumption than regular network topologies which implies an increase of the network lifetime [9].

Up to now, this kind of topologies has been implemented in WSNs but we want to apply them to the smart cities interconnection. So, in this paper, we propose the use of group based topologies for connecting the different services and subnets that monitor some environmental parameter. We will present the scenario where our proposal could be applied and the architecture design. Finally, the architecture will be simulated to see its operation.

This paper is structured as follows. Section 2 discusses some interesting works related to this proposal. Section 3 describes the proposed scenario and the interconnection system. Section 4 explains the architecture design and data management. Section 5 describes the mathematical model and the simulation results. Finally, in Sect. 6 presents the conclusion and future work.

2   Related Work

This section presents some interesting works related to proposed architectures to smart cities and interesting ideas of group-based topology proposals.

There are several approaches that try to explain how the Smart city architecture is deployed. For example, Gaur et al. [10] proposed a multi-level Smart City architecture based on semantic web technologies and Dempster-Shafer uncertainty theory and explained its functionality and some real-time context-aware scenarios.

Mitton et al. [11] presented a hierarchical organization for smart cities that permits to separately manage a high-level intelligence, achieving the abstraction of data developed according to the Sensor Web Enablement (SWE) standard. The solution is implemented using Contiki, an operating systems especially designed for sensors. The results shows this solution overcomes the limitations of SWE and gives the possibility of developing a platform for communicating heterogeneous sensors networks as the ones we could find in Smart cities.

Regarding to group-based topologies, in [7], Lloret et al. presented a group-based grid architecture using an efficient neighbor node selection. This architecture organizes logical connections between nodes from different groups of nodes allowing sharing resources, data or computing time between groups. Connections are used to find and share available resources from other groups and they are established based on node's available capacity. Suitable nodes have higher roles in the architecture and their function is to organize connections based on a node selection process. Nodes' logical connections topology changes depending on some dynamic parameters.

For example, Garcia et al. [8] showed how the organization of sensors in cooperative groups can reduce the global energy consumption of the WSN. Also, it is show that a cooperative network based on groups reduces the number of messages transmitted within the WSN, which implies a reduction in the energy consumed throughout the network, and, consequently, an increase in the life of the network.

Lloret et al. [12] presented in this work the design and simulation of a cluster-based architecture to structure topologies of WSNs to exchange information, data and services between all interconnected clusters. The results showed this protocols is scalable, secure and fault tolerant and it easily allows the joining of new clusters.

As far as we know, there are no similar proposals of protocols specially designed to interconnect small infrastructures in smart cities. For this reason, this paper presents an efficient protocol for Smart City Interconnection.

3 Proposed Scenario and Interconnection System Components

This section presents the network architecture and its operation as well as the different elements and nodes that compose the network.

3.1 Scenario Description

In the Smart City of this proposal, the protocol allows an intelligent communication between each IoT network, if each central node of the network (IoT Gateway) is intelligent and is also connected to an intelligent manager in the cloud (IoT Platform) through Internet.

Each Intelligent Network IoT (Smart Home, Smart Grid, Smart Health, Smart Factory) has a multiprotocol Gateway that allows you to manage and centralize all information regardless of the underlying technology of interconnection. Each Thing connected within the network performs exchange of requests and messages by protocol messages. These messages were written by an artificial intelligence (AI) algorithm in the Gateway, who used the tag for its type of parameter and then forwarded them to the Destination Things within the network (WLAN) or by the local network through Internet. In the cloud, an IoT platform is divided into sections with an identifier (Id) for each red connection converted into an interface that receives and classifies the information according to the types of parameters and then processes by artificial intelligence to share them and redistribute them in the other networks.

The platforms that are in the cloud, are vertically stacked as layers according to the type of service and is organized horizontally in interfaces according to the type of parameters, to give greater flow to the information and more processing capacity to the AI.

The operating philosophy of this protocol is based on two main functions; Monitoring of things and the exchange of "requests" through different types of messages. The requests or requests are processed by the IA, depending on the type of relationship established (M2M, P2M, M2P). That is, it is not just a remote control over Things; if not that the things are decided from the received request, if it activates or not the function that is required.

The data sent from the Things are organized in the platform by the AI in groups of parameters common to the IoT networks that are linked to the cloud. For example, if the group of parameters to be processed corresponds to an energy saving and consumption system, the service layer could be reinjected to the power grid, which is common for all intelligent networks.

In this way the messages issued by the Gateway of each network, would add to the package a header with information regarding the type of parameter and the AI would be responsible for deciding which service it belongs to and would also add it in the header. The body of the message would take the data processed by each protocol depending on its destination. In this sense, the function of the protocol is more relevant when the communication is established between the IoT Gateway AI and the IoT platform AI in the cloud.

In each intelligent network that will make up the smart city, things are connected to each other with different technologies depending on their use, bandwidth, processing capacity and distance. Therefore, the IoT Gateway has some of these technologies including Bluetooth 5 low cost (BLE 5.0) multiprotocol that allows the connection in mesh topology between technologies and protocols Thread, ZigBee, 6LowPAN and Wireless HART. The vast majority of interconnection protocols and technologies are compatible up to layer three of the vast majority of IoT architectures, which means that the work of the Gateway is based on establishing the type of relationship (M2M, P2M) and a common language between these technologies. This process is performed in the adaptation layer of the protocol between layers three and four (Figs. 1 and 2).

The data that originates in the Things are sent over protocols such as CoAP, MQTT, HTTP through any of the interconnection technologies and the Gateway manages them and forwards them using the IA. This will decide whether the packets are forwarded within the same network or outside the network based on the relationship, the resolution of a problem and a clear reason for the requests to be sent out of the network.

Once the data is sent out of the network, they travel on the protocol making use of another type of message where the information that will be served by the IoT platform in the cloud is packaged. Within the cloud, the AI algorithm is more complex and requires more resources to operate and managing the databases and permissions to give the necessary security to the entire system (Fig. 3).

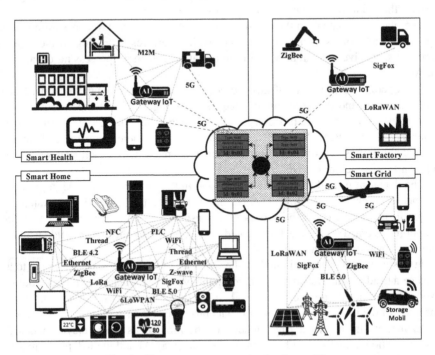

Fig. 1. Heterogeneous network of a Smart City

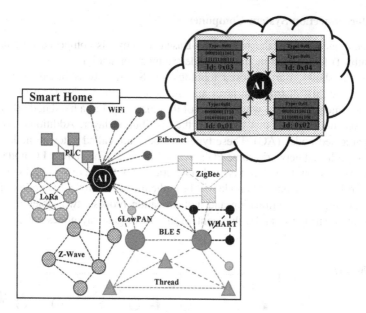

Fig. 2. Heterogeneous network of a Smart Home

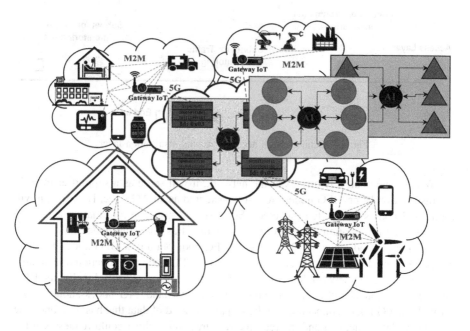

Fig. 3. Network integration of monitoring networks in a Smart City.

3.2   Interconnection System Components

As we mentioned before, the IoT Group-Based topology is composed by small networks (subnet) focused on monitoring a determined application.

As Fig. 4 shows, our proposed topology for Smart City is based on two-layer architecture, i.e., the distribution layer and the access layer. Each subnet in charge of measuring some parameters, which is part of the smart city, has a fixed node (FG) and a backup fixed node (BFG) that belong to the distribution layer. Additional nodes are called aggregated nodes (AG). These types of nodes are called gateway nodes.

In an established network, some FG nodes are known. When a new FG node joins a new network, it should be identified and authenticated with one or several FG nodes of other networks while a new AG node will be authenticated with the FG node of its own network. During the identification and authentication process, two tables (the access table and the distribution table) that contain the list of gateway nodes are created.

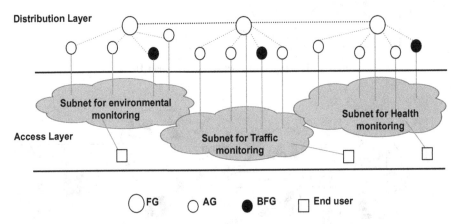

Fig. 4. Architecture of access layer and distribution layer

When a new gateway arrives to the network, it will serve as a support element in the distribution layer. BFG nodes are also considered as an AG node. However, it will be the FG node's designated successor. So, it should keep the information as an AG and the same information of the FG node. It will act as a backup node.

When a FG node fails, BFG becomes the FG node but a new BFG node should be designed. The BFG node designation is taken by the FG node as a function of available connections and the network load that the AG node is able to support. Finally, the BFG node will be considered as an AG node. On the one hand, AG nodes should learn, through the FG nodes connections in the subnet, the kind of data that has its subnet, the volume of data generated and the required resources this subnet could request. On the other hand, FG nodes are used for maintaining and managing the Smart City network interconnection. The FG nodes help to establish adjacencies between AG nodes which are used for forwarding data between the subnets that compose the access layer.

To create and maintain the distribution layer, there are two types of tables. Every gateway should maintain two tables:

(i) The access table is used by all gateways in the same subnet for communicating tasks. The FG node and all AG nodes in the same subnet form the access table. Each FG node maintains a unique access table.
(ii) There are two types of distribution tables. The FG nodes' distribution table is used to interconnect the FG nodes and interconnect AG nodes of different subnets.

Finally, the AG nodes' distribution table is used to forward the data from the end users of subnets to other AG nodes.

4 Protocol Design and Data Management

This section presents the proposed protocol and how the different elements manage the transmitted data.

As we can see in Fig. 5, the FG nodes are connected to other FG nodes from other subnet (black point lines) while the AG nodes are connected with FG of its own subnet (red point lines). At the same time, the AG nodes are connected to the selected AG nodes of the other subnets through solid black lines. Finally, there could be more AG nodes in the same subnet and they should be connected with the same AG node of the other subnet.

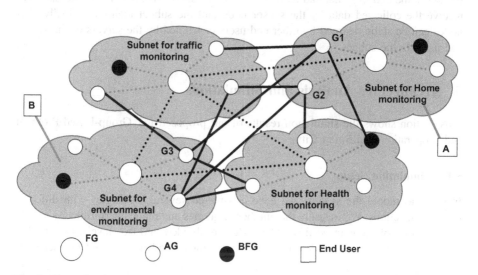

Fig. 5. Example of four subnets connected by the proposed Smart City interconnection (Color figure online)

When a new FG node joins the network, it can randomly establish the first connection with any FG node in this network. A FG node will try to become adjacent to at least one other FG node previously known. When FG nodes advertise their information with other FG nodes, they reply with what is lacking in their distribution tables. This process allows FG nodes to share routing information with adjacent nodes and to build its distribution databases. Independently, each FG node then runs the Shortest Path First (SPF) algorithm [13] on the distribution database to determine the best routes to a destination. The SPF algorithm adds up the cost, which is a value based on the hops to the destination, the available number of simultaneous supported connections, by the FG nodes involved in that path, to other FG nodes, and the available load of the FG nodes involved in that path. It also sends an identifier of its own subnet and what kind of data its subnet will be send, without affecting on the cost value. The FG node then, chooses the lowest cost path to add to its distribution table. If there are multiple paths to a destination, the lowest cost path is preferred.

When an end user sends a query, it is initially sent to its own subnet. If no result can be found, the search is sent to its network gateway (the AG node). The AG node looks up its distribution table and sends the search to the other AG nodes in its distribution table. It also looks up the type of multimedia file that can be searched (some networks allow audio searches only). That minimizes the waste of resources and bandwidth. Every AG node, receiving that query, sends the search to its subnet and will receive results. These results will be sent to the source AG node with an identifier of its network. The identifier will be used find the associated metric. Finally, the results will be sent to the end user that had requested it. As a result of this query, the end user will receive the collected data by the sensor node and the subnet identifier. Finally, AG nodes can be static, learned by other end users or learned by the servers or the super-end users in the subnet.

5 Architecture Analysis and Simulations

This section shows the simulation results of our proposed IoT Group-Based Protocol and it operation in a Smart City.

5.1 Simulation Setup

In order to model the system, we have considered several topologies with different nodes connections. We measure the number of queries and replies performed by a node as a function of the elapsed time. The nodes are divided into two levels, i.e., the FG nodes level and the AG nodes level. The behavior of both is modeled by means of number of queries and replies and time wasted. The notation used in our model is shown in Table 1:

Table 1. Notation parameters.

Abbreviation	Explanation
M	Maximum of P2P networks in FG and AG node's distribution table
m	Number of entries in FG and AG node distribution table
Q_{FG}	Query done by a FG node
Q_{AG}	Query done by an AG node
R_{FG}	Reply done by a FG node
U_{FG}	Update message from the FG node
DT_{FG}	FG distribution table
ATi	Access table of the 'i' subnet
Ci	Connections of the 'i' FG node

To model the FG nodes behavior, it is assumed that there is a FG node per subnet and m subnets interconnected. In addition, the FG node contains m entries (one per subnet) in its distribution table. The FG node also has n entries in its access table that correspond to the number of AG nodes.

- **Queries generated by a new entry:** When a new FG node joins the network, the neighbor FG nodes should update their distribution database, adding the new node. This update is propagated until the edge of the network. If we consider that every FG_i has C_i connections, then, the number of updates will be (see Eq. 1):

$$U_{FG}(DT_{FG_i}(\sum_{k=j \leq m}^{m \leq M} k)) \Rightarrow \sum_{i=1}^{C_i} U_{FG_i}(DT_{FG_i}(\sum_{k=j \leq m}^{m \leq M} k)) \tag{1}$$

Where 'm–j' represents the entries in the distribution table entries of the other FG nodes.

- **AG Queries to request AG distribution table:** When a AG node sends a request to a FG node, the AG node generates a message to every FG node in its distribution table. So, every FG node queried by the AG node will generate a reply. So, the generated replies can be modeled by (see Eq. 2).

$$Q_{AG}(\sum_{i=j \leq m}^{m \leq M} i) \Rightarrow \sum_{i=j \leq m}^{m \leq M} Q_{FG}(DT_{FG}(i)) \Rightarrow \sum_{i=j \leq m}^{m \leq M} R_{FG}(AT_i(elected)) \tag{2}$$

If the AG node is a new AG node, then, $j = 1$.

To check our model, we consider no processing delays and the same bandwidth for all nodes. So all propagations are done in t_p.

When a new FG node joins the network, the network should converge. The convergence time should be the elapsed time that FG/AG nodes need to update their distribution table. This time is also determined by the diameter of the network.

Assuming that our network has m FG nodes, when the new FG node requests the entry to the FG level, the convergence time will be calculated by Eq. 3. If consider a topology like a line, the total convergence time will be modeled by Eq. 4:

$$T_t = d \cdot t_p \tag{3}$$

$$T_t = (m - 1) \cdot t_p \tag{4}$$

Where d is the number of hops from the first to the last FG node.

At the AG nodes level, every new AG node must send a query to its FG node. This query generates m queries to other FG nodes. Those m queries will generate m replies to the first FG node and these m replies will be forwarded to the AG node. Finally, the AG node will send the m queries to the elected AG nodes of other networks and this fact will create m responses. In this case, the convergence will be modelled by Eq. 5:

$$T_s = (4 + 2 \cdot d) \cdot t_p \tag{5}$$

Where d is the number of hops from the first to the last FG node.

5.2   Simulation Results

In order to show how our protocol works, we have used four different topologies with different configurations where the number of connections, the degree of the nodes and the diameter of the topology values are varied to take measurements. The degree of the nodes is fixed in 56. It can be controlled by software when a new FG joins the system. The networks converge in $t_p = 0$. Each graph allows knowing the convergence of the interconnection system at FG nodes level how many replies are generated by an AG node the first time it joins the interconnection system.

Figure 6 shows the first topology. It is composed by 56 nodes, 2 neighbor nodes per node and the network diameter is 28.

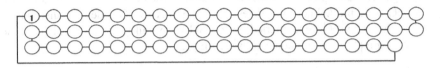

Fig. 6. Topology 1

Figure 7 shows the number of packets generated by Topology 1 and measured at the third AG node.

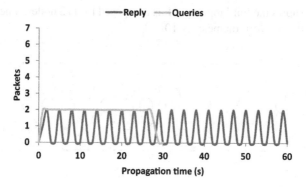

Fig. 7. Results of packets generated by Topology 1 and measured at the third AG node.

Figure 8 shows the second topology. It is composed by 84 nodes, 3 neighbor nodes per node and the network diameter is 15.

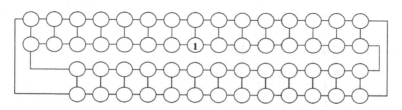

Fig. 8. Topology 2

Figure 9 shows the number of packets generated by Topology 2 and measured at the third AG node.

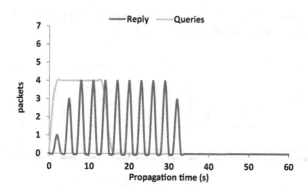

Fig. 9. Results of packets generated by Topology 2 and measured at the third AG node.

Figure 10 shows the third topology. It is composed by 112 nodes, 4 neighbor nodes per node and the network diameter is 10.

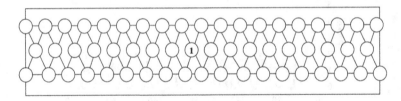

Fig. 10. Topology 3

Figure 11 shows the number of packets generated by Topology 3 and measured at the third AG node.

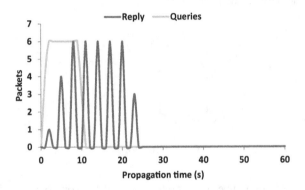

Fig. 11. Results of packets generated by Topology 3 and measured at the third AG node.

Figure 12 shows the fourth topology. It is composed by 140 nodes, 5 neighbor nodes per node and the network diameter is 10.

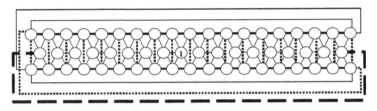

Fig. 12. Topology 4

Figure 13 shows the number of packets generated by Topology 3 and measured at the third AG node.

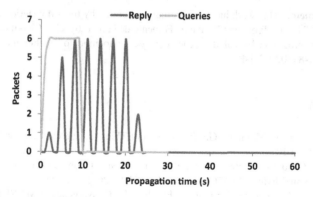

Fig. 13. Results of packets generated by Topology 4 and measured at the third AG node.

As results show, when the network is small and the nodes have few neighboring nodes, a large number of queries are generated. Consequently, the network generates a large number of replies (See Fig. 7). However, when the number of nodes and the number of neighbors is high (See Fig. 12), the network initially generates a high number of queries but, due to the composition of the group-based topology and our protocol, the amount of replies generated is much lower (See Fig. 13). The results show that the proposed protocol and architecture is easily scalable showing a low network load.

6 Conclusion and Future Work

The integration of different technologies, protocols and architectures through a centralized management in a Gateway or at the platform level in the cloud, are complex to manage, due to the large amount of information generated by all interconnected devices. These devices compose complex networks known as IoT solutions. So, the use of decision methods through artificial intelligence (AI) algorithms becomes evident.

Most of these things are programmable and have the ability to connect to the Internet, which means the possibility of integrating artificial intelligence algorithms into their systems making them smart, this makes the communication between Things, Gateway and Platform even more efficient, because all would be controlled by the AI. The AI would avoid making use of the main Internet connection channel, if it first evaluates and decides that Things (M2M) can solve a problem locally.

To interconnect all these systems is needed to develop architectures and protocols specially designed to this kind of applications and services. The group-based topologies are energy efficient and reduce the network load. So, the scalability of WSNs in Smart Cities is guaranteed.

As future work, we would like to implement this proposal in a real scenario and compare these results with the simulated ones. In addition, we want to implement secure systems to ensure the data privacy [14] and analyze the possibility of extending the proposed to Next Generation Wireless Networks [15] and cognitive networks [16].

Acknowledgement. This work has been partially supported by the "Ministerio de Economía y Competitividad" in the "Programa Estatal de Fomento de la Investigación Científica y Técnica de Excelencia, Subprograma Estatal de Generación de Conocimiento" within the project under Grant TIN2017-84802-C2-1-P.

References

1. Atzori, L., Iera, A., Morabito, G.: The Internet of Things: a survey. Comput. Netw. **54**(15), 2787–2805 (2010)
2. Lloret, J., Canovas, A., Sendra, S., Parra, L.: A smart communication architecture for ambient assisted living. IEEE Commun. Mag. **53**(1), 26–33 (2015)
3. Bellavista, P., Cardone, G., Corradi, A., Foschini, L.: Convergence of MANET and WSN in IoT urban scenarios. IEEE Sens. J. **13**(10), 3558–3567 (2013)
4. Schaffers, H., Komninos, N., Pallot, M., Trousse, B., Nilsson, M., Oliveira, A.: Smart Cities and the future Internet: towards cooperation frameworks for open innovation. In: Domingue, J., et al. (eds.) FIA 2011. LNCS, vol. 6656, pp. 431–446. Springer, Heidelberg (2011). https://doi.org/10.1007/978-3-642-20898-0_31
5. Zanella, A., Bui, N., Castellani, A., Vangelista, L., Zorzi, M.: Internet of Things for smart cities. IEEE Internet Things J. **1**(1), 22–32 (2014)
6. Gaur, A., Scotney, B., Parr, G., McClean, S.: Smart City architecture and its applications based on IoT. Procedia Comput. Sci. **52**, 1089–1094 (2015)
7. Lloret, J., Garcia, M., Tomas, J., Sendra, S.: A group-based architecture for grids. Telecommun. Syst. **46**(2), 117–133 (2011)
8. Garcia, M., Sendra, S., Lloret, J., Canovas, A.: Saving energy and improving communications using cooperative group-based wireless sensor networks. Telecommun. Syst. **52**(4), 2489–2502 (2013)
9. Azizi, R.: Consumption of energy and routing protocols in wireless sensor network. Netw. Protoc. Algorithms **8**(3), 76–87 (2016)
10. Gaur, A., Scotney, B., Parr, G., McClean, S.: Smart city architecture and its applications based on IoT. Procedia Comput. Sci. **52**, 1089–1094 (2015)
11. Mitton, N., Papavassiliou, S., Puliafito, A., Trivedi, K.S.: Combining cloud and sensors in a Smart City environment. J. Wirel. Commun. Netw. **2012**, 247 (2012)
12. Lloret, J., Garcia, M., Bri, D., Diaz, J.R.: A cluster-based architecture to structure the topology of parallel wireless sensor networks. Sensors **9**(12), 10513–10544 (2009)
13. Cormen, T.H., Leiserson, C.E., Rivest, R.L.: Introduction to Algorithms. MIT Press (1990). ISBN 0-262-03141-8
14. Sánchez, J., Corral, G., de Pozuelo, R.M., Zaballos, A.: Security issues and threats that may affect the hybrid cloud of FINESCE. Netw. Protocols Algorithms **8**(1), 26–57 (2016)
15. Ali, K.B., et al.: Enhanced IEEE 802.21 handover design for QoS support in next generation wireless networks. Adhoc Sens. Wirel. Netw. **34**(1–4), 221–243 (2016)
16. Wang, Y., Song, M., Wei, Y.: Complex network evolving model with preference and anti-preference for cognitive radio ad hoc networks. Adhoc Sens. Wirel. Netw. **34**, 99–128 (2016)

Optimization of the Dimensioning Process of a Very Low Enthalpy Geothermal Installation

Cristina Sáez Blázquez[✉], Ignacio Martín Nieto,
Arturo Farfán Martín, and Diego González-Aguilera

TIDOP Group, Department of Cartographic and Land Engineering,
University of Salamanca, Higher Polytechnic School of Avila,
Hornos Caleros 50, 05003 Avila, Spain
u107596@usal.es

Abstract. The implementation of the very low geothermal energy is not as extended as the rest of renewable energies. The high initial investment these systems usually require makes them unaffordable for most users. In this regard, this research tries to emphasize the importance of a suitable dimensioning of the whole geothermal plant. With that aim, three different calculation methods have been presented. One of them is based on manual calculations using standard values while the two remaining assumptions consider the use of specific geothermal software. Results reveal that the most suitable method is constituted by the implementation of optimized parameters in the geothermal software. These parameters are obtained from a series of previous analysis and laboratory tests. Applying the most appropriated procedure the initial investment is considerably reduced. Additionally, the electricity consumption of the heat pump is also lower using the mentioned calculation. In this way, the present research demonstrates that and adjusted and proper calculation process can make the geothermal system more attractive for a large number of users.

Keywords: Very low geothermal energy · Dimensioning ·
Optimized parameter · Geothermal software

1 Introduction

Climatic change is a vital importance issue that nowadays requires the development of new strategies to deal with it. One of the main causes of this phenomenon is the greenhouse gases emission which has exponentially increased during the last century. In 2016, at the United Nations Paris Agreement, 195 countries were involved to combat the climatic change [1]. In this regard, renewable energies play a fundamental role to reduce or eliminate the carbon dioxide emissions. According to the International Energy Agency [2], renewable energies will contribute to reduce the 32% of the global emissions during the period 2013–2050. However, one of the main problems most of these clean energies present is the dependence on the climatic conditions (solar radiation, wind velocity…). This fact could generate contradictions between the energetic production and the demand required by the user.

© Springer Nature Switzerland AG 2019
S. Nesmachnow and L. Hernández Callejo (Eds.): ICSC-CITIES 2018, CCIS 978, pp. 179–191, 2019.
https://doi.org/10.1007/978-3-030-12804-3_14

One of the renewable energies whose use is not dependent on the external conditions is the geothermal energy. This energy allows extracting the internal earth heat to use it in a certain use. In particular, the very low enthalpy geothermal energy can be used anywhere on the earth surface to produce sanitary hot water or to warm/cool a space. Since the earth temperature stays constant at the depth of 15 m, the climatological conditions do not affect the capacity of thermal exchange in this kind of installations [3–5]. Despite the large number of advantages these system present (reduced CO_2 emissions, climatic conditions independence, constant energetic supply…), its use is not widespread in the current moment and it is quite lower in comparison with the remaining green energies [6–9]. The principal reason of this fact is the initial investment these installations require. Although the amortization periods are considerably low, the high investments mean an important problem at the time of opting for its implementation [10, 11].

On this matter, an optimal dimensioning of the geothermal installation could achieve significant reductions of the global investment. In this research, three different calculation procedures were applied on the same study case to finally present an economic comparison. One of these methods is based on the optimization of the parameters that are part of the geothermal calculation while the rest of procedures use standard values. The structure of the manuscript includes a general description of the study case and each of the methodologies applied, and the corresponding sections of results, discussion and final conclusions.

2   Materials and Method

2.1   Study Case Description

As mentioned before, in this research the dimensioning of a very low geothermal installation was made by the implementation of several procedures. With that aim, in the first place, the initial conditions of the study case on which this research is focused are defined in Table 1.

Table 1. Study case description.

Study case characteristics	
Building surface (m^2)	180
Location	Province of Ávila (Spain)
Energetic demand (kWh)	35.000
Geology	Granitic materials

2.2   Methodology

Since nowadays, there is not specific regulation establishing a standardized method to calculate a very low enthalpy geothermal system, three different procedures were followed in this research for the dimensioning of the planned installation. Figure 1 shows each of the mentioned methodologies.

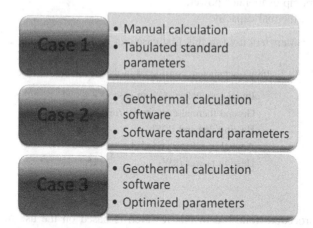

Fig. 1. Methodologies used in the geothermal calculations of the suggested installation.

Below, each of the procedures previously presented are thoroughly described.

Case 1

The first method is characterized by the manual calculation of the geothermal configuration. This procedure, based on tabulated parameters, is usually applied when the heating power is lower 30 kW since more accurate methods are not economically justified.

The sequence followed in this first case is:

- Determination, from tables, of the ground specific thermal capacity.
- Calculation of the heat pump evaporator power.
  For its estimation, the following expression is required.

$$P_e = P_c x (COP - 1)/COP \tag{1}$$

Where:

P_e = heat pump evaporator power.
P_c = heating power.
COP = performance operation coefficient of the heat pump.

- Drilling length calculation. The drilling length is obtained from the expression presented in Eq. 2.

$$L = P_e/C_t \tag{2}$$

Where:

L = drilling length.
P_e = heat pump evaporator power.
C_t = Terrain thermal capacity.

The initial parameters used in this first case can be found in Table 2.

Table 2. Initial parameters considered in the calculation of case 1.

Initial parameters used in case 1	
Ground thermal capacity (W/m)	55
Heating demand (kWh)	35.000
Annual operation period (h)	2.400
Heating power (kW)	15

Case 2

The second procedure followed in this research is based on the use of the specific software of geothermal calculations Earth Energy Designer *"EED"*, developed by Blocon Software. This program requires, from the user, the introduction of a series of characteristic parameters of the area and installation. In this second case, these parameters were taken from standard values that the software suggests. These values are shown in Table 3.

Table 3. Initial parameters introduced in EED software in case 2.

Initial parameters used in case 2	
Ground thermal conductivity (W/mK)	2,10
Grouting material thermal conductivity (W/mK)	0,70
Heat exchangers	Double-U
Working fluid	Mono-ethylene glycol
Drilling diameter (mm)	150
Annual operation period (h)	2.400
Heating power (kW)	15

Case 3

In the last case considered in this research, the geothermal calculation was equally made by using EED software. In this assumption, the parameters this software requires were experimentally obtained. In this way, the optimization of the geothermal dimensioning is based on a series of laboratory tests and works in the area projected for the study. Additional costs are not generated given that these tests are part of existing databases. The results of these tests that, can be found as scientifically publications, allowed defining the following parameters:

– Geological and thermal characterization of the materials where the building is planned to be set. By the geological exploration of the area and after laboratory measurements on the ground materials, the thermal conductivity of the subsoil was obtained. This property plays a fundamental role in this kind of systems since it determines the capacity of the ground to transmit the heat to the rest of geothermal components.

Given that the location of the geothermal system is known, consulting the geothermal map developed for the province of Avila, the thermal conductivity of the ground in the study area has the value of 3 W/mK. Figure 2 presents the mentioned geothermal map of Avila.

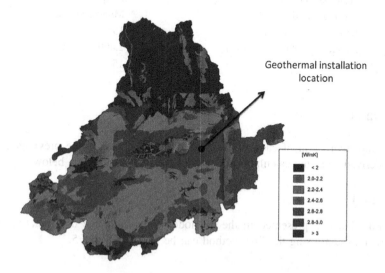

Fig. 2. Geothermal map of the province of Avila [12].

- Selection of the grouting material with the most suitable properties. This material is commonly used in geothermal drillings to guarantee the transmission of the heat from the ground to the working fluid. Based on previous researches [13], the most appropriate grouting material for the conditions of this study (assuming that there are not watercourses in the subsoil) is the mixture of aluminum cement-sand-aluminum shavings. Such material has the proper technical and mechanical conditions and reaches a thermal conductivity value of 2,789 W/mK.

- Heat exchangers design. After different laboratory tests, the helical heat exchangers presented the best results. However, its implementation is not appropriated for some locations given the drilling diameters they require. In this case, the ground is constituted by granitic materials and the current drilling methods do not guarantee to reach the diameter sizes required. For this reason, vertical heat exchangers were selected. Despite the double-U heat exchangers are the option usually chosen, laboratory tests showed that simple-U heat exchangers present the same results than the double-U ones [14]. Thus, the vertical simple-U heat exchangers were used in the calculation of the mentioned case 3.

As a result of the studies previously described, the initial values introduced during the process of calculation of EED software can be observed in Table 4.

Table 4. Initial parameters introduced in EED software in case 3.

Initial parameters used in case 3	
Ground thermal conductivity (W/mK)	3,00
Grouting material thermal conductivity (W/mK)	2,79
Heat exchangers	Simple-U
Working fluid	Mono-etilenglicol
Drilling diameter (mm)	150
Annual operation period (h)	2.400
Heating power (kW)	15

3   Results

By the implementation of each of the procedures described in the previous section, results derived from the calculation in each of the cases are shown below.

3.1   Case 1

Using Eqs. 1 and 2 presented in the methodology section, the configuration of the geothermal system using the first method can be found in Table 5.

Table 5. Geothermal system obtained using the procedure of case 1.

Installation configuration using case 1	
Evaporator power (kW)	11,67
Total drilling length (m)	212
Number of drillings	2

3.2   Case 2

Based on the introduction in EED of the parameters presented in the previous section for this second case, the software provides the design of the geothermal system (drilling length and number of boreholes) and the evolution of the fluid temperature during the period of the installation operation. From the multiple configuration suggested by the software, the first option was selected (Figs. 3 and 4).

The following Table 6 collects the design of the installation according to the calculation previously presented.

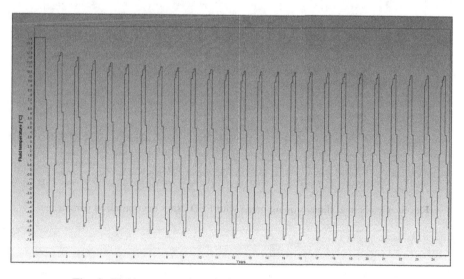

Config	No bh	Type	Spacing [m]	Depth [m]	Total length [m]	Land area [m²]	Length [m]	Width [m]	Comments
0	1	single		172	172	1	1	1	Chosen f...
0	1	single		172	172	1	1	1	Detailed ...
1	2	1 x 2 line	30	94	187	30	30	1	Chosen f...
1	2	1 x 2 line	28	94	187	28	28	1	Detailed ...
1	2	1 x 2 line	29	94	187	29	29	1	Detailed ...
1	2	1 x 2 line	30	94	187	30	30	1	Detailed ...
1	2	1 x 2 line	25	94	188	25	25	1	Chosen f...
1	2	1 x 2 line	25	94	188	25	25	1	Detailed ...
1	2	1 x 2 line	26	94	188	26	26	1	Detailed ...
1	2	1 x 2 line	27	94	188	27	27	1	Detailed ...
1	2	1 x 2 line	22	95	189	22	22	1	Detailed ...
1	2	1 x 2 line	23	94	189	23	23	1	Detailed ...
1	2	1 x 2 line	24	94	189	24	24	1	Detailed ...
1	2	1 x 2 line	20	95	190	20	20	1	Chosen f...
1	2	1 x 2 line	19	95	190	19	19	1	Detailed ...
1	2	1 x 2 line	20	95	190	20	20	1	Detailed ...
1	2	1 x 2 line	21	95	190	21	21	1	Detailed ...
1	2	1 x 2 line	17	96	191	17	17	1	Detailed ...
1	2	1 x 2 line	18	95	191	18	18	1	Detailed ...
1	2	1 x 2 line	15	96	192	15	15	1	Chosen f...
1	2	1 x 2 line	14	96	192	14	14	1	Detailed ...
1	2	1 x 2 line	15	96	192	15	15	1	Detailed ...
1	2	1 x 2 line	16	96	192	16	16	1	Detailed ...

Fig. 3. Geothermal dimensioning made with EED using the standard parameters.

Fig. 4. Fluid temperature evolution using the standard parameters.

Table 6. Geothermal design obtained using the procedure of case 2.

Installation design in case 2	
Number of boreholes	1
Total drilling length (m)	172
Medium fluid temperature (°C)	3,25

3.3 Case 3

As in the previous case, EED software provides the design of the drilling and the evolution of the working fluid. In this case, the optimized parameters were implemented. The following Figs. 5 and 6 show the described process.

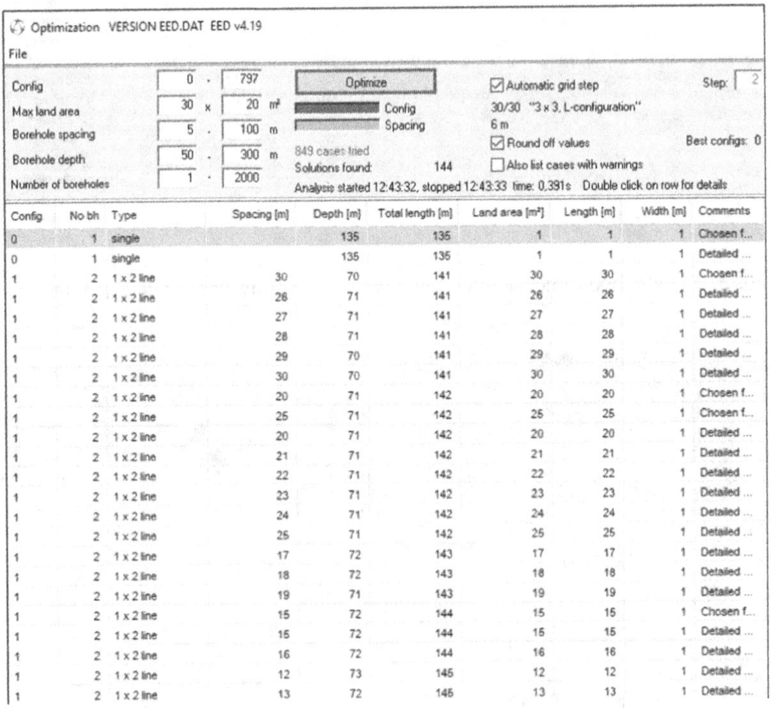

Config	No bh	Type	Spacing [m]	Depth [m]	Total length [m]	Land area [m²]	Length [m]	Width [m]	Comments
0	1	single		135	135	1	1	1	Chosen f...
0	1	single		135	135	1	1	1	Detailed ...
1	2	1 x 2 line	30	70	141	30	30	1	Chosen f...
1	2	1 x 2 line	26	71	141	26	26	1	Detailed ...
1	2	1 x 2 line	27	71	141	27	27	1	Detailed ...
1	2	1 x 2 line	28	71	141	28	28	1	Detailed ...
1	2	1 x 2 line	29	70	141	29	29	1	Detailed ...
1	2	1 x 2 line	30	70	141	30	30	1	Detailed ...
1	2	1 x 2 line	20	71	142	20	20	1	Chosen f...
1	2	1 x 2 line	25	71	142	25	25	1	Chosen f...
1	2	1 x 2 line	20	71	142	20	20	1	Detailed ...
1	2	1 x 2 line	21	71	142	21	21	1	Detailed ...
1	2	1 x 2 line	22	71	142	22	22	1	Detailed ...
1	2	1 x 2 line	23	71	142	23	23	1	Detailed ...
1	2	1 x 2 line	24	71	142	24	24	1	Detailed ...
1	2	1 x 2 line	25	71	142	25	25	1	Detailed ...
1	2	1 x 2 line	17	72	143	17	17	1	Detailed ...
1	2	1 x 2 line	18	72	143	18	18	1	Detailed ...
1	2	1 x 2 line	19	71	143	19	19	1	Detailed ...
1	2	1 x 2 line	15	72	144	15	15	1	Chosen f...
1	2	1 x 2 line	15	72	144	15	15	1	Detailed ...
1	2	1 x 2 line	16	72	144	16	16	1	Detailed ...
1	2	1 x 2 line	12	73	145	12	12	1	Detailed ...
1	2	1 x 2 line	13	72	145	13	13	1	Detailed ...

Fig. 5. Geothermal dimensioning made with EED using the optimized parameters.

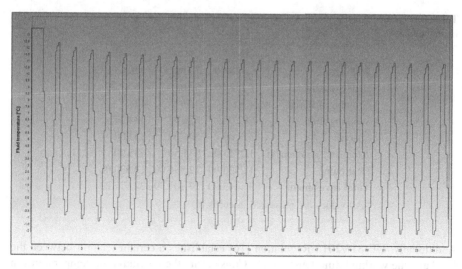

Fig. 6. Fluid temperature evolution using the optimized parameters.

Table 7. Geothermal design obtained using the procedure of case 3.

Installation design in case 3	
Number of boreholes	1
Total drilling length (m)	135
Medium fluid temperature (°C)	5,38

Results from the calculation showed in Figs. 5 and 6 have been collected in Table 7.

4   Discussion

Results show that the total drilling length is considerably reduced using the optimized parameters. Consequently, the number of geothermal components required is equally lower. This fact means the reduction of the initial investment of the global geothermal system. Table 8 shows the initial investment of each of the assumptions considered in this research. The economic estimation was carried out using the commercial catalogs of *Enertres, Raugeo y Alb* and considering that the drilling prize of the area was 44 €/linear meter.

Another difference among the scenarios considered in this research makes reference to the fluid temperature. This factor has a direct influence on the operation coefficient of the heat pump (COP). It also determines the relation between the power provide by the heat pump and the electricity consumption. The COP of the heat pumps selected in this research has the value of 4,7 for some specific working conditions (inlet fluid temperature of 0 °C and outlet temperature of 35 °C according to EN14511 Law [15]).

Table 8. Initial investment of the geothermal installation in function of the procedure implemented.

	Case 1	Case 2	Case 3
Drillings	9.328,00	7.568,00	5.940,00
Heat exchangers	7.252,00	5.505,47	2.752,73
Grouting material	4,90	3,50	4,00
Working fluid	682,00	553,32	434,29
Spacers	378,00	306,00	252,00
Accessory components	1.271,00	635,50	635,50
Heat pump	12.530,00	12.530,00	12.530,00
Total investment	31,445.90	27.101,79	22,577.23

* All values are presented in euros (€)

Additionally, UE 813/2013 Regulation [16] establishes a certain relation between the COP and the working fluid temperature. Considering the medium fluid temperatures in each of the assumptions, the real COP of the heat pump in each case was calculated. Finally, the electricity consumption and the annual electricity costs were also determined.

In the case 1, since the method do not allow to know the fluid temperature, a COP of 4,5 was assumed. A lower COP results from the elevated drilling length required using the procedure of case 1.

Table 9. Heat pump COP and electricity consumption associated to the heat pump use in each case.

	Case 1	Case 2	Case 3
Heat pump power (kW)	15,00	15,00	15,00
Energetic demand (kWh)	35.000	35.000	35,000
Real COP	4,50	4,85	4,94
Electricity consumption (kWh)	7.777,77	7.216,49	7,085.02
Annual cost (€)	945,70	877,45	861,47
Accumulative total cost, year 30 (€)	28.371,00	26.323,50	25.844,10

* The electricity prize considered was 0.12159 €/kWh.

As can be seen in Table 9, the difference in the annual costs among the three assumptions is mostly insignificant. However, beyond the economic field, the fluid temperature has a great importance on the heat pump operation. If this temperature was too low, the heat pump could not work properly and the thermal exchange with the ground could be damaged. For this reason, it is important to achieve the highest possible fluid temperatures and, it can be reached using an optimal geothermal dimensioning.

In the graphic presented in Fig. 7, the total cost (initial investment and outlay derived from the operation of the system at the end of the operation period) of the installation can be observed for each of the methods described here.

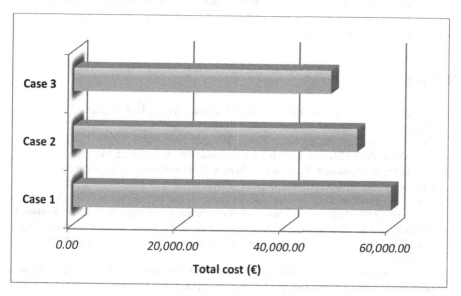

Fig. 7. Total cost of the geothermal system in the year 30 in function of the calculation procedure applied.

5 Conclusions

In the present research, the dimensioning of the geothermal installation was carried out implementing three different methods. According to the results presented above, some consideration can be established.

- The manual calculation constitutes the easiest but also the most imprecise alternative. Thus, the total drilling length is incremented 18.87% in comparison with the procedure of case 2 and 36.32% in comparison with case 3.
- Regarding the use of EED software, it is the most appropriate solution for a geothermal calculation. However, its use is usually recommended only when the heating power is higher than 30 kW.
- In addition to the use of EED software, the optimization of the geothermal parameters is also convenient. As shown in this research, when these parameters are correctly defined, the design of the system is adjusted and the total budget is considerably reduced.
- For the study case described here, the implementation of software EED using the optimized parameters reaches the reduction of the initial investment in 21.51% in relation to using standard values.

- The heat pump operation is also improved using the method of case 3. Thus, the electricity consumption of this device is also reduced meaning an additional economic saving in the long time period.

For the reasons presented, a proper geothermal dimensioning could mean an increase in the number of very low enthalpy geothermal systems making them more affordable for the general user.

References

1. United Nations Framework Convention on Climate Change. Historic Paris Agreement on Climate Change (2016)
2. Energy Technology Perspectives 2016 – Towards Sustainable Urban Energy Systems. OECD/IEA, Paris (2016). http://www.iea.org/etp2016/. Accessed 25 May 2018
3. Schellschmidt, R., Sanner, B., Pester, S., Schulz, R.: Geothermal energy use in Germany. In: Proceedings World Geothermal Congress (2010)
4. Lund, J.W., Freeston, D.H.: World-wide direct uses of geothermal energy 2000. Geothermics 30, 29–68 (2001). https://www.sciencedirect.com/science/article/pii/S0375650500000444#!
5. Fridleifsson, I.B.: Geothermal energy for the benefit of the people. Renew. Sustain. Energy Rev. 5(3), 299–312 (2001). https://www.sciencedirect.com/science/article/pii/S1364032101000028#!
6. Sarbu, I., Sebarchievici, C., Dorca, A.: Simulation of ground thermo-physical capacity for a vertical closed-loop ground-coupled heat pump system. In: International Multidisciplinary Scientific GeoConference Surveying Geology and Mining Ecology Management, SGEM 2017, Issue 42, pp. 557–565 (2017). https://www.scopus.com/sourceid/21100274701?origin=recordpage
7. Sliwa, T., Nowosiad, T., Vytyaz, O., Sapinska-Sliwa, A.: Study on the efficiency of deep borehole heat exchangers. SOCAR Proc. 2, 29–42 (2016). https://www.scopus.com/sourceid/5800184384?origin=recordpage
8. Nanaki, E.A., Xydis, G.A.: Deployment of renewable energy systems: barriers, challenges, and opportunities. Adv. Renew. Energies Power Technol. 2, 207–229 (2018). https://www.sciencedirect.com/science/article/pii/B9780128131855000005X
9. Fraga, C., Hollmuller, P., Schneider, S., Lachal, B.: Heat pump systems for multifamily buildings: potential and constraints of several heat sources for diverse building demands. Appl. Energy 225, 1033–1053 (2018). https://www.sciencedirect.com/science/journal/03062619/225/supp/C
10. Jeong, J., Hong, T., Kim, J., Chae, M., Ji, C.: Multi-criteria analysis of a self-consumption strategy for building sectors focused on ground source heat pump systems. J. Clean. Prod. 186, 68–80 (2018). https://www.sciencedirect.com/science/article/pii/S0959652618307820?via%3Dihub#!
11. Luo, J., et al.: Investigation of shallow geothermal potentials for different types of ground source heat pump systems (GSHP) of Wuhan city in China. Renewable Energy 118, 230–244 (2018). https://www.sciencedirect.com/science/article/pii/S0960148117311187?via%3Dihub#!
12. Blázquez, C.S., Martín, A.F., Nieto, I.M., García, P.C., Pérez, L.S.S., Aguilera, D.G.: Thermal conductivity map of the Avila region (Spain) based on thermal conductivity measurements of different rock and soil samples. Geothermics 65, 60–71 (2017)

13. Blázquez, C.S., Martín, A.F., Nieto, I.M., García, P.C., Pérez, L.S.S., González-Aguilera, D.: Analysis and study of different grouting materials in vertical geothermal closed-loop systems. Renewable Energy **114**, 1189–1200 (2017)
14. Blázquez, C.S., Martín, A.F., Nieto, I.M., García, P.C., Pérez, L.S.S., González-Aguilera, D.: Efficiency analysis of the main components of a vertical closed-loop system in a Borehole Heat Exchanger. Energies **10**, 201–216 (2017)
15. AENOR, UNE-EN 14511–1:2014, Acondicionadores de aire, enfriadoras de líquido y bombas de calor con compresor accionado eléctricamente para la calefacción y la refrigeración de locales. Parte 1: Términos y definiciones (2014)
16. Diario Oficial de la Unión Europea, REGLAMENTO (UE) Nº 813/2013 DE LA COMISIÓN de 2 de agosto de 2013 por el que se desarrolla la Directiva 2009/125/CE del Parlamento Europeo y del Consejo respecto de los requisitos de diseño ecológico aplicables a los aparatos de calefacción y a los calefactores combinados (2013)

Waste Generation Prediction in Smart Cities Through Deep Neuroevolution

Andrés Camero, Jamal Toutouh[(✉)], Javier Ferrer, and Enrique Alba

Departamento de Lenguajes y Ciencias de la Computación, Universidad de Málaga,
Málaga, Spain
andrescamero@uma.es, {jamal,ferrer,eat}@lcc.uma.es

Abstract. Managing the waste collection service is a challenge in the fast-growing city context. A key to success in planning the collection is having an accurate prediction of the filling level of the waste containers. In this study we present a solution to the waste generation prediction problem based on recurrent neural networks. Particularly, we introduce a deep neuroevolutionary technique to automatically design a deep network that encapsulates the behavior of all the waste containers in a city. We analyze a real world case study consisting of one year of filling level values of 217 containers located in a city in the south of Spain and compare our results to the state-of-the-art. The results show that the predictions of our approach exceeds all its competitors and that its accuracy is a key enabler for an appropriate waste collection planning.

Keywords: Deep neuroevolution · Deep learning ·
Evolutionary Algorithms · Smart Cities · Waste collection

1 Introduction

The World's population is moving from rural to urban areas and it is expected that this trend will continue. The number of inhabitants in cities will be about 75% of the World's population by 2050 [1]. The fast demographic growth, together with the concentration of the population in cities and the increasing amount of daily waste are factors that push to the limit the ability of waste assimilation by Nature. This fact has forced the authorities to examine the cost-effectiveness and environmental impact of our economic system.

The linear structure of our economy has reached its limits and the natural resources of our planet are drained. Thus, a more sustainable model of economy is needed. For example, the *circular economy* [2,3], which consists in the transformation of our waste into raw materials, proposing a new paradigm for a more sustainable future.

The unsustainable development of countries has created a problem due to the unstoppable waste generation. In addition, there are hardly any technological means to make an optimal management of the waste collection process.

© Springer Nature Switzerland AG 2019
S. Nesmachnow and L. Hernández Callejo (Eds.): ICSC-CITIES 2018, CCIS 978, pp. 192–204, 2019.
https://doi.org/10.1007/978-3-030-12804-3_15

Nowadays, the solid waste collection is carried out without a previous analysis of the demand, i.e. following a manually defined route. This approach has severe limitations, one of the most important is the variability in the amount of waste that needs to be picked up. This is especially critic in the case of selective collection (plastic, paper, glass,...), where the waste volume is smaller than in the organic case. Thus, when dealing with recyclable waste, the planning of the optimal collection routes is even more influential.

An alternative to tackle the planning of the collection routes is to determine which containers should be collected. Note that the recyclable waste collection process represents 70% of the operational cost in waste treatment [4]. Thus a reduction in the number of unnecessary visits to semi-empty containers will save money! Therefore, we aim to provide an alternative to predict if a waste container should be collected or not. Particularly, we propose to predict the filling level of the waste containers (all the containers involved in the operation at once) using a Recurrent Neural Network (RNN).

RNNs are top-notch at predicting time series, however as all Deep Learning (DL) techniques the selection of an appropriate network design is a tough task [5]. The use of automatic intelligent tools seems a mandatory requirement when addressing the design of RNNs, since the vast possible RNN architectures that can be generated defines a huge search space. In this sense, metaheuristics [6] emerged as efficient stochastic techniques able to address hard-to-solve optimization problems. Indeed, these algorithms are currently employed in a multitude of real world problems, e.g., in the domain of Smart City [7–11], showing a successful performance. Nevertheless, the use of such a methodology in the domain of DL is still limited [12].

In this article, we propose a hyper-parameter technique based on evolutionary computation and use it to design and train an RNN that predicts the filling level of the containers of a whole city. We test our approach using a real-world case study, presented by Ferrer and Alba [13], and benchmark our results against the results presented in the referred study. Therefore, the main contributions of this study are two:

- We define a deep neuroevolutionary technique to automatically design an efficient RNN.
- We use our proposal to design and train an RNN that predicts the filling level of the waste containers of a real city and benchmark our results against the state-of-the-art.

The remainder of this paper is organized as follows. The next section briefly reviews the state-of-the-art of smart waste management. Section 3 discusses about the use of DL to predict the waste generation rate. Section 4 presents a deep neuroevolutionary approach to design an artificial neural network-based predictor of the filling level of the waste containers. Section 5 presents the experiments carried out, results, benchmark, and analyses. Finally, Sect. 6 outlines our conclusions and proposes the future work.

2   Smart Waste Management

The waste collection is a process with uncountable variants and constraints which have led to a multitude of studies in recent years due to its importance. The works in the literature could be classified, among other ways, according to the waste type that is treated: *residential waste* commonly known as garbage [10,14], *industrial waste* where customers are more dispersed and the amount of waste is higher [15], *recyclable waste* [16] increasingly important for our society, where the collection frequency is lower than organic waste and *hazardous waste* where the probability of damage is minimized [17].

In the municipal solid waste collection [18], the authorities need global studies to quantify the waste generated in a period of time to be able to manage them. Particularly, the waste generation forecasting for Xiamen city (China) inhabitants was studied by [19]. The main difference with our approach is the granularity of the object under study. They predict the amount of waste produced by the whole city, in contrast, we predict every single container in a city (i.e. a disaggregated prediction of the whole city). This supposes a considerable increase of the complexity of the problem that is solved, because it is necessary to consider multiple aspects such as the location, the customs of the citizens, the population density of the area, etc. In the same research line, the impact of the intervention of local authorities on waste collection has also been studied [20], being this relevant in the medium-long term.

Regarding the location where the collection takes place, there exist multiple variants of the problem. There are *communal collections* where the local authority identifies a place shared by the community [11,21], in most cases a local waste facility for recycling. In the other side we found the *kerbside collection* [22] where the household waste is collected from individual small containers located near each house. The intermediate case studied here is the analysis of containers that give service to several streets and blocks of flats [23].

In previous works [13,24] the authors used machine learning techniques to predict the filling level of a container. Particularly, the authors used Linear Regression, Gaussian Processes and Support Vector Machines for regression to predict each container individually. In this work we present a unique RNN able to generate predictions for the whole set of containers instead of creating and training individual predictors for each container.

3   Deep Learning for Waste Generation Prediction

In this study, we focus on waste generation prediction by applying DL based on specific type of artificial neural networks (ANN), RNN. As other ANNs, this type of networks are composed of multiple hidden layers between input and output layers. RNNs incorporate feedforward and feedback connections between layers to capture long-term dependency in an input. Thus, RNNs have successfully applied to address learning applications which involve sequential modeling and prediction as natural language, image, and speech recognition and modeling [25].

In turn, they have been applied in Smart Cities problems that require time dependent prediction [12].

We apply supervised learning, which consists in an iterative process that requires a training data set (N input-output pairs). As this study deals with the prediction of the filling levels, the inputs are the current filling level each container and the outputs are the next (future) filling levels. Thus, for each input, the ANN produces an output (i.e., a tentative future filling rate) which is compared to the expected output by using an error (cost or distance) function. Then, a procedure is applied to reduce this error by updating the network until a given stop criteria is reached [26].

Minimizing such learning error is a tough task. Backpropagation [27] (BP), a first-order gradient descent algorithm, is the most widely used method to address such issue. In order to apply BP on RNN, the network has to be unfold [28], i.e., the network is copied and connected in series a finite number of times (known as look back) to build an unrolled version of the RNN.

Large ANNs (as unfolded RNNs) suffer from overfitting to the training data set, i.e., the error on the training set is driven to a very small value, but when unseen new data is presented to the network the error dramatically increases [29]. In order to address this issue, a technique called dropout, which consists in including a stochastic procedure to the training process, is applied [30].

The accuracy and the generalization capability of the RNN prediction depends on a set of configuration hyper-parameters: number of layers, number of hidden units per layer, activation function, kernel size of a layer, etc. Thus, a promising research line in DL proposes to find specific hyper-parameters configurations for an ANN to improve its numerical accuracy [31,32]. The results demonstrated that selecting the most suitable hyper-parameters for a given dataset provides more competitive results than using a generalized networks.

Since training an RNN is costly (in terms of computational resources) and the number of RNN architectures is infinite (or extremely large if we impose restrictions to the number of hidden layers or neurons), we are enforced to define a smart search strategy to find an optimal RNN.

Among the many potential optimization techniques to find efficient ANN hyper-parameterization, a few authors have already applied metaheuristics [33,34]. However, these solutions cannot be directly applied to deep neural networks (DNN), i.e. ANNs with one or more hidden layer, due to the high computational complexity of DNNs. Recently, new solutions specifically defined to address hyper-parameter optimization of DNNs by using metaheurisitcs are emerging: the deep neuroevolutionary approaches [5,12,35–37], showing competitive results in finding parameters that improve the accuracy and minimize the generalization error.

In this study, we focus on applying a deep neuroevolution approach to address the generation of container filling predictions. Our optimization method deals with the next main RNN parameters: the look back (i.e., how many times the net is unfold during the training), the number of hidden layers, and the number of neurons for each hidden layer.

4 Deep Neuroevolutionary Architecture Optimization

In this section we present the details of our proposal. First, we formally state the architecture optimization problem, and then we outline our deep neuroevolutionary approach to solve the problem.

4.1 Architecture Optimization

Optimizing an ANN consists in finding an *appropriate* network structure (architecture) and a set of weights to solve a given problem [26]. Particularly, we can analyze the *suitability* of an ANN by measuring its generalization capability, i.e. the ability to predict/classify new (unseen) data.

In our particular case, we are interested in optimizing the architecture of an RNN. Therefore, we decided to train an RNN using BP (i.e. we are finding an appropriate set of weights given a network structure) and measure the *mean absolute error* (MAE) of the predicted values against the observed ones. Equation 1 states the problem of finding an optimal architecture as a minimization problem, where N corresponds to the number of samples in the testing data set (X, Y), z_i stands for the predicted value of the i-th sample, and y_i corresponds to the ground truth of the i-th sample. Note that the RNN is fed with already predicted data $\hat{x}$, and that the architecture is constraint by B, H, and L.

$$\text{minimize} \quad \text{Fitness} = \frac{1}{N} \sum_{i}^{N} MAE(z_i, y_i) \tag{1}$$

$$\text{subject to} \quad B \leq \text{max\_look\_back} \tag{2}$$

$$H \leq \text{max\_hidden\_layers} \tag{3}$$

$$L \leq \text{max\_neurons\_per\_layer} \tag{4}$$

$$\hat{x}_i = \begin{cases} x_0 & \text{if } i = 0 \\ z_{i-1} & \text{if } i > 0 \end{cases} \tag{5}$$

4.2 Deep Neuroevolution

To solve the problem stated in Eq. 1 we designed a deep neuroevolutionary algorithm based on the $(1 + 1)$ Evolutionary Strategy (ES) [6] and on the Adam weights optimizer [38]. Our proposal is presented in Algorithm 1.

A **solution** represents an RNN architecture and it is encoded as an integer vector of variable length, solution $= < s_0, s_1, ..., s_H >$. The first element, $s_0 \in [1, \text{max\_look\_back}]$, corresponds to the *look back*, while the following elements $(s_j, j \in [1, H])$, correspond to the number of Long Short-Term Memory (LSTM) cells of the j-th hidden layer, subject to $s_j \in [1, \text{max\_neurons\_per\_layer}]$ and $H \in [1, \text{max\_hidden\_layers}]$. Note that the number of hidden layers is defined by the length of the vector. The number of neurons of the output layer is defined accordingly to the inputed time series, i.e. we add a *dense* layer (fully connected) with a number of neurons equal to the number of dimensions of the output.

Algorithm 1. Self Adapting (1+1)ES-based RNN architecture optimizer.

1: *solution* ← Initialize()
2: Evaluate(*solution, evaluation_epochs*)
3: *evaluations* ← 1
4: **while** *evaluations* ≤ max_evaluations **do**
5:     *mutated* ← Mutate(*solution, mut_element_p, mut_length_p, max_step*)
6:     Evaluate(*mutated, evaluation_epochs*)
7:     **if** Fitness(*mutated*) ≤ Fitness(*solution*) **then**
8:         *solution* ← *mutated*
9:     **end if**
10:     *evaluations* ← *evaluations* + 1
11:     SelfAdapting()
12: **end while**
13: *solution* ← Evaluate(*solution, final_epochs*)
14: **return** *solution*

First, the **Initialize** function creates a new random solution. Then, the **Evaluate** function computes the **Fitness** of the solution. Specifically, the solution is decoded (into an RNN), then the net is trained using the Adam optimizer [38] for *evaluation_epochs* epochs using the *training data set* and finally the fitness value is computed using the *testing data set*.

Then, while the number of evaluations is less or equal than *max_evaluations*, the evolutionary process takes place. Starting from a solution, the **Mutate** function generates a new **mutated** solution, which is later evaluated. The Mutate function consists in a two step process applied to the inputed solution. In the first step, with a probability equal to *mut_element_p* the j-th element of the solution is perturbed by adding a uniformly drawn value in the range [-*max_step,max_step*]. In the second step, with a probability equal to *mut_length_p* the length of the solution is modified by copying or removing (with equal probability) an element of the solution. Before returning the new solution, a *validation* process is performed to assure that the mutated solution is valid (i.e. its values complies with the restrictions).

Next, the fitness of the original solution and the mutated one are compared. If the fitness of the mutated is less or equal than the original solution, the mutated replaces the original solution.

As the last part of the evolutionary process, a **SelfAdapting** step is performed to improve the performance of the evolutionary process [39]. Particularly, if the fitness of the mutated solution improves the original one, then the *mut_element_p* and *mut_length_p* values are multiplied by 1.5, in other case these probabilities are divided by 4 [39]. In other words, if we are not improving, we narrow the local search space. On the contrary, while the solutions are improving (in terms of the fitness), we widen the local search space.

Finally, the evolved solution is evaluated (using *final_epochs* to feed the number of epochs of the training process) and returned.

5   Experimental Study

We implemented our proposal in Python 3, using the DL optimization library **dlopt** [40], and the DL frameworks **keras**[1] and **tensorflow** [41]. Then, we (*i*) selected a data set to test our proposal, (*ii*) optimized an RNN to tackle the referred problem, and (*iii*) compared our predictions against the state-of-the-art of urban waste containers filling level prediction.

5.1   Data Set: Filling Level of Containers

The data set analyzed in this article is the one used in [13,24], a real case study of an Andalusian city (Spain), where we highlight the benefits of our approach, being effective and realistic at the same time. Our case study considers 217 paper containers from the metropolitan area of a city. The choice of an instance of recycling waste (paper) is more attractive than a organic waste collection to show the quality of our approach because most paper containers do not need to be collected everyday like the organic waste, so they have a high variability in collection frequency.

5.2   RNN Optimization

We executed 30 independent times our deep neuroevolutionary algorithm considering the combinatorial search space defined in Table 1, using the data set described above, the parameters defined in Table 2, and a fixed *dropout* equal to 0.5. We use an 80% of the data to train the networks and the remainder data to test their performance (i.e., computing the fitness).

Table 1. RNN optimization search space.

Parameter	Value	Parameter	Value
min_look_back	2	max_look_back	30
min_neurons_per_layer	10	max_neurons_per_layer	300
min_hidden_layers	1	max_hidden_layers	8

The initial setup of the algorithm is taken from the related literature [12]. Considering that our proposal performs a self-adapting step, we do not performed a tuning of the parameters of the algorithm.

Table 3 summarizes the results obtained. The MAE, the mean squared error (MSE), the total number of LSTM cells, the look back, and the number of recurrent layers correspond to the statistics computed over the final solutions (30 RNN trained). We will refer to the solution returned by the algorithm as *solution*. The time corresponds to the statistics computed over the total time,

Table 2. ES parameters configuration.

Parameter	Value	Parameter	Value
mut_element_p	0.2	evaluation_epochs	10
mut_length_p	0.2	final_epochs	1000
max_step	15	max_evaluations	100

Table 3. ES-based RNN optimization results.

	MAE	MSE	LSTM cells	Look back	Rec. layers	Time [m]
Mean	0.073	0.014	450.667	5.933	5.433	96.866
Median	0.073	0.014	419.500	5.000	5.000	70.049
Min	0.071	0.013	127.000	2.000	1.000	33.216
Max	0.076	0.015	1252.000	16.000	8.000	405.339
Sd	0.001	0.000	227.661	3.648	1.906	75.488

i.e. the sum of the computation time of all the architectures evaluated, including the solution. The time is presented in minutes.

The results show that the algorithm is *robust* in regard to the MAE (and the MSE), however there is a noticeable variation in the architectures and in the time needed to compute a solution. In order to get insights into the relation between the architecture and the error we analyze the solutions and all the architectures evaluated during the optimization. Figure 1a presents the architectures (number of LSTM cells and layers) of the solutions along with their respective MAE and Fig. 1b shows the same information for all architectures evaluated. A small MAE (a darker dot) is desirable. It is important to remark that the MAE presented in both figures is *not comparable*, because in both cases the number of training epochs is different, therefore the results are expected to differ (at least in their magnitude).

It is quite interesting that the solutions are very diverse (see Fig. 1a), and that most of them use less than 500 LSTM cells. This is more interesting if we consider that the maximum allowed number of LSTM cells given the problem restrictions (see Table 1) is equal to 2400 and that many architectures evaluated have more than 500 LSMT cells (see Fig. 1b).

To continue with our analysis, we ranked all the architectures evaluated (excluding the solutions) into deciles and selected the top one (i.e. the best architectures evaluated). Then we plot the density distribution of the number of recurrent layers (see Fig. 2a) and of the total number of LSTM cells (see Fig. 2b). We also plot the density distribution of the solutions in both figures. The results show that both densities are relatively similar, therefore we intuit that there is an *archetype* that better suits to the problem. However, further analysis is required to validate this intuition.

---

[1] https://keras.io/.

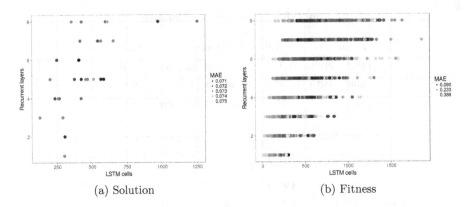

Fig. 1. Architectures evaluated during the optimization process.

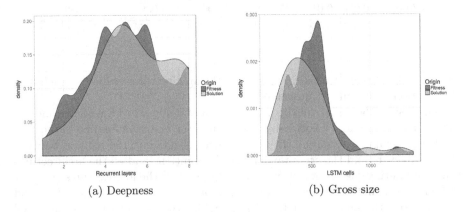

Fig. 2. The *best* solutions evaluated (fitness) compared to the final solutions.

5.3 Prediction Benchmark

To continue with the evaluation of our proposal, we benchmark the predictions made by the RNN against the results published in [13, 24]. In order to compare the approaches we compute the "mean absolute error in the filling predictions of the next month" (MM) using the solutions given by our algorithm, i.e. we predict a whole month using an RNN and summed up the predictions per container, then we compute the mean absolute difference between the predicted values and the ground truth. Table 4 summarizes the results of the MM computed using the solutions. Note that the MM results are better than the MAE (see Table 3).

We selected the median solution (in regard to the MM) and compared the results against the ones presented in [13, 24]. Table 5 presents the benchmark. In that previous work the authors proposed three time series algorithms used for forecasting the fill level for all containers. Particularly, they used techniques based on Linear Regression, Gaussian Processes, and Support Vector Machines for Regression called SMReg.

Table 4. MM statistics computed for the RNN solutions.

	Mean	Median	Min	Max	Sd
RNN	0.030	0.028	0.027	0.043	0.004

The results indicate that our proposal exceeds its competitors. Moreover, we performed a non-parametric Friedman's Two-Way Analysis of Variance Ranks Test that revealed RNN as the best algorithm, followed by the algorithm based on Gaussian Processes, the Lineal Regression and the SMReg as last algorithm in the comparison. Regarding the statistical significant differences, the values have been adjusted by the Bonferroni correction for multiple comparisons. There are significant differences between each pair of algorithms except for the particular comparison between Lineal Regression and SMReg. Thus, the RNN is significantly better than its competitors (in regard to the MM).

Table 5. MM statistics for the RNN solutions.

Method	Error
RNN	**0.028**
Gaussian processes	0.038
Linear regression	0.074
SMReg	0.095

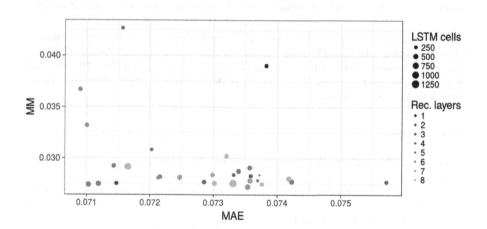

Fig. 3. Relation between the MAE and the MM.

Finally, to relate the results presented in this subsection (see Table 4) to the ones presented in the previous subsection (see Table 3) we plotted the relation between the MAE and the MM (please refer to Fig. 3). The figure also includes the architecture of the solutions (number of LSTM cells and number of recurrent layers). Something that caught our attention is that there is not an apparent linear relation between both metrics presented in the plot, however the summarized results presented for both metrics (see Tables 3 and 4) are robust in regard to the referred error measurement.

6   Conclusions and Future Work

Deep neuroevolution has emerged as a promising field of study and is growing rapidly. Particularly, the use of Evolutionary Algorithms to tackle the hyperparametrization optimization problem is showing unprecedented results, not only in terms of the performance of the designed networks, but also in terms of the reduction of the computational resources needed (e.g. the configurations are evaluated using a heuristic, therefore not all configurations are actually trained [42,43]).

In this study we present a deep neuroevolutionary algorithm to optimize the architecture of an RNN (given a problem). We test our proposal using the filling level of 217 waste containers located in Andalusia, Spain, recorded over a whole year and benchmark our results against the state-of-the-art of filling level prediction. Our experimental results show that an "appropriate" selection of the architecture improves the performance (in terms of the error) of an RNN and that our prediction results exceeds all its competitors.

As future work we propose to explore train-free approaches for evaluating a network configuration. Specifically, we propose to study the use of the MAE random sampling [42,43] to compare RNN architectures, aiming to reduce the computational power and the time needed to find an appropriate architecture.

Acknowledgements. This research was partially funded by Ministerio de Economía, Industria y Competitividad, Gobierno de España, and European Regional Development Fund grant numbers TIN2016-81766-REDT (http://cirti.es), and TIN2017-88213-R (http://6city.lcc.uma.es), and by Universidad de Málaga, Campus Internacional de Excelencia Andalucía TECH.

References

1. Bakici, T., Almirall, E., Wareham, J.: A smart city initiative: the case of Barcelona. J. Knowl. Econ. 4(2), 135–148 (2013)
2. Ghisellini, P., Cialani, C., Ulgiati, S.: A review on circular economy: the expected transition to a balanced interplay of environmental and economic systems. J. Cleaner Prod. 114, 11–32 (2016)
3. Tukker, A.: Product services for a resource-efficient and circular economy - a review. J. Cleaner Prod. 97, 76–91 (2015)
4. Teixeira, J., Antunes, A.P., de Sousa, J.P.: Recyclable waste collection planning-a case study. Eur. J. Oper. Res. 158(3), 543–554 (2004)
5. Ojha, V.K., Abraham, A., Snášel, V.: Metaheuristic design of feedforward neural networks: a review of two decades of research. Eng. Appl. Artif. Intell. 60, 97–116 (2017)

6. Back, T.: Evolutionary Algorithms in Theory and Practice: Evolution Strategies, Evolutionary Programming, Genetic Algorithms. Oxford University Press, New York (1996)
7. Ferrer, J., García-Nieto, J., Alba, E., Chicano, F.: Intelligent testing of traffic light programs: validation in smart mobility scenarios. Math. Prob. Eng. **2016**, 1–19 (2016)
8. Garcia-Nieto, J., Ferrer, J., Alba, E.: Optimising traffic lights with metaheuristics: reduction of car emissions and consumption. In: International Joint Conference on Neural Networks, pp. 48–54 (2014)
9. Massobrio, R., Toutouh, J., Nesmachnow, S., Alba, E.: Infrastructure deployment in vehicular communication networks using a parallel multiobjective evolutionary algorithm. Int. J. Intell. Syst. **32**(8), 801–829 (2017)
10. Nesmachnow, S., Rossit, D., Toutouth, J.: Comparison of multiobjective evolutionary algorithms for prioritized urban waste collection in Montevideo, Uruguay. Electron. Notes Discrete Math. **69**, 93–100 (2018)
11. Toutouh, J., Rossit, D., Nesmachnow, S.: Computational intelligence for locating garbage accumulation points in urban scenarios. In: Battiti, R., Brunato, M., Kotsireas, I., Pardalos, P.M. (eds.) LION 12 2018. LNCS, vol. 11353, pp. 411–426. Springer, Cham (2019). https://doi.org/10.1007/978-3-030-05348-2_34
12. Camero, A., Toutouh, J., Stolfi, D.H., Alba, E.: Evolutionary deep learning for car park occupancy prediction in smart cities. In: Battiti, R., Brunato, M., Kotsireas, I., Pardalos, P.M. (eds.) LION 12 2018. LNCS, vol. 11353, pp. 386–401. Springer, Cham (2019). https://doi.org/10.1007/978-3-030-05348-2_32
13. Ferrer, J., Alba, E.: BIN-CT: urban waste collection based in predicting the container fill level, Jully 2018
14. Garvin, B.J., Cohen, M., Dwyer, M.B.: Evaluating improvements to a metaheuristic search for constrained interaction testing. Empirical Softw. Eng. **16**(1), 61–102 (2011)
15. Sahoo, S., Kim, S., Kim, B.I., Kraas, B., Popov Jr., A.: Routing optimization for waste management. Interfaces **35**(1), 24–36 (2005)
16. Dat, L.Q., Truc Linh, D.T., Chou, S.Y., Yu, V.F.: Optimizing reverse logistic costs for recycling end-of-life electrical and electronic products. Expert Syst. Appl. **39**(7), 6380–6387 (2012)
17. Alagöz, A.Z., Kocasoy, G.: Improvement and modification of the routing system for the health-care waste collection and transportation in İstanbul. Waste Manage. **28**(8), 1461–1471 (2008)
18. Beliën, J., De Boeck, L., Van Ackere, J.: Municipal solid waste collection and management problems: a literature review. Transp. Sci. **48**(1), 78–102 (2014)
19. Xu, L., Gao, P., Cui, S., Liu, C.: A hybrid procedure for MSW generation forecasting at multiple time scales in Xiamen City, China. Waste Manage. (New York, N.Y.) **33**(6), 1324–1331 (2013)
20. Cole, C., Quddus, M., Wheatley, A., Osmani, M., Kay, K.: The impact of Local Authorities' interventions on household waste collection: a case study approach using time series modelling. Waste Manag. (New York, N.Y.) **34**(2), 266–272 (2014)
21. Tung, D.V., Pinnoi, A.: Vehicle routing-scheduling for waste collection in Hanoi. Eur. J. Oper. Res. **125**(3), 449–468 (2000)
22. Sniezek, J., Bodin, L.: Using mixed integer programming for solving the capacitated arc routing problem with vehicle/site dependencies with an application to the routing of residential sanitation collection vehicles. Ann. Oper. Res. **144**(1), 33–58 (2006)

23. Bodin, L., Mingozzi, A., Baldacci, R., Ball, M.: The rollon-rolloff vehicle routing problem. Transp. Sci. **34**(3), 271–288 (2000)
24. Ferrer, J., Alba, E.: BIN-CT: sistema inteligente para la gestión de la recogida de residuos urbanos. In: International Greencities Congress, pp. 117–128 (2018)
25. LeCun, Y., Bengio, Y., Hinton, G.: Deep learning. Nature **521**(7553), 436 (2015)
26. Haykin, S.: Neural networks and learning machines. Volume 3. Pearson (2009)
27. Rumelhart, D., Hinton, G.E., Williams, R.J.: Learning Internal Representations by Error Propagation. Technical report No. ICS-8506, California Univ San Diego La Jolla Inst for Cognitive Science (1985)
28. Jaeger, H.: Tutorial on training recurrent neural networks, covering BPPT, RTRL, EKF and the echo state network approach, vol. 5. GMD (2002)
29. Reed, R., Marks, R., Oh, S.: Similarities of error regularization, sigmoid gain scaling, target smoothing, and training with jitter. IEEE Trans. Neural Networks **6**(3), 529–538 (1995)
30. Srivastava, N., Hinton, G., Krizhevsky, A., Sutskever, I., Salakhutdinov, R.: Dropout: a simple way to prevent neural networks from overfitting. J. Mach. Learn. Res. **15**(1), 1929–1958 (2014)
31. Bergstra, J., Yamins, D., Cox, D.: Making a science of model search: hyperparameter optimization in hundreds of dimensions for vision architectures. In: International Conference on Machine Learning, pp. 115–123 (2013)
32. Jozefowicz, R., Zaremba, W., Sutskever, I.: An empirical exploration of recurrent network architectures. In: International Conference on Machine Learning, pp. 2342–2350 (2015)
33. Alba, E., Martí, R.: Metaheuristic Procedures for Training Neural Networks, vol. 35. Springer Science & Business Media, Berlin (2006)
34. Yao, X.: Evolving artificial neural networks. Proc. IEEE **87**(9), 1423–1447 (1999)
35. Miikkulainen, R., et al.: Evolving deep neural networks. arXiv preprint arXiv:1703.00548 (2017)
36. Morse, G., Stanley, K.O.: Simple evolutionary optimization can rival stochastic gradient descent in neural networks. In: Proceedings of the Genetic and Evolutionary Computation Conference 2016, GECCO 2016, pp. 477–484. ACM (2016)
37. Su, X., Yan, X., Tsai, C.L.: Linear regression. Wiley Interdisc. Rev. Comput. Stat. **4**(3), 275–294 (2012)
38. Kingma, D.P., Ba, J.: Adam: a method for stochastic optimization. arXiv preprint arXiv:1412.6980 (2014)
39. Doerr, C.: Non-static parameter choices in evolutionary computation. In: Genetic and Evolutionary Computation Conference, GECCO 2017, Berlin, Germany, 15–19 July 2017, Companion Material Proceedings, ACM (2017)
40. Camero, A., Toutouh, J., Alba, E.: DLOPT: deep learning optimization library. arXiv preprint arXiv:1807.03523, July 2018
41. Abadi, M., et al.: Tensorflow: a system for large-scale machine learning. In: OSDI 2016, pp. 265–283 (2016)
42. Camero, A., Toutouh, J., Alba, E.: Comparing deep recurrent networks based on the MAE random sampling, a first approach. In: Herrera, F., Damas, S., Montes, R., Alonso, S., Cordón, Ó., González, A., Troncoso, A. (eds.) CAEPIA 2018. LNCS (LNAI), vol. 11160, pp. 24–33. Springer, Cham (2018). https://doi.org/10.1007/978-3-030-00374-6_3
43. Camero, A., Toutouh, J., Alba, E.: Low-cost recurrent neural network expected performance evaluation. arXiv preprint arXiv:1805.07159, May 2018

Author Index

Printed in the United States
By Bookmasters